Trailblazers

For Réka and Dóra Dudley

TRAILBLAZERS

The First Women Elected to Government

PAULA BARTLEY

polity

First published by Polity in 2026.

Polity Press
65 Bridge Street
Cambridge CB2 1UR, UK

Polity Press
111 River Street
Hoboken, NJ 07030, USA

ISBN-13: 978-1-5095-6797-3 – hardback

A catalogue record for this book is available from the British Library.

Library of Congress Control Number: 2025949276

Typeset in 11 on 14pt Warnock Pro
by Cheshire Typesetting Ltd, Cuddington, Cheshire
Printed and bound in Great Britain by CPI Group (UK) Ltd, Croydon

For further information on Polity, visit our website:
politybooks.com

Contents

Introducing the Trailblazers

In 1907, a cross-dressing lesbian vegetarian stepped into male history. She was one of nineteen Finnish politicians, the first women in the world to be elected to the ruling body of any country. These women sparked a chain reaction that would ignite across the globe. More – many, many more – were to follow. This book is the story of some of the most extraordinary women – from Afghanistan to Zimbabwe – who trailblazed their way into a privileged male-only space. Some risked their lives; some paid with their lives.

The story begins in 1900. It is a story of women but also a story of politics and a chronicle of the world. It is not a tidy linear story of inevitable progress but a white-knuckle ride with some of the world's most extraordinary women. At the beginning of the century, politics was a man's world: men stood for election, men made the laws. All women had to do was obey. Life across the world was generally hierarchal and largely male-controlled. Unless they were of royal blood, there were no women – not one – in any government, in any country, in any part of the globe. Throughout Europe, Kings, Sultans, Grand Dukes, Princes – and one Queen – ruled their countries. Just by the virtue of their birth. There were significant numbers of Empires: the Ottoman Empire, the Russian Empire, the Austria-Hungarian Empire and the German Empire. These were all controlled by male despots, who also governed vast chunks of the globe. Queen Victoria, the only woman, reigned over the British Empire. It was the largest empire in history, spanning approximately a quarter of the earth, and governing over 400 million people.

Within European-controlled colonies most indigenous people lived under oppressive and discriminatory regimes. In pre-colonial days, African queens like the Madagascan Queen Ranavalona (1778–1861) and the Ghanian Yaa Asantewaa (1840–1921) had ruled their countries. All fought hard to protect their people's sovereignty and retain their independence. They lost. When they were colonised, native populations were not allowed to vote or hold office, and had little or no say in decision-making. They were forced to conform to laws they did not make. Colonial subjects faced discriminatory laws and policies which reinforced racial or ethnic hierarchies. Land ownership was restricted and access to education, health, employment was unequal. Life was grim. If indigenous people challenged colonial rule or demanded political rights, they faced repression and censorship. Freedom of speech was largely absent. Only two African countries remained free of colonial rule: Ethiopia and Liberia.

Change was coming. The twentieth century was marked by extensive global, social, technological and political transformations. It was a century that was both increasingly religious and increasing secular. Revolutions, two world wars, the Cold War, the decolonisation of Africa and Asia, the increasing power of America and the formation and collapse of the United Soviet Socialist Republic reshaped global politics. Women all over the world, at different times, in different jurisdictions and in different circumstances took advantage of the power vacuums created by these upheavals and demanded their rights to participate in governing bodies.

It was an age of increasing democracy. More and more countries adopted systems of government that gave citizens the right to vote and stand for government. New totalitarian systems emerged but the overall trend was clear: democracy was a growing global movement. Women, who comprise more than fifty per cent of the world's population, were at the heart of the century's most powerful political changes. Certainly, the twentieth century marked a radical shift in the landscape of politics, as women around the globe waged a determined struggle to claim their rightful place in government. Facing formidable obstacles and entrenched patriarchal systems, these courageous women shattered barriers and blazed a trail for future generations. This book examines the remarkable stories of the first women politicians who defied conventions, exceeded expectations, and left an enduring legacy of empowerment.

First, women needed the vote. At the turn of the twentieth century, women all over the world were denied this basic right. Activists fought hard to change this. There was a global campaign for women's right to vote, a movement characterised by a diverse array of strategies and tactics across different countries and regions. Some activists chose peaceful methods, others broke windows and burned down buildings. The trailblazing politicians of the twentieth century did not exist in a vacuum but stood on the shoulders of these brave suffrage campaigners who had gone before them.[1]

In November 1838, women gained the vote in the small and remote Pitcairn Islands; in 1881, the Isle of Man, a British Crown Dependency with its own Parliament, was the first Western country to grant votes for women; in 1893 women in New Zealand were given the vote, followed a few years later by Australia, Finland and Norway. In 1918, British women over thirty with property gained the vote; in 1920 all American women. Over the course of the twentieth century, women were gradually enfranchised. On 8 March 1999, Qatari women voted for the first time. Today, only men can vote for the Pope in the clergy-led Vatican City.[2]

Women usually won the right to stand for government at the same time as the right to vote. It took a long time for women to gain a parliamentary foothold in the older partial democracies: British women waited 654 years to enter the House of Commons, Swiss women waited 486 years and France, land of liberty, equality and fraternity, only let women take part in its assembly 157 years after the revolution.[3] Younger and newly independent nations like Pakistan, Mozambique and South Africa, full of optimism, and enthusiastic to build a new country, immediately gave women the right to enter government. The shift in power continues. At the start of the new millennium, women were still trailblazing their way into government. In 2000 the King of Bahrain appointed Dr Mariam Adhbi Al Jalahma, a married physician, to his Consultative Council.

The early years of the twentieth century were quite different from the later years and it is important not to imagine a seamless continuity. There was no unbroken straight line of progress. The arc of history did not always bend towards justice. Women's participation was neither inevitable, nor one of steady advancement nor always permanent. Sometimes, certain triggers were needed to spark off women's representation in government. In the twentieth century, war and revolution shook the very foundations of society, reshaping women's roles in powerful ways. *Trailblazers* will show how revolutions, by upsetting the status quo, introduced new opportunities for women. For example, in 1917 two revolutions swept away the old political order in Russia. In the second revolution, the Bolsheviks took power. Immediately they implemented legal reforms to improve the status of women by granting women equality in marriage and divorce and promoting gender equality in education and employment. For the first time in its history, Russian women enjoyed the right to vote and stand for election in the Soviets. They seized the moment. Women stood for and were elected to leadership positions in local soviets, legislative bodies and government agencies. Such bodies as these provided them with a platform to improve women's status further.

Wars, so devasting of human life, could also be a great force for progress.[4] Women's participation in war, as combatants, support workers, or resistance fighters, helped their fights towards political equality. The First World War led to the collapse of the old regimes of the Austro-Hungarian, Ottoman, German and Russian Empires and reshaped the geopolitical landscape of Europe. Autocracy – for the moment – was dead. Women in these former Empires welcomed these changes: they could vote and stand for Parliament. In addition, the principle of self-determination led to the emergence of new nation states which, no longer beholden to their conquerors, chose parliamentary democracy over despotic rule. New self-governing countries, like the former Austrian-controlled Hungary embraced modernity, immediately enfranchised all adults and encouraged women to stand for election.

A second global conflict, the Second World War, resulted in the deaths of millions and millions, the genocidal murder of Jewish people, the persecution of Roma and widespread destruction. Like the First World War, it spurred on democratic change. The defeat of Imperial Japan led to the restructuring of the country, with new power dynamics, a new political order and full democracy. Women benefitted. The aftermath of the Second World War, and its crushing of racist, antisemitic and oppressive regimes, also brought fresh hope to Jews and those still suffering under the domineering hand of colonialism. Israel became a newly created country, rising after the horrors of the Holocaust.

There were few women in African governments until the mid century. Why was this? Most African countries – Ethiopia and Liberia being the notable exceptions – were under the rule of mainly Britain, France, Germany or Portugal. Across colonial Africa, black women – and indeed men – were denied full participation in any governing body. The Second World War changed this by weakening European powers economically and militarily and making it difficult to maintain vast colonial territories. Empires were dismantled, some peacefully, others through armed struggle in which women played a significant part. And when countries broke off their colonial yokes, women were rewarded by being elected to government. For example, after decades of apartheid rule and a fierce armed struggle, the African National Congress held the first ever democratic elections and immediately gave black women the right to stand for Parliament.

In some former British colonies women's progress was restricted by race. Some confined women's vote to whites only. In Australia overt racism against the indigenous population led to the exclusion of Aborigines; in New Zealand the Maoris were not given equal rights; in Canada, the native population was excluded. In these countries, white women's rights were viewed as a safeguard against the rights of indigenous communities. Frighteningly, the distinction made between indigenous peoples and European immigrants reinforced the idea that citizenship was solely for whites.

The politicians in this book make up a diverse group. These were women from different geographical regions, different periods, different political parties, different religions, different ideologies, different classes. Some were fiery individualists, impatient to effect change; others quietly worked, often behind the scenes, to achieve a similar end. They had an important feature in common: all without exception were the first women to be elected. And all came to inhabit what was a previously male space.

So many – too many – of the women faced male resistance, often finding their trailblazing ideals squashed or undermined by men. So many – too many – of these first politicians confronted entrenched misogyny and gender bias, endured derogatory remarks and put up with sexist attitudes simply because of their biological form. Many just put on their fearless face and walked into their government chamber either alone, or with just a few other women, knowing that sometimes hundreds of men would be watching their every move. The women were resilient. For the most part, they were visionaries, often seeing new possibilities which others did not. Most displayed exceptional courage and determination in challenging the expectations of society and breaking into male-dominated spheres of government. Willing to confront opposition, discrimination and prejudice in pursuit of their political aspirations, so many of these pioneering women worked tirelessly to change the politics of their country. All had the odds stacked against them.

Another common thread that united them was their shared passion to transform their country into a better place. Most – but not all – were motivated by a strong sense of commitment to public service and a desire to improve the lives of their compatriots. Most – but not all – entered to address social injustice, promote gender equality and create a more inclusive society. Naturally, not all trailblazing women were heroines; a few were quite cunning schemers who wielded their influence to further their own agendas.

So many of these women were feminists, but feminism is like a benevolent Hydra with many heads attached to one body. Some women asked for equality with men of their class, their culture, or their religion; others wanted complete equality across the economic, social and political divides; still others, the equal yet different feminists, emphasised the differences between women and men, believing that women had unique, distinctive qualities and values such as compassion, nurture and care that they could bring to politics. With a couple of exceptions, the politicians in this book were woman-centred, focusing on the rights of women in jurisdictions across the world. The Indonesian Muslim politician who fought to make sharia law more female-friendly, the Spanish Catholic who fought for votes for women, the Russian atheist who shaped government policy, all wanted to improve the lives of the female sex.

A number of these first parliamentarians were former activists, committed to fighting injustice. Their actions challenged the stereotyped vision of a nurturing, gentle, submissive woman who stayed at home, cleaning, cooking and looking after her family. Some, like the French, Italian, Afghan and Iranian politicians, faced imprisonment, torture and sometimes death for their beliefs and actions. Most possessed a strong vision for social change, and had clear goals and strategies for advancing women's rights. All faced overt misogyny, were often accused of being unfeminine, too aggressive and much too self-assured. *Trailblazers* is thus often a story of the triumph of the human spirit over sometimes unbearable obstacles. Moreover, the women in this book shared another characteristic: they interrupted the narrative of masculinity merely by their presence in governments.

A few women achieved power through nepotism but most of the politicians in this book achieved it through a combination of determination and talent: to enter government, and to be the first to do so, often overcoming overwhelming opposition, showed a remarkable tenacity and sense of direction.

I am not trying to make these women better than they were. Not all were pleasant. Some wanted power to help the people of their country; some wanted power to help themselves; some were a complicated mixture of different motivations. Not all were saintly, and even the saintly ones sometimes had halos which slipped. A few were absolute devils. It is this messy, complex mixture that makes the story of women's entry into government so fascinating.

Trailblazers is an introduction to the numerous women who stepped for the first time into the governing bodies of their country. It is definitely not a comprehensive survey: not every woman, not every country is included. Instead, I have tried to provide a sense of the multi-dimensional and political diversity of the many extraordinary individuals who shaped the destiny of their own country, and indeed sometimes the world, usually for the better, occasionally for the worse. The book therefore has a wide geographical spread: Europe, the Middle East, Africa, Australasia, the Caribbean, the Pacific and the Americas are all covered. Within this spread, I have selected specific women from different countries, some small, some large, some powerful, some less so, both to capture the spectrum of politics and philosophies and to delve into the nuances of women's various experiences. This biographical approach will – I hope – allow for a deeper reflection on both the similarities and differences in the women's individual journeys, a theme that will unfold in the book. Undoubtedly these politicians played an integral role in shaping the political systems of their country, not only by shattering glass ceilings but by leaving an indelible mark on national, and occasionally international, politics. Collectively, they altered the course of history.

Trailblazers tells the story of forty-four of these pioneering women, sometimes rescuing them from obscurity even in their own countries. For instance, my very well-educated, clever and politically engaged Hungarian relatives had never heard of Margit Slachta, the first woman to be elected to their Parliament. For many women, I could find no books, few references and sparse Wikipedia entries. As a historian, I am used to archival work, the white gloves on my hands becoming grubbier by the day as I read sources which had not been seen since they were deposited. I had neither the money, the time, the language or the visas to travel across the globe, attempting to find information. So, I wrote to embassies and consulates. I discovered that I was using a new way of researching history, relying on the good will of staff across the world to tell me about the remarkable women in their country, provide original sources and put me in contact with librarians and others who could help. I have thanked them all in my acknowledgements. My research strategy is a story in itself, glimpses of which you will find in some of the chapters.

Chapter One

The First Trailblazers, 1900–1918: Finland, Russia, USA

Modern history was made in Finland. On 23 May 1907, the country astonished the world by electing nineteen women to its 200-strong Parliament, the Eduskunta. Previously, throughout the democratic world women had played no part in a governing body: parliament had been exclusively male. The women elected represented all social classes: from maids and factory workers to schoolteachers and noblewomen. As a non-Finnish English woman, how could I discover material about them? A quick email to the Finnish embassy resulted in an even quicker reply from Pirjo Pellinen, who supplied websites in Finnish. I was on my way. I chose Hilda Käkikoski from those elected, partly because I was intrigued to find out how and why a cross-dressing lesbian, feminist, and vegetarian teacher became one of the first women in the world to enter government.

Käkikoski lived at a time when Finland was part of the Russian Empire. The Russian Tsar had permitted Finnish women to vote and stand for election but had not granted Russian women the same rights. In 1917, this changed quickly and dramatically when the Tsarist autocratic system was swept away by two revolutions, creating new opportunities for women. Alexandra Kollontai, a socialist feminist with a Finnish background, was one of ten women appointed to the new Russian government.

Across the Atlantic, a quieter, slowly evolving revolution was underway. After a long campaign by suffrage activists, a few western states in the USA granted women voting rights and the right to stand for election to the federal government. Montana was one of these and it was here that Jeannette Rankin became the first-ever woman to be elected to the American House of Representatives.

Finland: Hilda Käkikoski (1864–1912)

Everything about Hilda Käkikoski shouted liberalism. Paradoxically, she stood as a Conservative candidate. She was a member of the Old Finnish Party (FP), a nationalist party which promoted the Finnish language and Finnish ideals. However, she did not fit in here easily either. Elected as an FP representative, she continually shocked her Conservative colleagues by her unconventional dress, openly lesbian lifestyle and her refusal to promote some of the Finnish Party programme.[1]

The election of these first nineteen women occurred unexpectedly. In 1906, Finland was still part of the Tsarist Empire until unrest in Russia, an unsuccessful war with Japan, and strikes in Finland forced the Tsar to concede power. In 1906 the Tsar granted Finland Home Rule. The Tsarist Grand Duchy of Finland, with its semi-feudal Diet of four estates, was replaced by a single chamber Parliament, elected by all adults over the age of twenty-three. It was a great leap forward.[2] Suddenly, the old-style autocratic system was replaced by a modern Parliament. From one of Europe's most unpromising countries for women's emancipation, Finland overnight became the most democratic.[3]

How does one become a trailblazer? Sometimes a political path is obvious, sometimes it is surprising. Nothing in Hilda's early life suggested a political career. Hilda Maria Sjöström was born on New Year's Eve 1864 in a small village, Porlammi, Lapinjärvi, Finland. Her father Johannes, a blacksmith from a Baltic-Finnic tribe known as Karelians, died of pneumonia when she was two. Her mother Liisa, from a Lithuanian background, remarried someone from the Swedish area who spoke no Finnish. As a young girl, Hilda was quite a tomboy, preferring to help her stepfather in his work rather than assist her mother with housework. Hilda was undoubtedly clever, and quite precocious, taking advantage of Finland's highly

Image 1   Hilda Käkikoski (1864–1912),
courtesy of the Embassy of Finland, London.

regarded education system. She enjoyed writing. When she
was thirteen her first article (on poachers) was published in the
local newspaper.

In 1874, aged fourteen, she won a scholarship to a girls'
school in Helskinki and cut her hair short. This was thought
eccentric. In the late nineteenth century long hair was not
merely a fashion statement but carried complex layers of meaning. It was a symbol of femininity and a marker of women's
adherence to social norms. Hilda's decision to break with these
traditions made an immediately obvious statement: she was
different. Her first year at the school was challenging. Hilda
had very little money. She boarded with poor families, could
not always afford food and was very lonely.

At the time, the language of government was Swedish.[4]
Hilda hated this. In her view, it was shameful that Finns were
forced to speak the Swedish language. Hilda, proud of her
Finnish heritage, changed her name to Käkikoski because
it sounded more Finnish than her own. Her birth name,

Sjöström, was of Swedish origin and Hilda's emerging Finnish nationalism rejected any association with the dominant country. After school she worked as a governess before enrolling in 1885 at the Finnish Graduate College university, which since 1870 allowed women to study and take their degrees. While an undergraduate, Hilda consolidated her feminism and her Finnishness.

In 1888, shortly after graduating as a teacher of Finnish language and history, Käkikoski began translating Martin Luther's sermons from German into Finnish. Encouraged by their success, she translated several other works, focusing on those written by women. Her writing career was given a boost by Zacharias Topelius, Professor of Nordic history, Rector of Helsinki University and a well-known Finnish poet and novelist. In 1894 Topelius invited her to his summer house in Koivuniemi where he encouraged her to write, often casting a friendly critical eye on her poetry. Hilda not only wrote poetry but also children's songs and short stories, and began a four-volume history of Finland.[5]

Patriotism was the guiding principle in Hilda Käkikoski's life. In 1895, now aged 31, she was awarded a doctorate in Finnish and Nordic history by the University of Helsinki and began teaching history and the *Kalevala* (the land of the Heroes) at folk schools.[6] Hilda loved the *Kalevala*, an epic poem about the creation of earth and the magical mythical development of Finland. It remains a significant part of Finnish culture: places, banks, a dairy company, a construction business and a jewellery firm are all named after one or another of the heroes and heroines of the poem. The poems, centring on good versus evil, light versus the dark, helped consolidate national identity. The Finns (of course) represented good and light; foreigners, the dark and evil. Writers and composers were inspired by the *Kalevala*: Tolkein's *Lord of the Rings*, Longfellow's *Hiawatha*, Sibelius' *Finlandia* and even a Donald Duck story were shaped by these folk tales.[7]

One can imagine the young, eccentric, unorthodox, enthusiastic Hilda captivating her students by reciting lines from the *Kalevala* about the strong women who inhabit the mythical tales.

In primeval times, a maiden, . . .
In a solitude of ether,
She descended to the ocean,
Waves her couch, and waves her pillow,
Thereupon the rising storm-wind
Flying from the East in fierceness,
Whips the ocean into surges,
Strikes the stars with sprays of ocean
Till the waves are white with fervour.

At university, Hilda had become interested in feminism and votes for women. In 1889 she joined the Finnish Women's Association (FWA), which had close ties with the Finnish Party, a nationalist party which promoted the use of the Finnish language. Soon she was writing for the association's magazine and in 1895 was elected its vice-president. The FWA had a wider agenda than suffrage, advocating equal rights in education, employment, an equal standard of sexual morality, all with a nationalistic emphasis. Here, Hilda fell in love with a few of her fellow women students and colleagues, all FWA members.[8]

For someone who was a member of the Conservative Finnish Party, Hilda had a remarkable sexual life. Women's organisations like the FWA provided Hilda not just with a platform for activism but a chance to socialise with women with similar beliefs, values and sexual orientation. Same-sex relationships were illegal in Finland, punishable by up to two years in prison. This did not stop Hilda developing relationships with several women. Her earliest was with another schoolteacher and activist, Fanny Pajula, with whom she lived for several years until

Fanny died in 1895. She was later romantically involved with married Hilda Ennola, American Frances Weiss, deaconess Hanna Masalin and political activist Helmi Kivalo.[9] Käkikoski proved an able speaker, touring the country as a representative of the FWA, often riding her bicycle to outlying districts to deliver her lecture 'Women's Issues as a Question of Life in the Fatherland', a mixture of feminism and nationalism. In her lectures, she emphasised the need for schools and universities to be open to girls, the right of women to work outside the home, and to enjoy the same overall rights as men. Girls, she argued, should have the opportunity to become teachers, doctors, judges and even shepherds if they wished. Her emphasis was always on women's right to vote. Is it right, she insisted, that one half of a nation was born to rule and the other half to be ruled?

In 1904, now aged forty, Hilda focused on her writing career, concentrating on history and women's rights. Her children's songs, poetry and short stories were popular. Soon her life was interrupted by a new political career: the Conservative-leaning Finnish Party nominated her as a candidate. She was concerned that she would have to give up her writing, especially her proposed four-volume history of Finland. Her mentor Danielson-Kalmar told her 'Now is not the time to write history, but to make history.'

In 1906 Hilda Käkikoski put her patriotism into practice by running for election as a representative of the Finnish Party. She spent five gruelling months travelling across the country, gathering support. Five women took turns travelling with her, making sure she was well fed and had a comfortable bed to sleep in. One wealthy merchant gave her a high-quality sledge and two bear claws, saying that Miss Käkikoski was a national treasure who needed to be looked after. Bears were revered in Finnish mythology as symbolising strength and courage, so in giving two claws to Miss Käkikoski, the merchant hoped to pass the bear's characteristics on to his admired would-be politician.

Käkikoski's election meetings, sometimes lasting five or six hours, focused on her passions: the constitution, temperance, chastity, suffrage, workers and peasant rights, votes for women and the importance of her mother tongue. The election campaign took place in winter. Käkikoski braved cold, frosty weather, travelling along snow-bound roads in her new sledge to meetings in outlying districts. Sometimes she spoke to small groups, at others to thousands of people. She began campaigning in her home village, Uusimaa, hoping to use her old school as an election base. When the teacher refused, she relocated her meeting to a freezingly cold house. Dressed in all her winter clothes she spoke to the villagers packed in tight, all standing because there was no room for chairs.

In March 1907 Hilda Käkikoski was elected MP for the Finnish Party, winning with the highest number of votes in her district, the province of Uusimaa, one of nineteen women and 181 men. Her party did not win the election but as the second largest was able to influence policy.[10] Once in the Eduskunta, Hilda focused on women's rights. She prepared carefully, only too aware that, as one of the first women ever to be elected to a governing body, the whole world was watching. She gathered information about women, visited school boards, researched the pay and conditions of women employed in the postal service and railways, before drafting her first parliamentary proposal for the right of women to apply for public office. Her passion was education. She spoke with colleagues about the need for youth clubs, folk schools and workers' colleges and of the need for universal compulsory education. She drafted the Finnish Party programme for the reform of elementary education, particularly the need for school meals. From her own experience, she knew that children could not concentrate if they were hungry. The money was granted for subsidised school meals.

Her other passion was women's rights, some of which clashed with party policy. Undeterred, Käkikoski worked across the party divide, joining the other women politicians to raise the age of marriage from fifteen to eighteen and increase mothers' rights over their children. She also worked for equal pay for teachers, women's eligibility for public office and women's freedom to work, all of which was contrary to Finnish Party policy. Her feminism had limits. In June 1907, she spoke against a proposal granting unmarried mothers child allowance. Käkikoski was – strangely hypocritical given her lesbianism – a strong advocate of chastity, asking Parliament to set a budget to promote it. She also devoted a large part of her parliamentary time to speak out against prostitution and venereal disease.

Hilda Käkikoski's tenure in the Eduskunta was short-lived: she did not stand in the 1910 election because of poor health. Finnish parliamentary independence was equally fleeting. Nicolas II's Prime Minister, Pyotr Stolypin, shut down the Finnish Parliament and Finland reverted to a monarchist dictatorship until the 1917 Russian revolution. In 1912, Käkikoski died, aged 48, with her four-volume history unfinished. She was buried in Karjalohja, alongside her companion Hilda Ennola.[11] She never lived to see an independent Finland.

Finland remained part of Russia until two revolutions severed the bond that connected them. In March, the abdication of the Tsar, the Grand Duke of Finland, meant that the country was no longer governed by Russia. No Tsar, no Grand Duke, no Russian control. On 2 November 1917, the new Bolshevik government affirmed the right of self-determination for the people in the Russian Empire. Finland immediately issued a declaration of independence. For the first time in centuries, Finland was a free and independent country.

Russia: Alexandra Kollontai (1872–1952)

A woman with a Finnish background, who believed in a different version of feminism from Käkikoski, was appointed to the newly created Bolshevik government: Alexandra Kollontai.[12] Alexandra was a completely different character, abandoning a life of noble idleness for the ordeals of a revolutionary. Kollontai achieved a trailblazing triple-first. She was one of ten women, all socialist revolutionaries, who were the first female politicians to take part in any Russian government.[13] She was also the first woman to serve in a government cabinet, and the world's first female Ambassador.

Kollontai was another surprise candidate for high politics. Born Alexandra Domontovich (1872–1952), she was from an aristocratic family, destined to get married to another aristocrat and spend her life looking after her husband and children. Her military father, General Domontovich, was a nobleman who proudly traced his ancestry back to the thirteenth century, a family that for centuries had served in the Tsarist Empire. The General had fought in the Russo-Turkish war, and had acted as a Military Consul in Sofia, Bulgaria. Her mother's social status was far removed from that of the General. Alexandra Masalina was from peasant stock, the daughter of a Finnish tradesman and a half-Russian and half-French woman. Her parents were rich, having made a fortune in supplying timber to St Petersburg, but the class bias in Russia meant that people frowned upon such a marriage. Alexandra, named after her mother, was their only child.[14]

Her aristocratic family background on one side and her rich peasant heritage on the other undoubtedly affected the young Alexandra. She was destined to stand apart. Her parents, keen for their daughter to fit in, ensured that she was well educated in music and languages, the prerequisites of a young lady in Russian society. As well as Russian, Alexandra was fluent in Finnish, French, German, Italian, English and Bulgarian. She could also speak Ukrainian. She spoke French with her mother, Finnish on her grandfather's Finnish estate and English with her nanny. Undoubtedly, her linguistic skills were exemplary. Alexandra's desire to attend university was dismissed by her mother, who argued that it was unnecessary for someone destined for marriage and motherhood.

At around the age of 18, in company with other aristocratic young women, Alexandra entered Russian society, attending balls, theatres, the opera and endless private parties. She was both beautiful and rich, 'ranked high in St Petersburg's brides' market' and could have married an equally wealthy aristocrat.[15] Her mother, keen to make a 'good match' for her daughter, was 'bent upon marrying me off at a very early age'.[16] Alexandra, as with her parents before her, chose someone considered particularly unsuitable: a penniless cousin and engineering student, Vladimir Kollontai. After fruitless attempts by her parents to stop the marriage, Alexandra married her love, and soon gave birth to her only son, Mikhail.

In 1896, the newly married Mrs Kollontai experienced a sudden and profound change of belief. Accompanying her husband, Vladimir, to one of the biggest textile factories in Russia, Alexandra witnessed at first hand the appalling working and living conditions of those employed there. She spoke passionately about their dwellings, of rooms filled with wooden bunks with rags piled on top, of men and women workers sleeping side by side, of windows boarded over. She was particularly upset when she noticed a little boy the same age as her son 'who was lying very still . . . the child was dead'.[17] Boris Pasternak's novel, *Doctor Zhivago*, later made into a film, conjures up the vile atmosphere and shocking conditions endured by workers in these factories.

By now, Alexandra was forging new friendships with social democrats and revolutionaries who encouraged her to read about social issues, took her to lectures and involved her in semi-legal societies. She was taking her first steps upon her revolutionary journey. In 1899, she left her husband to concentrate on her political work. She visited England where she met Sidney and Beatrice Webb and toured mainland Europe where she became friends with the luminaries of revolutionary politics: Rosa Luxemburg, Paul Lafarge, Karl Kautsky and George Plekhanov. Back home in Russia, and enthused by these experiences, Alexandra joined the illegal revolutionary Social Democratic Party (SDP) and began working underground, writing and distributing illicit leaflets, holding secret meetings and plotting revolution. In 1903 the SDP split into the Bolsheviks and the Mensheviks and Kollontai was forced to take sides. Plekhanov, a leader of the Mensheviks, persuaded her to join his faction; the other was led by Vladimir Ilyich Ulyanov, known as Lenin.

Alexandra Kollontai became a seasoned revolutionary, speaking at meetings, writing pamphlets and participating in subversive activities. Her first book, *The Life of the Finnish Workers: An Economic Study*, published in 1903, was the result of her love of Finland, 'whose independence and relative freedom were being threatened by the reactionary policy of the Tsarist regime'.[18] She used her personal links and her language ability to describe the exploitation, poverty and repression in Tsarist-controlled Finland. She emphasised the need to recognise and support the national aspirations of the oppressed people within the Russian Empire. When the Bolsheviks seized power, Alexandra's knowledge of Finland was used to frame its policy of national self-determination.

Kollontai was an engaging speaker, particularly on women's rights. Her mentors were Clara Zetkin and Rosa Luxembourg, both of whom saw socialism and feminism as inextricably linked. Kollontai shared the same political philosophy and throughout her life fought for the rights of working-class women. In 1907, inspired by the more experienced Luxembourg and Zetkin, she founded the first Working Women's Club, committed to drawing 'a clear line of demarcation between

the bourgeois suffragettes and the women's liberation movement of the working-class'.[19] Bourgeois feminists, she believed,
merely wanted equality with men of their class and had little
desire to upset the economic order or the class system. In
contrast, Kollontai insisted that only the demise of capitalism could bring about true equality for women. Her book, *The
Social Basis of the Women's Question*, fleshed out these ideas
and led to an intensive debate among feminists and their allies.

By this time, Kollontai had attracted police attention and in
1908 was forced into exile. First, she went to Germany where
she worked closely with Clara Zetkin. From then until 1917 she
was a revolutionary itinerant, a political refugee who earned
her living by speaking at socialist meetings across the world
on Marxist theory, feminism and the situation in her native
Russia. In the middle of suffragette violence and the increasing
demand for votes for women on the same terms as men (a
suffrage based on property qualifications) she and Zetkin were
invited by the British Socialist Party to speak on adult suffrage,
a less popular but a more democratic demand which was supported by women like the first future British Cabinet Minister,
Margaret Bondfield.[20] During her exile, Kollontai wrote the
most important book of her life, *Society and Motherhood*,
a volume of over 600 pages, analysing welfare legislation in
Europe and offering a radically new version of motherhood
and the family.

The outbreak of the First World War, the abdication
of the Tsar and two revolutions in her own country led to
Kollontai's revising her political position. She shifted from
Kerensky's Menshevism and became a Bolshevik. On 8 March
1917, International Women's Day, the women of St Petersburg,
Russia – factory workers, soldiers' wives and peasants – left
their homes and their work to protest in the streets about the
shortage of food and consumer goods, the high prices, and the
queues lengthened by the privations of war. Two days later
women invaded the military barracks, stole guns and persuaded

the soldiers to join them. Everyone in the city stopped work, prisoners were released from the city gaols, students left their university, police and soldiers went missing from their posts to join the protests. Kollontai commented that 'Russian women raised the torch of proletarian revolution and set the world on fire.'[21] The revolution spontaneously initiated by women proved unstoppable. In March Tsar Nicholas II abdicated; a month later Kollontai, along with many other revolutionaries, returned to Russia and was elected to both the Petrograd Soviet and the Central Committee. Not all Russians welcomed her return and she was subjected to vicious attacks. She was called the 'Valkyrie of the revolution' by her opponents, accused of taking German money to buy her elegant clothes, arrested by Kerensky's Menshevik Provisional Government and sentenced to hard labour for three months.[22]

Lenin called the uprising a 'petticoat rebellion', criticised the newly formed 'Provisional' government and led a second revolution which swept the Bolsheviks to power. Kollontai, now a committed Bolshevik, was elected People's Commissar for Social Welfare, the only woman elected to the Central Committee, the new government. She was the first female in the world to hold a ministerial post, and used her position to further the interests of women, helping to frame much of the Bolsheviks' social legislation.

As People's Commissar of Social Welfare, Kollontai was responsible for the war-disabled, orphanages, hostels for the homeless and the transfer of priests to the civil service. She was also tasked with setting up a free public health system. It was a challenge. The orphanages, ironically known as 'angel factories', were overcrowded, lacked sanitation and decent food and employed too few staff to look after often severely damaged children. Modern children's homes were to be set up in their place. Kollontai turned one previous 'angel factory' into a maternity home. She and her assistants cleaned and painted the dilapidated building, put up curtains, set up a nursery, a medical centre and a library. Hundreds of pregnant women registered to have their babies at the new home. On the day it was due to open, it was burned down, destroyed by people who detested Kollontai's politics.[23]

In November 1918, Kollontai and a few of her female comrades organised an All-Russian Congress of Women Workers and Women Peasants. When Kollontai asked the government for a venue which would accommodate around a hundred women she was told not to bother as few would turn up. In fact, most of her male comrades were unimpressed with Kollontai's commitment to women's equality. To their surprise, over a thousand women, mostly peasants in their sheepskin coats and felt boots who had made long and difficult journeys across war zones, came to listen to the women revolutionaries. In her speech, Kollontai spoke of setting up nurseries, laundries and canteens to set women free from domestic chores and endless childcare. The Congress was such a huge success that the Bolsheviks agreed to elect women in every factory and village to find out what women needed and report back to the Women's Commission headed by Kollontai. Shortly after, the government set up a new Women's Department, the Zhenotdel, an autonomous women's organisation. The Bolsheviks, influenced by Kollontai and the Zhenotdel, introduced equal pay and the right to an 8-hour day; made marriage secular, criminalised domestic violence, set the age of marriage at 18 for men and 16 for women and strengthened women's right to alimony payments; they legalised abortion (the first country in the world to do so) and abolished illegitimacy; they allowed women to own their families' farms. The Zhenotdel ensured that women factory workers were treated fairly and with respect. It also educated women politically, provided communal refectories and laundries, and set up creches in the belief this would free them from domestic chores.

Alexandra Kollontai spent these years promoting women's rights. In her pamphlet *The Family and the Communist State* she spoke of how the revolution would spark off new gender relations based on comradeship, equality and respect rather than on outdated notions of male superiority. Many traditional Russians were outraged when she reinterpreted female sexuality, basing it on women's desire rather than traditional expectations of male satisfaction. And when she put her beliefs into practice by having an affair with a younger man who was beneath her in the social hierarchy, she shocked many in the male-dominated Bolshevik party.

The Zhenotdel was active not just in European Russia but in Uzbekistan, part of Soviet Central Asia. Here, in a majority Muslim area, women were secluded, wore a veil outside the home, and were forbidden to meet men outside the family group. Under the direction of Kollontai, the Zhenotdel set up women-only clubs, creches, medical facilities and cultural events. They also organised women-only shops where women could shop and sell their products unaccompanied. These policies were successful: over thirty women's clubs and 43 women-only clubs were opened. In 1926, over a six-month period, seventy-one thousand women saw a medical consultant. Encouraged by these successes, in 1927 the government decided to celebrate International Women's Day by encouraging women to throw off their veils. On 8 March around seventy thousand women burned their veils in public. This challenge to male power, particularly the authority of Islamic clerics, spectacularly backfired: women were attacked and sometimes murdered. Soon Uzbek women became afraid to walk in the streets, put their veils back on and returned to the home. The women's clubs, shops and co-operatives closed.[24]

By now, Kollontai was moving away from Bolshevik policies, critical of their interference in the economy and their unwillingness to consult with the trade unions. She joined the Workers Opposition, was dismissed from her directorship of the Zhenotdel and was heavily criticised for her ideas on love and the family. In 1922 the Zhenotdel had its funding drastically cut, its local groups disbanded and its plans for equal pay and other women-centred policies ignored; in 1930 it was dissolved. Abortion was banned and divorce laws were tightened.

At this time, Stalin was consolidating his power, often by eliminating his opponents and those seen to threaten his authority. Realising her own life might well be in danger, Kollontai asked Stalin to find her a new role, preferably in a remote area. Stalin, realising that murdering the popular and leading revolutionary was not a good idea, gave Kollontai the post of Soviet trade representative to Norway, thus launching her career in the diplomatic service. In February 1924, she negotiated a treaty with Norway and was rewarded by being appointed the country's USSR Ambassador, the first woman in the world ever to be appointed to this top post. She had been bred with diplomatic skills. White linen tablecloths, sparkling chandeliers, well-polished silver and heightened ambassadorial elegance did not intimidate her. She knew when and how to use her knife and fork. Her aristocratic background, her knowledge of languages and her natural charm entranced the staff of the various embassies. Her incongruities were captivating: here was a beautiful and enchanting aristocratic woman who spoke the words of a revolutionary. More crucially, she negotiated treaties in which Russia benefitted.

In 1926, in the middle of an internecine battle between Stalin and Trotsky, Kollontai was moved to Mexico. From 1927 to 1930 she returned to Norway as Ambassador, before being sent to Sweden, where she remained until 1945, well away from the centre of power, and well away from Stalin's vicious purges. In 1934, when the USSR joined the League of Nations, Kollontai was assigned to the Legal Committee, where she tried to persuade the League to adopt the principle of civil equality and to repeal discriminatory laws. In 1940, she negotiated the Finnish-Soviet peace treaty which ended the war between the two countries: Finland lost significant territory and was forced to agree to lease the Porkkala Peninsula to the Soviet Union for fifty years.

However, Stalin's bloody Terror, a period of mass repression and vindictive political persecution of anyone who might or might not prove a threat, took its toll on the health of Kollontai. She had seen her friends arrested, disappear, put in prison and murdered by the state for so-called disloyalty. Not surprisingly, she feared the worst for herself and her family. In 1942 she suffered two strokes which left one side of her body paralysed. She spent the rest of her life in a wheelchair. Ten years later she died.

Undoubtedly, Kollontai was an idealist visionary. Well versed in both Marxist and feminist theory, she was able to marry socialism and feminism into a new theoretical and practical philosophy. Her writing skill was legendary: 47 of her various articles are held in the Marx Memorial Library, London, helpfully translated into English by one of its members.

America: Jeanette Rankin (1880–1973)

Jeanette Rankin was a feminist who had more in common with Käkikoski than with Kollontai. She, like Käkikoski, was a natural Conservative, but one who sat uneasily within its ranks, and one who was not afraid to challenge the policies of her party. In November 1916, for the first time in its history, Americans elected a woman to the House of Representatives: the 36-year-old Jeanette Rankin became the Republican representative of Montana, a state which had granted votes for women two years earlier. This was four years before most white American women were allowed to vote and a life-time away before Native Americans and women of colour were able to cast their ballots.[25]

Jeanette Rankin was born in Montana, nine years before it officially became a state of the USA. The northwest American county was a frontier state, a land of cowboys, ranchers and miners, pioneers drawn to the vast prairies, lured by its mineral wealth and willing to appropriate land from the indigenous population. Three years before Jeanette was born, the US army was defeated at the Battle of the Little Bighorn, known as Custer's last stand, by an alliance between three Native American warrior groups. It was a pyrrhic victory: within a year white Americans had asserted control and Native Americans were forced onto reservations. Jeannette was old enough to be aware of the massacre of every child, woman and man at the Indian mission not far from where she lived. She saw the husband of the local schoolteacher wearing a Native American scalp on his belt.

White settlers in the American west practised gender equality: taming the land was a struggle, both in terms of guarding against the Native Americans whose lands they had stolen, and in terms of tilling, planting and reaping crops from the virgin soil. The fifteen-year-old Jeanette must have heard about legendary 'Black Mary', otherwise known as 'Stagecoach Mary', who in 1895 was the first woman, and the first African-American, to work for the US Postal Service, driving a stagecoach across the state of Montana to deliver mail. Mary was fearless, protecting herself from bandits and wild animals with a range of guns, often hidden under her apron.

Jeanette's parents were pioneers. Her father, John Rankin, had left Ontario, Canada, to come to wild, unexplored Montana in search of gold. His prospecting was unsuccessful and he turned to the building trade, constructing the first bridge across the river as well as a church, shops and houses for the new settlers. Soon he had made enough money to buy a ranch, marry the local schoolteacher, Olive Pickering, and start a family. Their first-born was Jeannette. In about 1885 the family moved into the town where John built an imposing three-storey house with hot and cold running water, a wood-burning stove and a bathroom with a zinc tub, unheard of luxuries in Missoula. Each summer Jeannette spent her holidays at the ranch, where she helped with the typical household tasks of cleaning, sewing, canning fruit and vegetables, looking after the chickens and caring for her five younger siblings. She also chopped wood, built fires, helped with the farm machinery and built sidewalks.[26]

With her father's encouragement, she studied at Montana State University, Missoula, living at home while she did so. In 1902 she graduated with a BSc and looked around for a career. She tried teaching, she tried dressmaking and in 1904, when her father died, she moved to Boston where her brother was studying. Boston was a city of two halves: Harvard and the slums. For the first time in her life, Jeannette witnessed white poverty, disease and squalor, where children went hungry and adults were worn out from a lifetime of low pay, long hours, unhealthy working conditions and living in overcrowded tenements.

Back at home she had a crisis of identity. Bored, and not knowing what to do with her life, she left for San Francisco where she spent four months at the Telegraph Hill Association, a settlement house which helped impoverished female immigrants and their children. Here she realised her life's ambition: to be a social worker. For this she needed something other than a BSc. In 1908 Jeannette enrolled at the New York School of Philanthropy, taking morning lessons in economics, sociology and public speaking and spending the afternoons and evenings in the Bowery, a downtrodden part of the city, full of disreputable tenements, saloons, pawnshops and prostitutes. Her studies convinced her that poverty could be ended by efficient government.

It was here too that she discovered a new direction: votes for women. The college was composed mainly of women, most of whom were dedicated suffragists. Jeanette set to work, all the time learning how to canvass, organise a campaign, fundraise, engage in debates and reach out to male voters to persuade them to support votes for women. In 1911 she was offered a post at \$50 a month with the New York Woman Suffrage Party. One of her jobs was to stand on a soap box in the middle of a street and speak up in support of votes for women, good practice for the rough and tumble of political life. From here she became a roving activist, travelling in trains and coaches across the country and gaining support for women's suffrage. She was so successful that in 1913 she was appointed Field Secretary for the National American Suffrage Association, which meant even more journeys, criss-crossing the country to visit around fifteen states.

In her home state of Montana, she visited every mining village and settlement, blazing 1,300 miles in 25 days on the suffrage trail, often across unwelcoming territory.[27] Her campaign eventually led to victory: in 1914 Montana joined ten other states which allowed women to vote and stand for Congress. One of her biographers claims that 'the triumph of the suffragists in Montana was her creation . . . she was the driving force. She had been the first to see the opportunity, she was the chief propagandist, the leading organiser, the architect of the victory.'[28] She was developing the attributes of a good leader.

Jeannette Rankin realised that if a woman was elected to Congress, she could fight for national women's suffrage within it. In 1916, now well known because of her suffrage activism, she took her next political step by announcing her candidacy as a Republican. When asked about her political leanings she commented, 'I never was a Republican. I ran on the Republican ticket.'[29] Indeed, she ignored her party's programme and ran on a platform promoting woman suffrage, child welfare, labour and agricultural reform, and peace.

Her suffrage campaign experience helped: she was a good public speaker, had high-level organisational skills, was an assiduous worker and knew that she needed to get out and speak to voters. She travelled all over the state by car and trains across the plains, over mountains, captivating listeners on street corners and railway stations, knocking on doors to speak to housewives, meeting men at factory gates, chatting to men outside saloons and pool halls, holding meetings in one-room schools and at pot-luck suppers. She attributed her success to the women of Montana: she gained votes from Democrats as well as Republicans, from women keen to elect the first female Congresswoman.

In November 1916, after 140 years of a male-only Congress, the first female legislator was appointed. In her press statement Rankin promised to represent all American women, introduce laws for an eight-hour day, equal pay for equal work and a federal suffrage amendment. It was not a classic Republican speech.

Wearing a dark blue silk suit with a white collar and cuffs, Miss Rankin entered Congress for the first time. In one hand was a bunch of purple and yellow flowers given to her by suffragists, the other held the arm of a Montana colleague who accompanied her down the Congressional aisle. Both sides of the House, Democrat and Republican, jostled to shake her hand and all cheered her as she entered and sat down. She was, after all, making American history. When she stepped forward to take her oath, both Republicans and Democrats stood to applaud her.

These flattering gestures were not to last. Immediately, she stepped into a hotbed of controversy. Most of Europe was at war and Americans wanted to support their friends. On 2 April 1917, just a few days after Rankin's very first day in Congress, President Wilson asked permission to go to war against Germany to make the world safe for democracy. On 6 April, after a few days of intense debate, the vote took place. As the only woman to enter the House, 433 male eyes were upon Congresswoman Rankin. She voted against war, one of a small minority of fifty. It was a brave decision, as she was pressurised by suffragists, by political allies, by her family and her best friends to vote in favour of the war. She knew the weight of history was upon her, often weeping during the debate, knowing that her decision would generate headlines. When she arose to vote she made a simple statement: 'I love my country, but I cannot vote for war.' The fearless – or maybe foolhardy – decision to stand up for her beliefs was a hall mark of her identity. She was vilified by the press, her colleagues, and leaders of the suffrage movement. Her refusal to capitulate led to widespread condemnation: one newspaper stated that she was 'a dagger in the hands of the German propagandists, a dupe of the Kaiser, a member of the Hun army in the United States, and a crying schoolgirl'.[30] Jeanette Rankin knew that her Congressional career was over.

Throughout her life, Rankin remained a committed pacifist. In her opinion, the deaths of people could be avoided by diplomacy. War, she insisted, was not a way to deal with world problems: too many young bodies were blown up, too many bodies buried in strange lands, too many parents bereaved. 'There can', she argued, 'be no compromise with war; it cannot be reformed or controlled; cannot be disciplined into decency or codified into common sense; for war is the slaughter of human beings, temporarily regarded as enemies, on as large a scale as possible.'[31] She had once stated that 'a person can be shot, but an idea cannot. Killing is the antithesis of life . . . a dead enemy cannot become our friend. And the ideal dies within us when we violate it.'[32]

Meanwhile, the Congresswoman from Montana still had two years left to make a difference. Jeanette Rankin's relatively less controversial focus was votes for women. She entered politics through the suffrage movement and throughout her life lived and breathed feminism. On 24 September 1917 she stood up in Congress to support a Democratic resolution to set up a Committee on women's suffrage. Congress agreed and appointed Congresswoman Rankin to the Committee. On 3 January 1918 the House Committee on Woman Suffrage began its hearings. Six days later, President Wilson agreed to a Federal amendment to give women the vote and asked Jeanette Rankin to open the debate. Her passionate speech referred to Wilson's statement about protecting European democracy. 'How shall we explain to them the meaning of democracy', she argued, 'if the same Congress that voted to make the world safe for democracy refuses to give this small measure of democracy to the women of our country?'[33] The motion passed the House, only to fail in the Senate. Nonetheless, the tide was turning. Miss Rankin's first term in Congress may not have brought about any immediate change but she shifted the political weather. A year later, the Nineteenth Amendment to the United States Constitution awarded votes for women. Every woman in every state now had the right to vote.

When the Amendment passed, Jeannette Rankin was not in Congress. The representative from Montana had lost her seat, largely because of her anti-war stance. The peace issue took over her life. In 1919 she attended the Women's International Peace Conference in Switzerland, a meeting which formalised the Women's International League for Peace and Freedom (WILPF). The conference coincided with the publication of the terms of the Treaty of Versailles. The seeds of future wars, the WILPF argued, were sown by its terms. Today it is the oldest active women's peace organisation in the world, with sections in 37 countries. Its commitment to women and minority rights, an end to the arm's trade, and economic and social justice rang out throughout the twentieth century.[34]

Rankin spent most of the 1920s and 1930s working in peace organisations from her one-room secluded home in Georgia. Jeannette was not poor. She received an allowance from her brother and an annuity from her late father but she lived as if she was deprived: her house had no running water, an outside lavatory, no heating and no home comforts. Here, in her out-of-the-way cottage, she founded the Georgia Peace Society. In the 1920s she was appointed a paid organiser for the National Council for the Prevention of War, once again touring the country promoting her ideas.[35] Jeanette Rankin was able to do this both because of family financial support and because she remained single – she said she had no wish to be a 'baby factory'. Some believe she was a lesbian: she was certainly woman-centred, maintaining an intimate long-lasting friendship with the journalist and author Katherine Anthony. Miss Rankin raged against those who financially benefitted by war. She characterised war as a 'rich man's war fought by poor men'. Dead men, she argued, made money for certain businesses. The profit made by the United States Steel Corporation during the First World War was one billion dollars, equal to the pay of two million soldiers.[36] In her view, the greed of munition manufacturers – whom she called merchants of death – would lead to further war. The immense profits made from cannon, guns, ammunition, tanks, aircraft and naval ships, all consumables that needed replacing, encouraged munition makers and those who financed them to portray war as a patriotic enterprise, rather than a menace to society. Preparation for war leads to war, she argued, further suggesting that if a country was to have peace, then they must prepare for it. It was not a typical Republican speech. Moreover, most Americans disagreed too, believing that war was essential to protect freedom. They praised famous military men, erected statues of famous warriors, and made movies celebrating the killing of enemies. It was hard to sustain the arguments for peace.

By the mid-1930s parts of the world were at war: Japan invaded China; the Italians invaded Ethiopia; there was a civil war in Spain; Adolf Hitler and his German Nazis took over Austria and had further expansionist aims. Together, these extreme right-wing governments threatened world peace. On 5 June 1940, Jeanette Rankin, fearful that America might be drawn into another world conflict, stood for a seat in Congress. Her slogan 'Prepare to the limit for defence, keep our men out of Europe', appealed to many.[37] After a 22-year gap, Jeannette Rankin was again a Congresswoman, elected by Montanans who agreed with her pacifist sentiments. Once in Congress, she used her time to speak up against war. But once again, the American tide was turning, particularly when Hitler invaded Belgium, Denmark, France, Poland and the Netherlands and was bombing Britain. America, shocked by Nazi aggression, now favoured intervention.[38]

On 8 December 1941, one day after Japanese warplanes bombed the American navy base in Pearl Harbor, Hawaii, the President asked the House of Representatives to declare war. The House voted 388–1. Only one voice spoke against war: sixty-year-old Jeannette Rankin. The rest of the representatives booed and catcalled; each time she rose to speak she was shouted down. When she cast her vote, she said 'As a woman I can't go to war, and I refuse to send anyone else.'[39] This time the backlash was more vitriolic than before: venomous letters, irate phone calls, unsympathetic comments from passers-by were hurled at her. She was called a 'bitch', 'old fossil', Hitler aid' and a 'disgrace and a traitor'.[40] Denunciations from the press followed, all accusing her of a lack of patriotism. The Cowpokes Union telegraphed to say 'in view of the way you botched up the last branding we would like you to have you saddle up your bronc, tie your bed roll on behind and just ride home'.[41] This one act of defiance had made her a target of public hate.

When Miss Rankin finished her term in Congress she decided not to run again. She knew she would lose. Once more, it seemed as if her political career was over. She may have dropped from public view but Jeanette continued with her peace campaign, read the works of Gandhi, visited India and travelled the world. In the late 1960s, the war in Vietnam put Jeanette Rankin back in the public eye. As bodies piled up, pressure built up against the war. In January 1968, now aged 87, Rankin led 5,000 women, all dressed in black, to Capitol Hill, Washington, to oppose the Vietnam war. As ever, she viewed war as based on male arrogance and brute force, a force which was oppressive to women.

On 18 May 1973, Jeannette Rankin died, aged 92. In her will, she left a small house and money in trust to a neighbouring black family. The rest of her estate was set aside to help 'mature, unemployed women workers'. The fund has awarded more than 1.8 million dollars to more than 700 women over the age of 35. Today she is remembered mainly as a peace activist. However, she wanted to be remembered 'as the only woman who ever voted to give women the right to vote'.

What do a nationalist, a revolutionary and a pacifist have in common? War and/or revolution affected all three women, providing power vacuums which enabled two of them to be elected. All considered themselves feminists. It is not the object of this book to offer an analysis of the various types of feminism – there is a large body of literature that examines this. However, what this chapter confirms, is that feminism takes various forms. The socialist feminism of Alexandra Kollontai would perhaps be abhorrent to both Hilda Käkikoski and Jeanette Rankin. And yet, each of these politicians challenged patriarchal norms, shared a common belief in equal rights and opportunities for women and reversed the general expectations of the period.

Their defiance came at a cost: both Kollontai and Rankin were either sidelined or lost power because they dared to question the masculine nature of their respective governments. Undoubtedly, all these women were unconventional, out of step with the norms and expectations of their respective cultures. All cared less about what society thought about their sometimes odd behaviour but cared deeply about the conditions and injustices affecting women's lives, and the need to create change. All challenged not just conventional norms of femininity but also the ideas of their own political parties, leading to them being marginalised or – as in the case of Jeannette Rankin – considered persona non grata. Regardless of the nature of their feminism, these three women marked a path through the dense thickets and brambles of male-only forests that would indicate the way for other women to follow. [42]

Chapter Two

The Aftermath of War, 1918–1930: Britain, Canada, Germany, Austria, Hungary, China

Open graves full of mud and the remains of fallen soldiers. Shells crashing around day and night, shaking the nerves of men trapped in the trenches. The constant threat of bullets and gas; the constant itch of fleas. Death in the First World War was everyday life. Like some wars, this one was a catalyst for change, dissolving old systems and offering new styles of government. Certainly, the aftermath of the First World War transformed the map of Europe, redrew national boundaries and marked a transformative period for women's rights. A new world order emerged as the familiar norms of society were disrupted by the emergence of women in governing bodies. Several countries with a long-established secure parliamentary system, often with a constitutional monarchy, expanded their democratic base and gave women the vote. In Belgium, Denmark, the Netherlands and Sweden full suffrage was granted, in Britain privileged women over the age of thirty, and in Canada women, except those from the First Nations, were given the vote.[1] At the same time, for the first time in their histories, women were allowed to stand for Parliament.

The collapse and the defeat of three great imperialist powers, Austro-Hungary, Germany, and the Ottoman Empire, led to the creation or restructuring of countries. New democratic republics were formed in Armenia (1919), Czechoslovakia (1918), Estonia (1920), Georgia (1919), Latvia (1922), Lithuania (1918) and Poland. The Imperial dynastic regime of Austria-Hungary broke up into two separate countries. Germany's Emperor was dethroned and forced into exile. The Ottoman Empire was disbanded. In one defeated nation after another, new forms of government were created from these former autocracies. Democracy emerged, wobbled and then collapsed in the countries of these old Empires, but not before they had, in a spirit of modernisation, elected women to their legislative bodies. The First World War, which had been hailed as a war 'to make the world safe for democracy', had seemingly achieved its aim, and women were to be part of it.[2]

Meanwhile, in the Far East, different but equally transformative changes were taking place. Just before the First World War, the Chinese Qing (Manchu) dynasty had been overthrown by a revolution, marking the end of over 2,000 years of imperial rule. A Republic was declared with Sun Yat-sen as its President, committed to modernising his country and championing democracy. His ideals were not implemented, largely due to the tumultuous politics of the country. However, Yat-sen kept one promise: he appointed the first woman to his Kuomintang government.

Britain: Constance Markievicz (1868–1927)

The first woman to be elected to the British Parliament was a gun-toting revolutionary, who was in prison for leading a violent uprising: Countess Constance Markievicz.[3] How did this happen? How did an aristocratic woman come to be in this situation?

Constance, the daughter of Lady Georgina and Sir Henry Gore-Booth, was born at 7, Buckingham Gate, London, in a prestigious area close to the Palace. Her father, Sir Henry Gore-Booth, was an Anglo-Irish aristocrat who owned Lissadell House, one of Ireland's great houses. Situated on the west coast of Ireland in County Sligo, next to the sea, mountains and woodland, Lissadell is a grand Georgian neoclassical Greek country mansion. It was here, on an estate of thousands of acres, that Constance and her four siblings, spent their childhood and teenage years living an idyllic rural life, walking by the sea, riding horses, hunting and mixing with

Image 2   Constance Markievicz,
courtesy of Library of Congress, USA.

the social and intellectual elite of Ireland. Constance followed
aristocratic convention: she and her sister Eva went on the
Grand Tour, where they 'rowed on the Rhone, heard Wagner
at Bayreuth, and studied painting and sculpture in Italy'.[4] In
1887 Constance was presented at Court to Queen Victoria. The
beautiful, wealthy and charming Miss Gore-Booth had 'come
out' and was now officially ready for marriage.

Less than three decades later, the British government condemned Countess Constance Markievicz, as she was now known, to death by shooting. How and why did this pretty, enchanting young aristocrat defy the social conventions of her class and sex and find herself in prison and condemned to death?[5]

Her political journey began in London. In 1892, aged 24, Constance enrolled at the Slade School of Fine Art, an exclusive college, with a world-leading reputation and world-famous alumni. Constance's peers at the Slade included Augustus and Gwen John, G K Chesterton and William Rothenstein. It was here that Constance became conscious of urban poverty, of the relentless privations of working-class Londoners. She also grew aware of gender discrimination and joined the National Union of Women's Suffrage Societies. Back home in Ireland, on Christmas Eve 1896, Constance and her sisters Eva and Mabel set up the North Sligo Women's Suffrage Association. About a year later Eva moved to Manchester and in 1903 founded, with Esther Roper, the Lancashire and Cheshire Women Textile and Other Workers' Representation Committee (LCWT), a women's suffrage group targeted at working-class women. Initially, Constance was active here too but later left for Paris.

In Paris, Constance studied at the Academie Julian, Montmartre, the only art school in Paris to accept women. Here she met her future husband, Casimir, a Polish count six years younger and 6ft 4in tall. In September 1900, the couple married and Constance became Countess Markievicz. They were a striking couple. At their wedding Casimir wore his Russian court uniform of white trousers and a black tunic with gold braids on his collar and cuffs; Constance wore a dress of white duchesse satin with an orange blossom bodice, a large pearl necklace and diamond tiara.[6] It was a conventional wedding service, entirely appropriate for young aristocrats, except that Constance promised to love and honour her husband but not obey. In November 1901 she gave birth to a daughter,

Maeve. Two years later, the young family moved to Ireland and Maeve was raised at Lissadell by her grandparents, leaving Constance with the time to paint . . . and start a revolution.

At first the young couple were part of Dublin's 'Castle set' of young aristocrats, a socially elite circle who attended dances held by the Viceroy Lord Aberdeen and his wife Ishbel. At Aberdeen's Lace Ball held to promote Irish women's craft skills, Constance wore a 'gown of emerald green chiffon over silk, which was entirely veiled with beautiful Limerick lace, caught with black velvet rosettes'.[7] No one commented on the incongruity between the cost of the gown and the seamstress's wage. Meanwhile, Constance was also moving in bohemian artistic circles, where she gradually became attracted to Irish nationalism. Her aristocratic life initially clashed with her new political focus. The first time she attended a Inghinidhe na hÉireann (Daughters of Ireland) meeting she shocked the members by arriving dressed in a silk ballgown and wearing her diamonds: she had come straight from a function at Dublin Castle, the administrative centre of the British government and the residence of the British Viceroy.

In 1908 Countess Markievicz launched her republican career. She joined Sinn Fein, the revolutionary women's organisation Inghinidhe na hÉireann (Daughters of Ireland) and wrote regularly for the women's nationalist journal *Bean na hÉireann* (Women of Ireland). In 1909 she set up the Fianna Éireann, a para-military boys' brigade, which became a feeder organisation for the Irish Citizen Army, forerunner of the IRA. Constance, skilled in hunting foxes and pheasants, taught the boys how to use guns, practising with small Winchester rifles and small revolvers until they were competent enough to shoot a moving target, maybe even a British soldier.

Gradually, Constance abandoned her old aristocratic unionist past in favour of a new identity as a feminist, a socialist and a Republican. In 1911, Countess Markievicz showed her passionate, tenacious side by demonstrating against the newly

Image 3   Constance Markievicz,
courtesy of National Library of Ireland.

crowned King George V and Queen Mary who were on a state visit to Ireland. She was arrested but released without charge. Her new life as a rebel was secured.

In 1914, Britain declared war on Germany, a war opposed by Irish nationalists. Constance wrote and distributed anti-war leaflets, anti-recruitment handbills and pro-German leaflets. She took every opportunity to incite rebellion. On 24 April 1916, Easter Monday, Constance Markievicz, now a Staff

Lieutenant in the newly established Irish Citizen Army, prepared for revolution. The 'floating land mine', as her husband
called her, was ready to act. The plan was to encircle the city,
take it by force and wait for the rest of Ireland to join the
uprising. Dressed in a dark green tunic, tweed knee breeches,
black stockings and heavy boots, and armed with an automatic
revolver and Mauser rifle, Constance walked into St Stephen's
Square, the main square of Dublin. Here she and her Citizen's
Army dug trenches in the green, commandeered houses and
requisitioned the College of Surgeon's building as headquarters. On the first morning, Markievicz allegedly killed a police
officer. One contingent, led by James Connolly, took over the
Post Office, and announced the birth of the Irish Republic. The
rebellion had begun.

Six days later it ended. On 30 April, after a week of intense
fighting, Constance surrendered to Captain de Courcy Wheeler,
an officer married to one of her cousins. Her trial was brief, a
court martial, a military court with no jury. On 4 May 1916,
Constance was accused of taking part 'in an armed rebellion
and in the waging of war against His Majesty the King . . .
being done with the intentions and purpose of assisting the
(German) enemy'.[8] She was sentenced to death by being shot.
This was later commuted to life imprisonment. Her sister,
Eva Gore-Booth, believed that her pleas to the British Prime
Minister Asquith to overturn her sister's death sentence had
helped.

Countess Markievicz was imprisoned in Kilmainham Gaol.
Her cell was damp, airless and dark, furnished with a pallet
bed, a table, a stool and a bucket which served as a lavatory.
Each day, she was woken up at 6:30 and given two cups of tea
and five ounces of bread. Constance then spent the morning
either scrubbing, laundering, making rope, cooking or mend-
ing clothes. At midday she was served two ounces of meat
with gravy, two ounces of cabbage, one potato and three slices
of bread. All meals were eaten alone. It was a far cry from the

luxury of Lissadell. In her cell she heard British firing squads shooting her comrades. Most of the leaders of the Easter Rising were shot: eight men died this way in just three days. Over 1,000 people lost their lives in the Rising. The Easter Rising had not been universally popular but the harshness and callousness of the British response shifted public opinion. James Connolly, one of the leaders, a good friend of Constance, was unable to stand because of a previous war injury. He was shot dead while sitting on a chair. It was a tragedy of Shakespearean intensity: the British army, 'in blood, stepped in so far', felt unable to stop its violence. Anti-war and anti-British sentiments hardened. Sinn Fein grew in strength, remodelling itself as a revolutionary party committed to over-turning British rule and establishing an Irish Republic.

On 17 June 1917, all political prisoners were released. Now 49 years old, Constance Markievicz returned to Dublin, and to a heroine's welcome. She was now both broke and home-less, looking emaciated and much older. As soon as she gained her freedom, Constance resumed work, making speeches all over the country, helping reorganise the damaged Sinn Fein and recruiting volunteers into a rebel army. Her freedom was short lived. In May 1918 the British authorities rearrested the Countess in a round-up of the Sinn Fein leaders. This time she was incarcerated in HM prison Holloway, a women's prison, where she was allowed painting materials, books and food from outside.

In November 1918, while she was still 'inside', there was a British General election. Sinn Fein contested every seat in Ireland: Constance Markievicz was selected to run for Dublin St Patrick's Division. And won it magnificently. Countess Constance Markievicz thus became the first woman to be elected to the British Parliament. All the other seventeen female candidates, including famous former suffragettes like Christobel Pankhurst, lost. The suffragists and suffragettes, who had campaigned for the vote for over a century and had faithfully served their country in the war, witnessed a convicted traitor – albeit once a former suffragist – who had fought against the British become the first woman to be elected. It was a bizarre outcome, a pyrrhic victory for these activists.

Every one of the 73 Sinn Fein MPs elected refused to take a seat in the House of Commons – they did not want to swear allegiance to the King. Instead, they set up their own Parliament, the Dail Éireann. Headed by Eamon de Valera, it issued a Declaration of Independence and demanded the British withdraw from Ireland. Constance, while still in prison, was given a Cabinet post: Minister of Labour in Ireland's new – and illegal – Parliament.

On 7 March 1919, the Countess was again released. She was still considered a 'danger to the public peace and a leader of the most extreme faction of Sinn Fein' but the authorities found it too embarrassing to have the first and only woman elected to Parliament serving time in a British prison.[9] Undeterred by the prospect of rearrest, Constance went straight to Dublin and resumed her fight for Irish Independence. Once more, her freedom was brief. In June 1919, she was incarcerated for the third time, sentenced to four months in Cork prison, for making a seditious speech and inciting rebellion. By now, the Irish campaign for independence was gathering pace. The Irish Republican Army launched a guerilla campaign against the police and British soldiers, setting off a brutal war with atrocities committed on both sides.

In October 1919, after being imprisoned for over two years, the Countess was again released from gaol. She still had no permanent home and spent her life sleeping in the homes of sympathisers, avoiding capture by the British forces, attending meetings, serving in the illegal Dáil as Minister of Labour, and plotting revenge against the British army. In September 1920 she was arrested again for treason and sentenced to two years hard labour. In November the IRA assassinated fourteen men thought to be undercover British agents; in reprisal the

British army fired on a crowd watching a football match in Dublin. Constance heard the shooting from her cell, writing to her sister Eva that it 'lasted twenty minutes . . . there were machine guns going'.[10] On 2 December 1920 she was court martialled, accused of conspiracy to murder British police and army officers. On Christmas Eve, now 52 years old, Constance was sentenced to two years hard labour, this time in Mountjoy prison. She was eventually released on 24 July 1921 when a truce was agreed between the Republicans and the British government. When the Anglo-Irish treaty partitioned Ireland into two, the southern counties became the Irish Republic. With Ireland an independent country, her Dublin constituency was abolished and Constance Markievicz ceased to be an MP.

Countess Markievicz, as with many Republicans, did not agree with the division of Ireland. A civil war between the two factions of Sinn Fein broke out. It was brutal. In November 1923 she was arrested for the last time, went on hunger strike in prison and was released on Christmas Eve. By 1926 she was disillusioned with Sinn Fein and helped create the Fianna Fáil party. On 15 July 1927, Constance, who had given away most of her inherited wealth, died in a public ward from peritonitis caused by a burst appendix. Before she died, Constance must have been aware that the first woman to take her seat in the British Parliament was another privileged aristocrat: Nancy Astor.

Canada: Agnes Macphail (1890–1954)

In 1921, in another former British colony, a 'salty spinster stepped out of her schoolroom' to become the first woman to be elected to the Canadian House of Commons.[11] She was Agnes Macphail,[12] aged 31, elected to represent the United Farmers of Ontario, a party founded in 1914. Agnes was unlike Constance Markievicz: unglamorous, steadfast, non-violent, unexciting and unprivileged. Like Constance, Agnes encountered male prejudice, though her experiences were of a different kind.

Agnes was born on 24 March 1890 in a tiny dilapidated farmhouse in Proton Township, Ontario. Her parents, Henrietta (nee Campbell) and Dougal Macphail, were farmers of Scottish ancestry who worked hard to try to make the poor soil of their farm productive. Agnes was proud of being from country stock, proud of her Scottish heritage, proud of belonging to a pioneering family. She loved her Ontarian landscape, enjoyed working on the family farm and remained rooted to country life all her life. Nonetheless, Agnes had no wish to be trapped in a marriage, no wish to be a farmer's wife with a brood of children. Instead, she trained as a teacher, taught in a range of rural schools and joined the United Farmers of Ontario, where her interest in politics began.

In March 1922, this country woman from a log cabin overcame the limitations of her background and entered the all-male Parliament. She looked around at the wooden panelling, sat on her allocated green velvet seat and joined the other elected representatives in the capital city's majestic House of Commons. All eyes followed her, one woman in an ocean of men. She was overwhelmed – and nervous. Initially she was greeted warmly by her male colleagues; someone placed red roses on her parliamentary seat[13] and most of the Cabinet crossed over to welcome her. On her first day, Agnes dressed soberly, in a plain blue serge dress, all too aware that her appearance would cause comment. Derogatory comments about her dress and appearance became common, mostly seeking to undermine her. Her plain dresses, horn-rimmed glasses and sensible shoes led newspapers to portray her as a school-marm spinster, safe, unconventional and boring.

The newspaper pundits were wrong: Miss Mcphail's progressive causes and unorthodox beliefs constantly challenged the white male chamber. She may have entered politics to represent the farming community and champion the rights of farmers, but she also fought for the rights of others. She was a self-professed feminist, pacifist, prison reformer, and champion of immigrants and other marginalised groups. Soon she became a target of the rough and tumble of parliamentary adversarial politics, and found that her acerbic wit helped to undermine her opponents. Clearly some MPs thought she should not be in the Canadian House of Commons. One shouted 'Go get a husband', only to be embarrassed when Macphail retorted 'How do I know he wouldn't turn out like you?'[14] Agnes found the House of Commons so hostile that she lost 20 pounds in weight.[15]

In the 1920s, Agnes was Canada's most famous champion of women's rights in Parliament. 'I am a feminist', she declared, 'and I want for women the thing men are not willing to give them – equality.'[16] She introduced the first equal pay legislation, fought for family allowances and women's access to divorce. She argued that men should equally share the running of the home and the care of their children.

Agnes Mcphail trailblazed reform in Canada. One of her achievements was her push for the humane treatment of convicts. At the time, disobedient prisoners were shackled for long periods with their hands above their heads, flogged with leather straps, restricted to a diet of bread and water and placed in solitary confinement in a darkened cell. Some were 'hosed down' in a special lockup. Here, high pressure water was directed at the convict until they apologised; those deemed to be insane were ducked in tubs of water. She branded the Canadian prison system as brutal, stupid and ineffectual.[17] Agnes made three key suggestions: firstly, prison should reform convicts not merely punish them; secondly prisoners should be employed in useful tasks, thirdly prison wardens should be trained officials adept at implementing her reform programme. In 1938, because of her incessant demands, a Royal Commission on Prison Reform proposed a complete revision of penitentiary institutions. The report was based on the recommendations of Agnes Mcphail.

Agnes was a tireless defender of her farming community. During the Great Depression of the 1930s, when farmers faced repossessions, she was convinced that socialism might help them. She co-founded the Co-operative Commonwealth Federation (CCF) which suggested nationalising the key industries, and creating a welfare state with old age pensions, health insurance and unemployment insurance. When Agnes was asked who would pay, she replied that 'there are some birds of passage, rather wealthy birds, who fly to the Bahamas' to avoid taxes. Agnes wanted these birds to return to the country that had made them rich – and pay their dues.

Agnes, as a life-long pacifist, worked hard for world peace. On 26 March 1928, she proposed a motion in the Canadian House of Commons for the establishment of a Department of Peace. She also suggested that an annual peace prize be awarded for the best work in the cause of peace. War, she argued, was disastrous for the victors as well as the vanquished: it cost too many lives and too much money that could be better spent raising people's living standards.[18] In an emotional speech to the Commons, a speech which echoes across the centuries, Agnes insisted that 'if we prepare for war, we get war; if we prepare for peace, we get peace. . . . war settles nothing. It causes other wars by arousing hatreds. It brings unemployment, poverty, misery, crime and death.'[19] Like Jeanette Rankin, she was an active member of the Women's International League for Peace and Freedom. In 1929 she was a delegate to the Prague Congress where she was elected on to the International Executive for her work in speaking out against war. Later that month, she travelled to Switzerland as the first Canadian woman to be a delegate to the League of Nations, founded ten years earlier to foster world peace. Here nationals of 53 countries met, 'prejudices were broken down, friendships founded on understanding are built up . . . conflicts become more difficult; judicial methods of settling disputes become possible and natural'.[20] Agnes Macphail was appointed to the Disarmament Committee.

Her optimism was idealistic: global disarmament did not happen and within ten years the world was once more at war. In 1940, Agnes Mcphail lost her seat. She died, aged 63, on 13 February 1954. Her dedication to public service and women's rights cemented her place as a significant figure and trailblazer in Canada. Various awards, scholarships, schools and public buildings bear her name in honour of her achievements.

Germany: Clara Zetkin (1857–1933)[21]

We have Clara Zetkin to thank for the only women's event that is celebrated internationally. On 8 March each year women across the globe observe International Women's Day (IWD). In over 25 countries – from Armenia to Zambia – it is a national holiday. In China, Madagascar and Nepal, women are awarded a half-day or day's holiday, a benefit reserved for women only. Men are expected to remain at work. In 1910, at a socialist women's conference in Copenhagen, Clara raised the idea of an International Women's Day to celebrate the fight for women's equality. Delegates from seventeen countries, including three of the first Finnish women MPs, accepted the proposal. A few years later it was agreed that 8 March would be International Women's Day.

Clara Zetkin was a German socialist and feminist.[22] In January 1919, aged 63, she was elected as an Independent Social Democrat representative, one of the first women to be elected to the Reichstag, the German Parliament. Germany, after a bitter defeat in war and the abdication of Kaiser Wilhelm II, had just become a democracy. A new constitution declared the country a parliamentary republic – the Weimar Republic – with all adults over the age of twenty able to vote. Under a system of proportional representation, thirty-seven women were elected.

Clara was born in Wiederau, a rural village in Saxony, Germany. She was the eldest of the three children of Josephine and Gottfried Eissner, a Protestant teacher. Her mother was French, proud of her revolutionary heritage and keen to teach the principles of equality, fraternity, egalité to Clara and her siblings. In 1875 the family moved to Leipzig where Clara was enrolled at the Leipzig Teachers' College for Women, an institute connected to the women's movement and run by feminists. Here she met members of Germany's newly formed – and shortly to be illegal – Social Democratic Party (SDP). In 1878 Clara, now aged 21, joined the SDP, became involved in underground politics and fell in love with a Jewish Russian émigré, Ossip Zetkin. At the time, as in the UK, women were forced to take the citizenship of their husband and because Clara had no wish to lose her German citizenship, the two remained unmarried. Instead, Miss Eissner renamed herself Mrs Zetkin and began her career as a revolutionary feminist committed to dismantle all forms of inequality through a socialist revolution.[23]

In 1880, Clara's lover was arrested and deported as an undesirable alien. Two years later, Clara joined him in his small one room apartment in Montmartre, Paris, both trying to eke out a living from teaching, translating and writing articles for the socialist press. In June 1885, the couple were evicted for not paying rent and all their possessions confiscated apart from the clothes they were wearing. On the streets, and without money, the couple were rescued by Russian émigrés who fed and housed the homeless couple. Before long, the couple had two sons, Maxim and Konstantin, and tried to settle down. However, the burden of household chores and looking after two active boys left Clara with little energy. She missed important deadlines for articles, excusing herself by complaining that she was 'seamstress, cook, washing woman etc . . . in addition come the two little rascals, who won't leave me in peace . . . if I want to bury myself in the character of Louise Michel [an anarchist and Paris communard], then I have to wipe the nose of No 1 . . . then it's time to feed No 2'.[24]

In June 1889, her beloved Ossip died and a year later Clara returned to Germany, safer now that the right-wing Otto von Bismarck had been dismissed and his anti-socialist law expired. By now, the tuberculosis that had killed Ossip was also coursing through her body, a body already weakened by the deprivations of poverty. She spent three months in a sanatorium in the Black Forest and arranged for formal schooling for Maxim and Konstantin. She was now a single mother, totally responsible for the care of her two energetic sons. According to both friends and foes, Clara was an 'exceptionally dedicated, loving and self-sacrificing mother, as well as charming playmate'.[25] Her mothering focused on intellectual nimbleness, physical fitness and compassion. She taught her sons English, French, natural science and read them classic literature; gave her boys cold baths and lots of exercise to toughen them up physically; and taught them the ideals and moral values of socialism. Her sons distributed her leaflets, helped in her election campaigns and were taken on demonstrations. Clara wanted to live socialism, not just theorise about it, always demanding integrity and honesty in both her personal and political life.

In 1898 George Zundel, a portrait painter and comrade who was eighteen years younger, moved into her apartment. A year later the two married but Clara retained her name of Zetkin. The marriage of a well-known activist to such a young man caused a great deal of worry to the conventionally minded socialist leaders.[26] Clara wryly noticed the difference between their theory and practice. Most of the male leaders avowed equality yet remained patriarchal, often disapproving of their own wives and daughters working outside the home or participating in politics.

Until 1908 Clara worked for the socialist cause covertly because women were prohibited from belonging to a political party. However, women were able to lead women's groups. Clara's editorship of the socialist women's journal *Die Gleichheit* (Equality) between 1891 and 1917 gave her great opportunities to reach out to working-class women. In 1914 its circulation was over 100,000, with key women activists such as Alexandra Kollontai regularly writing for the paper. Clara Zetkin was now confirmed as one of the most influential socialist feminists. In her view, capitalism was the source of women's oppression and the subjection of women could only be ended by a socialist revolution. She criticised the feminism of the moderate and largely middle-class women's movement because it ignored class inequality. In her view socialism and feminism were inextricably linked: there could be no socialism without women's emancipation; nor could there be women's emancipation without socialism.

The First World War split the left in Germany. The SDP supported the war effort; Zetkin was opposed. She argued that 'national differences are not between the masses of the nation but exclusively between the ruling classes'. Patriotism, she insisted, was 'the ideological blanket, which disguises its economic interests'.[27] Clara joined the Women's Peace Party and took part in the 1915 International Women's Peace Conference at The Hague where she spoke out against the war, asking 'who profits from this war? Only a tiny minority', i.e. the manufacturers of machine guns, tanks, torpedo boats and other weapons of war. Disillusioned with the SDP and its commitment to Germany's war efforts, Zetkin left the party to form the Independent Social Democratic Party, the ISDP. Zetkin's opposition to the war was dangerous and in 1916, after several arrests, she was placed in 'protective custody'.

Politics was perilous in the febrile atmosphere of post-war Germany. Clara's close friend and colleague Rosa Luxembourg was arrested, tortured, brutally murdered and her body dumped in a canal. On 29 January 1919, the newly elected Clara was the first woman to speak in the Reichstag, delivering a blistering attack on the way the government had treated members of Luxembourg's communist group; in March she wrote an article eulogising her friend. A few months later, possibly in honour of her friend, Clara Zetkin left the ISPD and joined the Kommunistische Partei Deutschlands (KPD), the communist party which had been set up by Luxembourg. Recognised for her political talents, she was appointed to the executive of the Comintern, the Communist International run by the USSR. From this time onwards, Clara Zetkin spent large amounts of time in Russia, away from threats of violence.

Clara was no saintly socialist. She possessed a volatile temper. 'Amiability', she once confessed 'is not one of my weaknesses' and 'sometimes even with the best of intentions I cannot manage without an "explosion".'[28] When chairing women's conferences, Zetkin would silence opponents, throw away any resolution with which she disagreed and only let those with similar views speak. Her mitigating factor was her charm, her warmth and her kindness.

By 1930 the Reichstag had descended into, often violent, chaos. Democracy was physically falling apart. In July 1932, the 75-year-old Clara Zetkin, returned to Germany for her last time. As its most senior member, she opened Parliament. Her health was compromised. She had cataracts, problems with her heart and liver, and suffered from catarrh and bronchitis, which left her incapacitated for weeks at a time. Now nearly blind, ill and frail, she was carried in on a stretcher and helped up the stairs to the platform. Here, leaning on a cane and with two sturdy women by her side, she delivered a forty-minute attack on Hitler and the Nazi Party.[29] By the time Hitler became Chancellor, Clara was back in Russia.

In that same year, the seriously ill Zetkin engaged in her last political fight. In an article, *Save The Scottsboro Boys,* she condemned the decision of an Alabama court, which, despite all evidence of their innocence, had declared nine Afro-American young men guilty of rape. It was 'the shameful judgement of the worst racial hatred', and she appealed to progressives all over the world to fight against this judicial murder.[30] 'Rise up', she pleaded 'to rescue these eight young individuals, who shall be dragged by the executioner onto the pyre of the electric chair.' The article went viral. Zetkin was alive to hear America's Supreme Court reverse the convictions. She died in June 1933 and her ashes were later buried in the Kremlin Wall.

Austria: Adelheid Popp (1869–1939)

After the First World War, optimism was in the air across much of Europe. On 11 November 1918 – Armistice Day – the Emperor of Austria abdicated. The next day the 'Republic of German Austria' was proclaimed, universal suffrage was introduced and women were allowed to stand for Parliament. Eight women were elected, seven from the left-wing Social Democratic Workers' Party (SDP) and one from the Christian Social Party. Mostly from working-class backgrounds, these women entered Parliament to fight against social injustice and gender discrimination. However, the collapse of the Austrian Empire left the country in disorder. Adelheid Popp, a semi-literate, working-class woman, entered this turbulent political scene keen to fight for the rights of the underprivileged within the Austrian Parliament. How did she do it?

Adelheid Dwořak was born in Inzersdorf near Vienna into a working-class Catholic family. As a child and a young girl, she knew only hunger and poverty mixed with exploitation. Her father Adalbert was an alcoholic; her mother Anna was worn out and depressed after giving birth to fifteen children and watching ten of them die in childhood. Her father was a brute who beat his wife so hard that she often fled half-dressed to hide at a neighbour's house. The children had no dolls, no toys, no fairy stories, no sweets. There were no tender words, no kisses or hugs, no love. On the one occasion the family bought a Christmas tree, her father destroyed it on Christmas Eve in a mad fit of drunkenness. Adelheid was six years old when her tyrannical and abusive father died. She was not sad, even though his death threw the already impoverished family into even greater distress. In a bid to create a better life, Adelheid's mother moved her family to Vienna where they shared a small windowless room with no natural light and no heating. The family very nearly starved.

Forced to leave school at ten years old, Adelheid began work as a domestic servant, then as a seamstress and factory worker. She left home at 6 a.m. and returned at 8 p.m.[31] She learnt first-hand about exploitation: she worked long hours for inadequate pay, was sexually harassed, suffered constant hunger pains and lived in squalid insanitary accommodation.[32]

Offended by these injustices, the teenage Adelheid and her brother attended a Social Democratic Workers' meeting. When the two arrived, men were standing shoulder to shoulder, rubbing their hands and stamping their feet to keep warm in the unheated hall. Here, she came to understand that poverty was not the fault of the individual but a consequence of an unjust system. She was the only woman present. It was a pivotal moment. From then on, Adelheid coupled her emerging socialism with feminism: women, she realised, were at the very bottom of a very unfair economic system. At the age of seventeen her passionate speech about the conditions of women workers drew her to the attention of leading socialists. She was, according to Eleanor Marx, 'patronised by Victor Adler, lionised by August Bebel and adored by Freidrich Engels'. In February 1894 she married the Social Democratic leader Julius Popp at Vienna City Hall, with Victor Adler acting as best man. The couple had two sons, Felix, who died in 1925 of an infectious disease, and Jultschie, who died in the First World War.[33]

Adelheid, who had only three years of schooling, could read but not write very well. Nevertheless, she created one of the largest socialist women's movements in Europe. In 1891, she founded and edited the SD women's paper *Arbeiterinnen-Zeitung* (*Working Women's Educational Society*) dedicated to the struggle for women's rights. It published articles promoting women's education, suffrage, better working conditions and a reform of the marriage laws. In 1893, she played a key role in organising one of Austria's first-ever women's strikes, rallying around 700 women to demand shorter working hours and better conditions.

Under the Austrian monarchy, women were forbidden to take part in politics. In 1895, spied upon by the secret police, Adelheid was arrested, put on trial and sentenced to fourteen days in prison for publishing an article entitled 'Free Love and Bourgeois Marriage'. The authorities accused her of degrading the institution of marriage. Undeterred, in 1909 she published the *Autobiography of a Working Woman*, one of the most widely read socialist books, a polemic which was translated into English and other languages.

When she entered Parliament in 1919, Adelheid Popp was a well-seasoned and well-known political agitator, known to be keen to abolish the nobility and committed to promoting working-class women's interests, among them reform of the marriage laws, abortion and equal pay.

In 1933, she left the Social Democrats for health reasons. Tragically, she witnessed her life's work disappear. In 1934 she was in hospital when the extreme right-wing Dollfuss-Schuschnigg authoritarian government crushed the Social Democrat Party, banned all other political parties, swept away all human rights laws and abolished the elected assemblies. There was a mass arrest of socialists. In 1938, after Dollfuss had been murdered and Schuschnigg forced to resign, a Nazi government was established. Hitler declared Anschluss: Austria was now absorbed into Germany.

Adelheid began to witness her life's work evaporate. She died on 7 March 1939, just a few months before the start of the Second World War.

Hungary: Margit Slachta (1884–1974)[34]

The First World War created opportunity in a neighbouring country. In 1918 Hungary declared its independence when the Austro-Hungarian empire collapsed. The country was now significantly smaller, as the Treaty of Trianon, signed by a reluctant and defeated Hungary, took away two thirds of its territory and sixty per cent of its population. At first, life in the newly reconstructed independent Republic of Hungary augured well. Its first decree declared universal suffrage, setting the voting age for women at 24 and men at 21, and seemingly cementing the country as a constitutional democracy. It proved illusional. Hungary was battered by both internal and external events. In March 1920, a communist revolution briefly upset the new social order, followed by an authoritarian, conservative, extreme nationalistic and then fascist regime which lasted until after the Second World War when Soviet Russia took over.

Into this political maelstrom stepped Margit Slachta, a Catholic feminist nun, who was the first woman to be elected to the Diet of Hungary, the country's Parliament.[35] She found herself caught between the pincers of Fascism and Communism. Tortured and imprisoned by the Fascists for saving Jews from persecution and intimidated by the Communists for her Christian faith, she was forced to flee her homeland and seek sanctuary in the United States of America.

Margit was born in Kassa (today Košice, Slovakia), to upperclass Catholic parents: her father Kálmán descended from a Polish aristocratic family, her mother Mária was the daughter of land-owners. Margit, the second eldest of six girls, studied at a Catholic college and graduated as a language and history teacher. In 1908, when the rest of the family moved to the United States, Margit stayed in Hungary, gave up teaching and trained as a social worker, where she helped young offenders and prisoners straighten out their lives.

Margit was a deeply committed Christian and a feminist. She became a nun, joining the Social Mission Society, a religious order of women committed to working with the under-privileged. Soon, she realised that social work could not solve the underlying difficulties facing the underprivileged but having a political voice in Parliament might. Margit was no retiring silent nun, hiding away behind convent walls, but an activist and tireless fighter for women's rights. In 1914 she became editor of *Christian Woman*, a forum for Catholic feminists, and in 1918 set up the Christian Women's Camp, a group within the Christian Social People's Party, to promote women in politics. She called for women's right to education; for equality in the workplace; for participation in public life. Margit combined her Catholic belief and its inherent traditionalism with a modern agenda of women's self-determination. She was described as a 'preserving innovator'.

In 1920 Margit was the first – and only – woman to be elected to the Hungarian Diet as a member of the Christian National Unity Party. In an interview shortly after her election she insisted 'that the interests of the family must be brought into national politics . . . I will fight for (better) pay . . . for a solution to the housing problem'.[36] While in Parliament she delivered 28 speeches addressing women's rights and inequality in Hungary. She promoted higher taxes to pay for welfare reform, fought against price rises, tried to restrict the consumption of alcohol and – in true Christian fashion – proposed placing a cross on the dome of Parliament. In 1922, when the Parliamentary session ended and after only two years in Parliament, Margit was deselected as a Christian Party MP because of her radical views on women. She was also dismissed from her convent and had her vows annulled.

In 1923, now aged 24, Margit set up the Society of Social Sisters, an order of nuns similarly committed to helping the poor and the vulnerable but also to campaign politically. Now in charge, Margit rejected the traditional nun's habit of a wimple, veil and long black dress, and instead wore a simple uniform of a long grey tunic and white blouse. They were called the 'grey sisters'. Hers was a practical Christianity, providing help to the vulnerable, training women for social work and working politically to change the law. From a young age, Margit Slachta realised that charity alone could not reduce poverty and that it needed political intervention to structure a more equal society.

One of Margit's bravest actions was her fight against the persecution and murder of Jewish people. In 1938, she was a fierce critic of Hungary's first antisemitic laws, which limited the number of Jewish people in the professions, government and commerce to twenty per cent, then a year later to five per cent. Two hundred and fifty thousand Jewish people lost their jobs. In 1941, a law forbade Jews from marrying Gentiles. Each year it worsened. Jewish Hungarians had their legal rights removed, their possessions confiscated, relocated to substandard houses and were forced to wear a yellow star. They were beaten up and murdered by their fellow citizens. From the outset, Margit was an open critic of Nazism and its vile creed. She called it Satanism. Her journal *Voice of the Spirit* published articles opposing these laws and condemning the treatment of the Jewish population. In 1943 the government suppressed her paper but Margit continued to publish and distribute it illicitly. Margit saw antisemitism as a direct contradiction of the Ten Commandments and of Christian beliefs. Continually, she criticised the persecution 'in the name of Christianity, but against the spirit of Christianity' by 'creatures who call themselves human'. In her view, the Hungarians complicit in these atrocities violated the norms of her Christian faith.

In 1940 Hungary joined the Second World War on the side of Nazi Germany. Soon Jewish Hungarians were arrested and deported to death camps. Slachta told her nuns that their Christian beliefs and values meant that they should protect the Jewish population. She raised her voice 'to protest that in our country such mass official atrocities can happen and we do this as human beings, as Christians, and as Hungarians. . . . As Christians, we see in it the most serious violation of the commands of God and our religion.'[37] She was a lone voice, crying in the wilderness. The rest of the Christian community largely remained silent.

Margit tried to persuade the leaders of the Christian world to intervene. She wrote to the Hungarian Bishops asking them to excommunicate those Catholics participating in the persecution of Jewish people. She protested to Magdolna Purgly, the wife of Admiral Horthy, the antisemitic pro-German Regent of Hungary and later Nazi puppet, and asked her to stop the deportation of Hungarian Jews. In 1943, Margit visited Pope Pius XII and asked him to object to the persecution of Jewish people. 'I had never felt as I did then, my face was burning, my hands, usually dry, were clammy and tears were welling up in my eyes.'[38] He listened, expressed sympathy but, as was the case with others, did little.

Slachta knew she was alone in her fight. She forged baptismal certificates and identity papers for Jewish people under threat, sent food to the ghettos and sheltered people in her convents. She was tortured, imprisoned and only narrowly escaped the death penalty. A few of her religious colleagues were taken prisoner, brutalised and thrown in the river Danube. Under Slachta's guidance her order rescued more than 2,000 Hungarian Jews.

After the Second World War, when Hungary was again defeated, Margit returned to parliamentary politics. She was re-elected to the Diet as an independent member, and remained there between 1945 and 1948. Once more, she emphasised the need for women to have economic and political power, all within a Christian framework. By now, Hungary was a satellite of atheistic Soviet Russia, which nationalised church institutions, suppressed religious orders and persecuted the Christian churches. Margit's fierce, uncompromising Catholicism brought ridicule, scorn and repression. In June 1948, she delivered her last speech, criticising the government's plans to nationalise church schools. The Bill was passed. In protest, Margit refused to stand for the national anthem at the end of the Parliamentary session, an act that was seen as disrespectful and she was suspended for six months. Her life was yet again in danger. She was now an enemy of the state, and, fearing arrest, was forced to flee Hungary. She was never allowed to return.

In 1969, Margit Slachta was selected as one of the Righteous among the Nations by Yad Vashem, the remembrance centre in Jerusalem, Israel, dedicated to preserving the memory of the six million Jews who were murdered, and honouring both the survivors and those who risked their lives to help Jews during this time.[39] In 1974, Margit died in a convent of the Social Sisters in Buffalo, New York, where she had lived in exile. In her will she asked to be buried in Hungary. At 4 p.m., Tuesday, 7 December 2021, Margit Slachta's body eventually came home when she was reburied in the National Graveyard. Her legacy lives on: today her Sisters of Social Service are active in nine countries across the globe.

China: He Xiangning (1878–1972)

At the age of seven, He Xiangning made her first bid towards independence. Her father, a man of high status, wanted his daughter to have her feet bound, which meant tightly wrapping her feet to alter their shape and size. For this, her toes would be curled under the sole of her foot and the arch of her foot broken to make sure her feet remained small. Some girls had their feet broken by a hammer to bend them into shape. These so-called lotus feet were a status symbol, a traditional mark of feminine beauty and a way to capture a husband. Small feet were a mark of social standing, implying that a woman was not required to work. It was a cripplingly painful experience for women, whose mobility was severely impaired and who would be prone to constant foot infections. Despite her father's insistence, the seven-year-old Xiangning refused to have her feet bound, repeatedly cutting off the bindings at night. It was her first feminist action, probably fuelled by the stories she had heard of the Taiping Heavenly Kingdom Movement where female soldiers in the Taiping army travelled the world and fought against injustice. With big feet.

Revolutions, as well as wars, open power vacuums which create opportunities for women like Xiangning. For over two thousand years, China was ruled by imperial dynasties. The last of these – the Qing dynasty – which had provided sovereigns since the seventeenth century, was overthrown. Political turmoil increased when the Empress Dowager Cixi, who had effectively controlled China for fifty years, died, and was replaced by a two-year-old boy. Rebellions, invasions and wars shook up the dynasty, forcing the new Emperor to abdicate. Into this turbulence stepped Sun Yat-sen and his revolutionaries. In 1921, He Xiangning, sometimes known as Shuangqing Louzhu, was appointed to Sun Yat-sen's Kuomintang government as Minister for Women's Affairs.[40]

The situation in China remained volatile. And Xiangning was in the middle of the political tornado. On the morning of 20 August 1925 Xiangning's husband died in her arms, shot by an assassin. She narrowly missed being murdered herself. Why did this happen? And how could I find out? Fortunately, one of my neighbours is from Shanghai and helped me trace source material in Chinese.[41]

Born into a wealthy landowning family in Hong Kong, it was expected that Xiangning would follow Chinese customs, look pretty, have her feet bound, learn poetry, be adept at calligraphy and marry a suitable husband chosen by her parents. Her father, He Binghuan, owned a lucrative business dealing in tea and property, while her mother managed a traditional home. However, Xiangning wanted a life beyond material goods. The

Image 4 He Xiangning with her son, 1909.

ninth child of a doting father, she persuaded her father to allow
her to study alongside her brothers. She became a diligent
student.

In 1897, 22-year-old Xiangning agreed to an arranged
marriage to Liao Zhongkai, a Westernised Chinese who had
been born in California, educated in Hong Kong and – most
importantly for her parents – wanted to marry someone with
normal-sized feet. It proved to be a good match. Zhongkai
encouraged his wife's passion for learning, provided her with
books and taught her about Chinese art. In 1903, Xiangning
sold her jewellery and the rest of her trousseau and joined her
husband in Japan where he was studying. She took Japanese
classes and enrolled at Mejiro Women's University.

The young married couple soon became involved in student
politics, dedicating themselves to the revolution. Its leader,
a future President of China, Sun Yat-sen became a close
ally. Xiangning was one of the first women of Sun Yat-sen's

Revolutionary Alliance (later the Kuomintang), a party committed to the overthrow of the Qing dynasty. The young couple
used their apartment as a secret meeting place where revolutionaries came and plotted against the repressive regime. While
in Japan Xiangning studied at an art school, which developed
her skill to design and make revolutionary flags and emblems
for the Kuomintang (KMT). Meanwhile she gave birth to two
children: a daughter called Dream Wake, and a son named
Cheng Zhi.

In 1911, Xiangning returned to Hong Kong, after a nine-year
absence. It was the eve of the revolution, a revolution which
ended two thousand years of imperial rule. The Qing dynasty
had fallen. The couple were joyful, but their joy was short-lived
when an army general seized control. Their lives were now in
danger and, once again, they fled to Japan. In 1916, after the
general was deposed, they finally returned to China to protect
the revolution from the warlords who were threatening to de-
stabilise the new regime. The situation in China was volatile as
competing warlords sought to maintain control: the burning,
killing, looting and plundering was making China ungovern-
able. To help finance Sun Yat-sen's army against the warlords,
Xiangning co-founded *Women Devoted to the Needs of Soldiers
Leaving for War*, raising funds by selling her paintings. She
visited soldiers on the frontline, encouraged women to join the
Red Cross and collected as much money as she could for the
newly established first Chinese republic.

Sun Yat-sen, with Soviet Union support, established a
government in Canton and in 1924 appointed Xiangning as
Minister for Women. She was a staunch feminist and worked
tirelessly to promote gender equality. One of her first initiatives was to organise the first ever Chinese celebration
of International Women's Day. During her three years as
Minister, she fought for the complete equality of women edu-
cationally, legally, socially and economically. She established
hospitals and evening schools targeted at women and their

needs. She promoted many legal changes: the abolition of child brides, concubinage and the bonded servitude of female children. In addition, Xiangning tried to protect the rights of working women by advocating paid maternity leave.

In March 1925 Sun Yat-sen died of liver cancer. The lives of Xiangning and her husband were endangered. The right-wing section of the Kuomintang plotted to kill them. Five months after the death of Sun Yat-sen, their enemies struck. On the morning of 20 August, as the couple arrived for an important committee meeting at the Kuomintang headquarters, her husband Liao was shot four times and dropped to the ground. Xiangning held her bleeding husband in her arms, only to watch him die on the way to hospital. After her husband's funeral, Xiangning hung a large banner 'The Spirit Lives On' outside the front of her home, saying she was willing to 'sacrifice the whole family if it is for the good of the country'.[42]

Xiangning continued her political career. In October 1925 she founded an organisation to help peasants, a women's ambulance group to rescue injured soldiers and visit the frontline troops to comfort the army. In December, Xiangning formed the China Federation of Women, attracting women across the social spectrum to defend the democratic revolution. In January 1926, she was elected member of the Central Executive Committee, also serving as head of the Women's Department. She, and other left-wing member of the KMT, stood together with the Communists to implement social and economic reforms which would benefit the peasants.

When a new leader of the KMT, Chiang Kai-shek, emerged and the KMT lurched rightwards, she and Sun Yat-sen's widow emerged as his most outspoken critics. When Chiang Kai-shek repressed communists, she spoke passionately in their defence, making it clear that the Communist Party 'was our friend . . . We must fight together with them, attack the enemy, and complete the national revolution.'[43] She constantly reiterated that the guiding principle of the revolution was to support the peasants and workers. Chiang Kai-shek disagreed and in April 1927 went on a mission to murder communists and other revolutionaries. On one occasion, they imprisoned the communist leader Zhou Enlai, who had been arrested and faced certain death. Xiangning persuaded them to release him. This was to have positive outcome in future years when China became a communist republic and Zhou Enlai its first Premier. At the end of 1928, recognising that the KMT was turning to the right and was not the party it had once been, Xiangning resigned from her position as a Central Executive Committee member.

Realising that political activity might well be dangerous, Xiangning self-exiled, firstly to France, then to Germany, where she stayed with Sun Yat-sen's widow, Song Qingling. In 1931, she returned home because of a threatened Japanese invasion, shouting from the rooftops to ask the Chinese people to put their country before factional politics and unite against the Japanese enemy. At the same time, she denounced Chiang Kai-shek's complicity, his dictatorial regime and his policy of non-resistance. In one poem, she stated 'you call yourself a man, but you are willing to be bullied by the Japanese. The Chinese will lose their land and mountains without a fight, and all of posterity will be ashamed. We women are willing to go to the battlefield and die. Let us exchange our women's clothing for your military uniforms.'[44] On 28 January 1932, the Japanese invaded. Immediately, Xiangning acted: she appealed to Chinese overseas for funds; she founded a hospital for wounded soldiers; she raised money and medicine to support the resistance; and braved gunfire to visit the front lines. By now, she called for national unity, a winding-up of the hostility between the communist and the KMT, and an end to the civil war, all to help China in its struggle for survival.

In November 1937, Shanghai fell to the Japanese, forcing Xiangning to flee to the British colony of Hong Kong. In 1941, when Hong Kong was invaded, she was forced to leave there too. During the war, she became an itinerant revolutionary, promoting the anti-Japanese war effort, raising money, medicine and clothing for the soldiers who fought against the invasion of their country.

After the war ended and Japan defeated, He Xiangning returned to Hong Kong. Her home became a meeting place for revolutionaries opposed to Chiang Kai-shek. In 1948, He Xiangning, now thoroughly disillusioned with the KMT, founded the Revolutionary Committee of the Chinese Kuomintang (Minge). She immediately threw herself into the people's liberation struggle, this time with a united party with clear, unambiguous goals.

On 1 October 1949 Mao Zedong announced the People's Republic of China in Tiananmen Square, Beijing. Xiangning was invited to Beijing where she was warmly welcomed by Zhou Enlai, grateful for helping him when he was imprisoned and who recognised her as an important political figure. She was elected as a member of the Central People's Government and awarded various positions: Vice Chairperson of the CPPCC, Vice Chair of the Standing Committee of the National People's Congress, Chair of the Overseas Affairs Committee, Honorary Chair of the All-China Women's Federation. In 1953, Xiangning was elected member of the Constitution Drafting Committee. Here she had a chance to reconstruct a new China. In the same year, she was elected Honorary President of the All-China Women's Federation in recognition of her leadership of the women's movement before the revolution. Foot-binding was made illegal, and the ban enforced.

In 1959 widespread famine, caused by a combination of natural disasters and poor agricultural policies, swept across China. It was kept secret. Traditionally grandparents were served first, then men, then women. Three years later there were hardly any girls under the age of ten left in one province; the 1964 census showed that 4.7 million more girls died than boys. Deaths from this avoidable famine ranged from 45 to 60 million. I can find no record of what Xiangning thought about this, or what she thought about other repressive polices like the cultural revolution.[45] On 1 September 1972, aged 94, she died of pneumonia. Zhou Enlai, Song Qinling and other party leaders attended her funeral. Flags were flown in Tiananmen Square and other prominent places. Several museums and memorials in China are dedicated to her life and work, including the He Xiangning Art Museum in Shenzhen. Five years after her death, the Chinese government introduced its one-child policy, designed to curb the country's population.

The First World War reshaped the global map. In Europe, new nation states were created, older ones like Hungary re-emerged and well-established countries like Britain were shaken by nationalist uprisings. Democracy had seemingly triumphed over autocracy. In the after-math of the conflict, women stepped into the political vacuum, asserted their presence and demanded a voice in shaping the new world order.

All the politicians in this chapter were committed feminists, all fought for the rights of women. Their feminism, like that of the women in the previous chapter, took various forms. For some, like He Xiangning, Clara Zetkin and Adelheid Popp, feminism was tightly bound up with their socialist beliefs; for Constance Markievicz it was tied up with nationalism; for Agnes McPhail it emerged from her liberalism, and for Margit Schlacta it formed part of her Christian faith. The courage of these women also unites them. Each one challenged the patriarchal norms of her country, sometimes facing not just ridicule but persecution, imprisonment and death threats.

European women were to be caught up in one of the century's most challenging periods, witnessing first the emergence of democracy, then its collapse as a frightening new world order emerged. Britain and Canada also suffered from the worldwide Depression but democracy remained intact. China remained outside this maelstrom. He Xiangning was able to surf the left-wing wave of revolutionary socialism that swept through China, surviving the communist take-over, the purges of the Cultural Revolution, and becoming a key figure in the Chinese Communist Party.[46] He Xiangning had died before China's one-child policy, a policy which resulted in mass female infanticide, was enforced. Who knows what she might have thought about it?

Chapter Three

The Great Depression, 1930–1940: Spain, Turkey, Brazil, New Zealand

On 29 October 1929, America's Wall Street Crash precipitated a worldwide economic crisis. Banks collapsed, businesses went bust, currencies lost their value, consumer spending plummeted and unemployment rocketed. International trade collapsed as nations raised tariffs, restricted imports and put forward protectionist policies. Capitalism seemed to be disintegrating. This new decade was to be a tumultuous one for democracy as economic instability undermined faith in elected governments and authoritarianism re-emerged. These new autocratic regimes curtailed freedom of speech, persecuted opposition and controlled public opinion by suppressing the press. In Europe, Fascism raised its ugly head. Women's subjugation in these authoritarian regimes was legitimised. For women in these countries, it was an inauspicious time to be a politician. In these challenging times, brave women continued to confront male political supremacy, using newly opened power vacuums to promote their candidacy. Politicians like the Spanish Clara Campoamor, the Turkish Fatma Memik, the Brazilian Carlota Pereira de Queirós and the New Zealander Elizabeth Reid McCombs all championed women's equality, sometimes facing opposition from friends as well as foes. [1]

Spain: Clara Campoamor (1888–1972)

In January 1930 Spain entered a new era. The dictator Primo de Rivera was overthrown, King Alfonso fled to Rome and in 1931 a second Spanish Republic was proclaimed. Socialists gained control of the government and proposed a new constitution. In June, before women were allowed to vote, three women – all left-wing feminists – were elected by an all-male electorate to the Cortes (the Spanish Parliament), marking a significant moment in the country's political history. One of them was Clara Campoamor,[2] elected as a Radical Republican Party MP for a Madrid constituency. She played a pivotal role in transforming Spain into a full democracy. It was not to last. When the newly fledged democracy was overthrown by a military coup, Clara's life was endangered and she became a refugee, roaming the world seeking sanctuary. It was a price she was willing to pay to keep her political integrity. Clara was lucky to remain alive: at one time she was nearly thrown into the sea when travelling on a ship escaping capture. I know this because the Spanish Embassy kindly sent me contact details for Archivo del Congresso de los Diputados (the Spanish archives), which sent me links to a range of unpublished documents. Sonia Morcillo-Garcia, an Hispanic specialist at Cambridge University Library, provided the rest.

Growing up in the final decades of nineteenth-century Spain, Clara's life trajectory was unpromising. She was born on 12 February 1888 in Madrid to Pilar Rodríguez, a seamstress, and Michael Campoamor, an accountant.[3] In 1896 Clara's father died, leaving his wife with three young children – Manuel, Clara and Ignacio – to raise as a single mother. Clara was eight. When she was thirteen, Clara was forced to leave full-time education to contribute to the family income. Between 13 and 21 Clara worked as a seamstress, a shop assistant and a telephonist to supplement her mother's earnings. Determined to escape from her restricted world, Clara found work as a 'cable girl', learned to type and gradually made her way up the secretarial ladder. In 1909, aged 21, she was appointed to the telegraph office of the Ministry of the Interior, a new job in a different city which increased her independence. During this time, she also worked as a secretary to the editor of the left-wing newspaper, *La Tribuna*. Here, she began forming her own political ideas, which, combined with her experiences of economic hardship, lit a fire in her for social justice.

Clara, who had left school early, aimed to be a lawyer. It would be expensive as Clara had to find the cost of tuition, buy pricy textbooks and have enough money for general living expenses. In 1921, now aged 33, Clara took a step that would completely change her life, and with it the history of Spain. For the next three years, she studied for her baccalaureate and a law degree, all the time working to finance her studies. With remarkable resilience and tenacity, she enrolled at the University of Madrid and financed her studies by part-time work as a teacher, a secretary and a translator. In 1924, Clara gained her law degree and became the second woman to join the Madrid Bar Association. From then on, Clara's two great passions were the law and politics. She founded her own law firm, focusing her professional practice on fighting for women's rights. Single women who were claiming paternity, married women who were seeking marital justice, women who were raped, all found a sympathetic ear and a lawyer who would defend them.

Clara believed in women's ability to dismantle the prejudices and the machismo of pre-Republican Spain. There was much to reform: women suffered educational and political injustice, discrimination at work and marital inequality. In law, the Spanish Civil and Penal Code stipulated that wives must obey their husbands. Transgressors were punished. Married women could be imprisoned for two to six years if they were found guilty of adultery; their wages and money belonged to their husbands; and they needed their husbands' permission to buy goods and run their own business.

Clara had an unstoppable determination to fight for women's rights. She joined or set up a range of organisations: in 1922 the feminist and suffrage group, the National Association of Spanish Women and the Spanish Society of Abolitionism (to end prostitution); in 1929 the International Federation of Women in Legal Careers; in 1930 the Spanish Women's League for Peace; in 1931 the Women's Republican Union. All these groups had one end: to improve women's lives.

When she was elected to the Cortes, Clara set to work to reform the law. She was appointed to two parliamentary committees, one on labour and social security and the other on the constitution. As a well-established and respected lawyer, Clara used her legal knowledge to help prepare a new constitution for the recently formed Republic. She called for an end to sexual discrimination, the legal equality of sons and daughters, equal divorce rights and universal suffrage.

As a suffrage activist, Clara wanted votes for women enshrined in the new constitution. She had a clear sense of direction and a vision for Spain's future. In front of 470 men and two women, Clara proposed that in article 36 of the 1931 Constitution 'citizens of either sex, over 23 years of age, will have the same rights in elections', arguing that 'you cannot build a democratic republic without half of the citizenship'. It was highly contentious but Clara was not afraid to take risks. Her biggest disappointment, besides the misogyny of her own party, was the opposition of her friends and left-wing feminist colleagues, Victoria Kent and Margarita Nelken. Over many years, all three women had fought together for women's rights, had stood side-by-side to further the socialist cause. However, Kent and Nelken refused to support votes for women, arguing that women would be too influenced by the clergy of the conservative Catholic Church and would vote against progressive reforms. Clara's motion passed by 40 votes, but only with the backing of right-wing politicians who believed that votes for women would favour them.[4] Despite left-wing and feminist opposition, Spanish women now had the right to choose their politicians. Clara's persistence in overcoming obstacles, her resilience in withstanding the disapproval of her comrades, and her ability to work independently was to have a lasting impact on Spanish politics.

Women also benefitted from a range of legislative reform promoted by this resolute feminist lawyer. Clara called for reform of the marriage and divorce laws, new laws giving equal rights to children born in and out of marriage, labour legislation, maternity rights and equality in marriage. In December 1932, prompted by a letter from several women's organisations asking for the abolition of prostitution, Clara called for an end to prostitution and trafficking in women and girls. She denounced the 'houses of tolerance' i.e. state-regulated brothels, arguing that the State should not legalise vice, nor receive taxes from brothels, nor continue its medical examinations of prostitutes. Many feminists from across Europe – Nancy Astor in Britain, Angelina Merlin in Italy – were similarly trying to reform laws which disadvantaged prostituted women.

In 1933, there was a general election. Clara lost her seat. Left-wing parties were swept away by the advance of the right wing. The Radical Republican Party blamed its defeat on Clara's advocacy for votes for women. It became clear to everyone that left-wing support for women was conditional, driven by political expediency rather than a genuine commitment to justice. In 1936, when most women voted for a left-wing coalition and led it to an overwhelming victory, no one apologised to Clara.

In 1936 Clara saw her dream of a democratic republic destroyed. In July, the Spanish army led by General Franco rebelled against the democratically elected Republican government. Civil war broke out between Fascist rebels and the legitimate government. Clara, whose life was in danger, went into exile. She fled with her 79-year-old mother and fourteen-year-old niece, but was prevented from leaving Spain on an Argentine ship by orders of the Spanish government. Instead, she was forced to board a German ship full of fascists bound for Mussolini's Italy. The sailors threatened her and intimidated her throughout the voyage and once tried to throw her overboard. By now Clara realised that the war drums beating in her own country were a prelude to a death march that was about to begin in Europe.

The trio crossed Italy to Switzerland. They stayed in Lausanne, where her friend Antoinette Quinche gave the family refuge. In 1938, after her mother died, the fifty-year-old Clara left Europe aboard a British Royal Mail ship for a new and unknown country: Argentina.[5] In Argentina, Clara felt more at home: she did not have to learn a new language and felt comfortable in the Spanish culture, able to write and publish her work. Here she published *Creole Heroism*, a collection of personal anecdotes revealing the heroism of refugees and their fight for survival in exile. In 1948 she rented a house in Buenos Aires and took care of five of her brother's children while he was exiled in France. In 1955 a military coup overthrew the Argentian government. Clara, who feared a reprise of Spain, left for Switzerland, the last stage of her 'endless exile', constantly suffering the desolate impotence of never quite belonging and of constantly suppressing her energetic fighting spirit for reform. She felt uprooted, de-rooted.

As an expatriate Republican, Clara hoped that Franco would be deposed and that Spain would return to a democracy. Like many refugees, Clara thought her exile would be temporary, and banished the thought that she might die a refugee in a country that was not her own. She 'longed for Madrid, its clear sky, its streets that were veins of her own body, so beloved since the earliest childhood, that she knew almost as much as the wrinkles of her own face'.[6] Clara was forbidden to return unless she publicly apologised for remarks against the Roman Catholic Church and gave the dictatorship the names of those opposed to it. She was condemned to live out her days in an alien land.

In 1972, Clara died of cancer aged 84 in Lausanne. She wanted her ashes to be returned to Spain, to be buried in her homeland. Her good friend, Antonia, arranged for one of Clara's relatives to cross the French border at night and take

Clara's ashes back home to be buried secretly in a grave in San Sebastian. Three years later Franco died and Spain reverted to a democracy. Today Clara Campoamor is honoured in Spain for persuading the predominantly male Cortes to grant votes for women, thus bringing full democracy to Spain. She has a European Union building in Brussels named after her.

Turkey: Fatma Memik (1903–1991)

Further east, another transformation was taking place as Turkish women leapfrogged over countries such as France, Italy and Switzerland to grant women the right to vote and the right to be lawmakers. For me, as a researcher, Turkish was even more inaccessible than Spanish. The language was impenetrable. Fortunately, the Turkish Embassy responded to my pleas and pointed me towards various sources. I discovered that in 1935 seventeen women entered the Grand National Assembly of Turkey. These stylishly dressed women, all with their heads uncovered, sat together in the back rows. All were very excited, knowing that they were making Turkish history. Turkey, a newly constituted Republic formed in 1923 from the defeat and disintegration of the Ottoman Empire and the abolition of the caliphate, was synonymous with the shift away from religious control of the state. Mustafa Kemal Atatürk, Turkey's first President, dismantled the Islamic legal system, ended religious control of the government and instituted many reforms, including a secular constitution, a ban on polygamy and full civil and political equality for women. The wearing of fezzes and turbans in public was made illegal for men. Women civil servants were banned, and all Turkish women were discouraged, from wearing the hijab. Atatürk was determined to drag Turkey into the modern age, seeing traditional religious leaders as standing in his way, and in the way of progress.

EDİRNE
Dr. Fatma Memik

Images 5 and 6   First women elected to the
Turkish Parliament, 1935. Source: Creative
Commons.

Atatürk was slow in introducing full democracy. In
1934, women were granted the vote and the right to sit in
Parliament. Twelve of the new lawmakers were former teachers,[7] two were farmers,[8] one was a writer,[9] one an inspector[10]
and one a physician: Dr Fatma Memik. All were assiduous,
attending Parliament on a more regular basis than men. Most
sat quietly, raising and lowering their hands as votes were
taken. They all caused little trouble; being a member of the

Assembly was unconventional enough. Some, however, spoke up.[11]

Fatma, now aged 32, was the youngest woman deputy, elected for the Republican People's Party, a party founded by Kemal Atatürk.[12] Between 1923 and 1945, Turkey was a one-party state and the party picked all the candidates. A small number of seats were allocated to women. When Kemal Atatürk nominated Fatma as a candidate, she was guaranteed a seat in his Parliament. The President wanted her as a representative of women and liked her because she spoke French, was a distinguished medic and an enlightened woman. In a post-election interview, she said 'this is such a great revolution that I could not believe it if I had seen it in my dreams. That is why I have been in a deep excitement for several days. What a great honour and a great compliment for me, my heart is full of gratitude.'[13]

Fatma was born in 1903 in the village of Akviran to Cemile Harum and Şakir Bey, a baker and flour merchant. At the time, Turkey was the centre of the Ottoman Empire. Once one of the world's greatest imperial powers, controlling large parts of eastern Europe, North Africa, and the Middle East including modern-day Israel and Palestine, it was beginning to crumble. Fatma and her family were unaware of this trend. She began her education at a local primary school but in 1910, aged 8, she moved to Istanbul with her father so she could attend the Bayezid girls' school and later the Bezmialem Valide Sultan School. Obviously very clever and studious, in 1923 she began medical studies and in 1929 graduated the top of her class.

Fatma was a high-flying medic. Between 1929 and 1931 she specialised in internal medicine, focusing on the prevention, diagnosis and treatment of adult diseases, at the Foundation Gureba Hospital. After a short spell at the Hybeliada Tuberculoss Sanitorium, she quickly worked her way up the medical tree. In 1934 she returned to the Gureba Hospital as head of the polyclinic. A feminist and activist for women's rights, her blend of feminism, coupled with her experience as a physician, gave a distinctive character to her work as a politician.

Fatma won the Edirne constituency in three successive elections. Her experience as a physician helped her work effectively as a member of the Health and Social Welfare Commission. She also took part in the Labour Law Commission set up to reform working conditions. Fatma was especially interested in improving the working lives of women. Above all, she took her role as a local MP seriously. In this role, she championed public health measures, particularly in her Edirne constituency. In May 1939, in a discussion about the budget of the Ministry of Health, she informed Parliament that the Evros river in her region overflowed, fields were submerged and crops destroyed because of an inadequate water system. Inevitably, this led to a great shortage of food, seed and animal feed. Nearly seventy thousand animals, she informed Parliament, were starving, with farmers threatening to dispose of their livestock because they could not afford to keep them. Malaria spread across the area. Dr Fatma Memik established mobile medical teams to help those with the disease and to prevent others from catching it, but people still died unnecessarily. As a medical doctor, she knew only too well that a clean, safe and regular water supply was essential. Fatma therefore asked the government to clean up the rivers, drain the swamps, construct flood defences and rebuild the ancient and inadequate sewage and water system.[14]

Fatma helped her constituents in other ways. In 1935, she submitted a report to Parliament asking that the trans-orient railway be nationalised. At the time, the railways were owned and run as concessions by foreign companies who charged high prices. It was not fair, she believed, for foreign companies to extract profit at the expense of ordinary Turkish people. More particularly, she wanted the vegetables and fruit produced in her constituency to be transported easily and at a reasonable price.

Fatma was committed to women. She was equally committed to medicine, and took every opportunity to help women progress in this field. In June 1937, she spoke in favour of building a new medical facility at Ankara, remarking 'I would like to ask your permission to express my gratitude and thanks to my esteemed elders and professors, who twelve years ago fought hard for the development of Turkish girls in the field of health . . . on behalf of my colleagues, Turkish women.'[15] As well as her parliamentary work, Fatma continued with her charitable and medical work. She was a member of the Topkapi Fukaraperver committee, the Women's Protection Agency, the Child Protection Agency, and worked as a volunteer doctor. In 1938 she attended the International Child Protection Congress in Belgrade. In her medical life she was known as the 'Doctor who practises for free', and the 'mother of the poor' because she helped those who could not afford to pay. After her political career ended in 1946, she returned to medicine.

Brazil: Carlota Pereira de Queirós (1892–1982)[16]

On 13 March 1934, a woman's voice was heard for the first time in the Brazilian Chamber of Deputies. Two years earlier, women had been granted the right to vote and the right to stand for office. 'As well as being a female representative', she told the Assembly, 'I am, like all those who are here, a Brazilian, integrated into the destinies of her country and forever identified with its problems . . . Today men and women must work together, simultaneously, using all our resources to increase Brazil's potential.'[17] The woman was Carlota Pereira de Queirós. Her country, a former Portuguese colony and the fifth largest in the world, was in economic and political chaos. The price of coffee, which was the mainstay of the economy, had crashed alarmingly and an armed insurrection had recently overthrown the constitutionally elected government. Carlota, a Brazilian feminist, was determined to act as an interlocutor for both her country and for women.

Carlota was born on 13 February 1892 in São Paulo to José and Maria Pereira de Queirós. She came from a privileged and politically influential family: her paternal grandparents were wealthy landowners, her grandfather a leading member of the Republican Party and founder of the newspaper *A Provincio de São Paulo*. Carlota was well educated, studying at the Escola Normal da Praça where she was awarded a teaching diploma. Between 1912 and 1922 she worked as a kindergarten teacher. She became disillusioned by teaching and, probably helped by family money, switched careers. In 1920, now aged 28, she enrolled at medical school and in 1926 graduated. Her thesis *Studies on Cancer* won the Miguel Couto Prize, the highest award in her field of haematology. Carlota was undoubtedly intelligent and tenacious, determined to jump over the overwhelmingly male medical barriers that confronted women. Her talent was recognised. As soon as she graduated, she was appointed to manage the paediatric clinic at the school's Faculty of Medicine. In 1928 she became head of the clinical laboratory and founded and managed paediatric clinics in both Rio de Janeiro and São Paulo. A year later, in 1929, she was commissioned by the government to travel to Europe, where she spent time in Switzerland, France and Germany, studying infant dietetics.

In 1930, the lawyer and politician, Getúlio Vargas seized power, overthrowing the constitutionally elected government. In 1932, Carlota joined the insurrection, largely based around São Paulo, against his 'government'. It was a revolution which challenged the centralisation of power by Vargas and demanded a new constitutional framework. Known as the Constitutional Revolution, it soon became violent as the rebels and government troops clashed and intense fighting broke out. Carlota, along with 700 other women, organised a Department of Assistance to the Wounded to care for the men who were injured, as well as running a 'Sewing Workshop' which made uniforms for the rebels. It was here that she gained political visibility, and it was here that her path towards parliament was laid. After 87 days of fighting, with 934 deaths recorded officially, the rebels conceded defeat by the better equipped and larger government forces.

The insurrection was squashed by Vargas. However, the government was forced to concede a new constitution. Carlota's state of São Paulo was permitted to elect representatives for a new Constitutional Assembly. The political leaders of the two main parties who had led the revolt were in exile so a new party was formed. Carlota was chosen to be one of the 22 candidates. Immediately she launched her campaign with a manifesto asking women to support her candidacy.

On 3 May 1933, Carlota became the first and only woman to sit among the 253 parliamentarians in the newly constituted National Constitutional Assembly, nominated as a representative of the United São Paulo Party. In July 1934, the constitution was ratified and Carlota was re-elected to Congress as a member of the Constitutional Party of São Paulo. Carlota insisted that she was received as an equal in the Constitutional assembly without experiencing any misogyny from her male colleagues. 'Not in a single moment', she commented 'did I feel myself in the presence of enemies.'

From the start, Carlota fought for women's and children's rights, for an end to poverty and for educational reform. The first decree in the new Brazilian Assembly was framed by Carlota: it ruled that public funds must be ring-fenced to reduce poverty and its problems. Carlota used her medical knowledge, to advance her cause. She was a member of the Education and Health Commission, where she wrote the proposal for the creation of social services. This led to compulsory funding for social assistance, the construction of the Casa jo Jornaleiro (an organisation which provided a safe space for homeless young boys who sold newspapers on the streets) and a children's biology laboratory which encouraged children to engage with science.

The 1934 constitution which Carlota had helped frame was short-lived. In 1937, Getúlio Vargas closed Parliament, created a new constitution and banned all political parties. During this period, Carlota returned to medicine. She organised the first social service course for women and continued to work for a variety of women's organisations. She published educational texts including work on Froebel and Montessori, and medical texts on haematology. In 1942 she became the first woman to join the National Academy of Medicine. In 1950 she founded the Brazilian Academy of Medical Women; between 1961 and 1967 she served as its President. She died, aged ninety, in São Paulo. Carla's life was without drama, but it was not inconsequential. A Carlota Pereira de Queirós Citizen Women Diploma is awarded annually to five women who have defended women's rights.

New Zealand: Elizabeth Reid McCombs (1873–1935)

Meanwhile, in the New World, the image of an MP was a white man in a suit. In 1893, New Zealand was the first country to grant women the right to vote. It was to be another twenty-eight years before they could stand for Parliament, and another forty-three years before the first woman was elected. In 1933, Elizabeth McCombs was elected the country's first woman MP.[18]

Born on 19 November 1873 at Kaipoi on the South Island of New Zealand, Elizabeth was one of seven sisters and the eighth of nine children of Irish-born Alice Connolly and Scottish-born Daniel Henderson. The children were brought up Presbyterians, a Christian Protestant non-conformist sect committed to social reform. In 1886, when Elizabeth (Bessie) was thirteen, her 55-year-old alcoholic father died. Her mother struggled to feed, clothe and house her young family. Three years later, Elizabeth left school, her education possibly curtailed through lack of money.

When Elizabeth lost her father, her elder siblings adopted a parental role and cleared a political path for their younger sister. Her two sisters Christina and Stella were feminists committed to improving the lives of women and encouraged Elizabeth to become a member of a small socialist club. From there it was a short step to join her sisters on the committee of the Progressive Liberal Association, a socialist group committed to women's rights. In 1898 she took her first step to political independence as a founding member of the Canterbury Children's Aid Society, an organisation set up to secure stringent laws to protect children, to rescue children from undesirable homes, to help care for destitute and neglected children and to set up free creches and nursery schools. In 1901, the Society noted that 'fresh cases are constantly being brought under its notice; poverty, ignorance, immorality and drunkenness on the part of parents result in much suffering to great numbers of children'.[19] Years later, long after Elizabeth had died, the Society was prosecuted for child sexual abuse.

All her life, Elizabeth – possibly because of her late father's alcoholism – was an unswerving prohibitionist. For her, drink was the root of most problems. In 1902 she was the first President of the Young People's No License League, an organisation which mirrored its parent body by advocating the prohibition of alcohol. She also joined the New Zealand Women's Christian Temperance Union (WCTU), a women's international movement, which promoted temperance, Christianity and the abolition of the sale of alcohol. Each member pledged total abstinence and to work for the complete prohibition of alcohol. It adopted the slogan 'lips that touch wine shall not touch mine'. Drink and feminism were often interlinked. WCTU groups across the world often headed the women's suffrage movement, organised petitions and suffrage meetings, distributed suffrage leaflets, lobbied politicians and wrote articles and pamphlets in support of votes for women. In 1893 they were successful in New Zealand. Throughout her life Elizabeth was teetotal, belonging to several prohibition groups. When she died, she was President of the WCTU Sumner branch.

Politics brought Elizabeth a man she could kiss. In 1903, she married another socialist and teetotaller, the Irish-born James McCombs, whom Elizabeth had met at a Progressive Liberal Association meeting. The two shared a political and religious ideology: both were committed Christians, committed socialists, committed to women's rights and committed to the abolition of alcohol. They were active members of the Christchurch Socialist Church and the Fabian Society. In 1913, James founded the Social Democratic Party and became one of its first MPs; in 1916 this merged with other left-wing groups to become the New Zealand Labour Party, with James as President and Elizabeth as a member of the executive. Elizabeth stayed at home with the children on the South Island while James sat in Parliament in North Island's Wellington. Fortunately, New Zealand Parliaments did not sit throughout the year. It convened, said one, after the cows dried up and before the milking season began, allowing James to return home during the long recess. He served as MP for nine years.

Elizabeth, now a mother with two children – Patricia and James – and taking care of two orphans, was a trailblazer in her own right. She was the second woman to be elected to the Christchurch City Council (1921), one of the first to be appointed a JP (1926) and was the first woman to Chair the Electricity Committee (1929). In these roles she promoted her unique brand of 'domestic feminism', building creches and women's lavatories, sponsoring cheap electricity for housewives and improving nurses' working conditions in the local hospitals.

In 1933, James died of a heart attack. The recently widowed Elizabeth, though grief stricken by the sudden death of her husband, stood as Labour candidate in the by-election that followed. She was now sixty years old and her children were grown up. Her late husband had won with only a small majority of 32 whereas Elizabeth, with the help of women's groups, was elected with an overwhelming majority, winning 6,344 of the 10,347 votes, over sixty per cent of the vote. 'I am glad to think', she said in her election address, 'that the first woman to be elected to the Parliament of New Zealand is a member of the Labour Party because the Labour Party has always stood for equal rights . . . for men and women.'[20] Members of over 50 women's organisations held a reception for her and she received over 1,000 congratulatory letters from women of all political and religious persuasions. Parliament had to make concessions: 'No women allowed' signs were taken down; MPs had to refer to Members rather than Gentlemen and the government was forced to build a new lavatory for its first female MP.

The first woman to be elected to Parliament was no parliamentary novice. Elizabeth had helped her late husband in his work as an MP. She had helped him fight two unsuccessful elections and was well acquainted with the workings of Parliament. With a robust record of political reform, she was confident and capable of navigating the all-male assembly. The public galleries were crowded when Parliament convened, full of people who wanted to witness the historical performance of New Zealand's first woman law-maker. MPs from all sides applauded and people in the galleries cheered when she entered the House. Two bouquets of flowers were placed on her desk. She did not disappoint. Newspapers reported that she showed no sign of nervousness when she delivered her initial speech, a 'reasoned address, characterised by fluency and neat marshalling of facts'.[21] In fact, Elizabeth had commented that 'I would like to warn honourable members that

women are never satisfied unless they have their own way.'[22]
She had had to overcome a deeply misogynistic culture. One
newspaper reported that 'women, taken as a sex, are notoriously illogical. Argument to the fair sex usually means harping
on one string and getting cross if the argument is routed.'[23] The
paper conceded that Mrs Elizabeth McCombs was different.

Following her election she remarked, 'I do hope that the
women of New Zealand will realise that where they are
concerned . . . I shall be their representative first.'[24] She kept
her promise. During her short term in Parliament, Elizabeth
championed equal pay, fought for women's unemployment
pay, advocated more women in the police force and tried to
raise the age of marriage from 12 for girls and 14 for boys to an
equal age of 16. She managed to change the Nationality Laws.
Under existing law, women who married a foreigner took on
the nationality of her husband and was thus denied many of
her rights as a New Zealander. The minister, after hearing her
arguments, added a new clause allowing women who married
'aliens' the right to declare their own nationality.

Elizabeth ensured she kept her large parliamentary majority
by working hard in her constituency: she opened the season at
the croquet club, the YWCA garden party, the bring-and-buy
fair at the Opawa school, an event at the local rowing club,
a ceremony at the Soldiers' Settlement Scheme, the annual
meeting of the Federation of Women's institutes, opening
flower shows, and countless Labour Party events.

In 1935, after only two years in Parliament, the 61-year-old
Elizabeth McComb died. Her obituaries point to overwork
as the cause, all speaking of the way she sacrificed her life
to women's rights and to helping the most vulnerable. Flags
were flown at half-mast across the country; thousands lined
the route of her funeral procession. Three hundred trade union
officials, in groups of four, marched in front of the coffin. The
streets of Christchurch were crowded when Bessie McComb's
coffin was paraded through the city's streets. A Memorial

Garden – the McCombs Memorial Garden – was created in honour of the two Labour politicians.

Terence McComb, her son, succeeded to her parliamentary seat. New Zealand's Parliament was once again all-male and predominantly white. In 1949 the first Māori woman, Iriaka Rātana, who was heavily pregnant with her seventh child, was elected a Labour MP. In 2022 women outnumbered men – 60 women to 59 men – for the first time. 'About blimmin' time' said a Green Party MP. In that same year, New Zealand elected its first woman Prime Minister, Jacinta Ahern, a Labour Party MP.

Every woman in this chapter broke new ground by marking a way through the forest of masculinity. They all forged new paths, fostering change and progress, sometimes through persuasion rather than conflict. At the beginning they shared a cautious optimism that women's political rights were advancing globally. However, in the 1930s, the world-wide Depression created economic dislocation and widespread poverty, thus curtailing the efforts of all these social reformers. Countries responded to these challenges in various ways. Women suffered, particularly in those regimes which became autocratic. As Joan W. Scott points out, there is a connection between authoritarian regimes and the control of women, arguing that rulers 'have legitimised domination, strength, central authority and ruling power as masculine' and made laws which put women in their desired place.[25] Certainly, the fragility of democratic institutions was revealed when repressive regimes took over by force and squashed opposition. In Spain, the triumph of its authoritarian regime with its masculinised ideology, rolled back the gains women had made. Women were pushed out of political life and relegated to domestic roles. In Brazil, state intervention ameliorated the effects of the international downturn but it did so at the expense of democracy, and often at the expense of women. Turkey espoused democratic principles and provided new opportunities for women to take part in the body politic, but in practice a strong, centralised one-party rule suppressed opposition. There was no democratic wobble in New Zealand. A few months after Elizabeth McComb's death, the country elected its first Labour government, which swiftly established a welfare state, extended benefits for families, set up community-based health care, free education, unemployment benefits and policies to protect working people.

Chapter Four

War and Peace, 1940–1950:
Italy, France, Japan, Pakistan, Israel

On the night of 12 March 1945, fascist 'authorities' executed two sisters, Vera and Libera Arduino, for taking part in the Italian resistance. Women anti-fascists placed a bouquet of yellow mimosa tied up with a red, white and green ribbon, the colours of the Italian flag, on their tomb. The mimosa was a symbol of Clara Zetkin's International Women's Day. It was a message of solidarity.

Soon after the murder of the Arduino sisters, the leader of the Fascists, Benito Mussolini, and his mistress, were arrested and shot. Their bodies were taken to Milan and hung upside down for public display in the Piazzale Loreto. The Fascist era was over. On 8 May, when Germany surrendered, the war in Europe ended. A few months later, on 2 September 1945, the global conflict finished when the Japanese surrendered.

The Second World War was the most devastating conflict in history, resulting in unparallelled destruction, a genocide and claiming more lives – some estimate 70 million – than any other war. It marked a significant shift in global power, hastened the collapse of the British Empire, enforced democracy on defeated countries, created new nations and re-drew national boundaries. The defeat of Nazism and Fascism – with their racist ideology and masculinised politics – renewed and strengthened democratic ideals, and it was widely accepted that universal suffrage was inevitable. Women benefitted from this powerful new commitment to democracy.

Italy: Angelina Merlin (1887–1979)

Post-war Italy, as with most of Europe, experienced acute economic and social crisis: agricultural production was sixty per cent down, industrial production had decreased by one-third, the 350 per cent war-time inflation had battered the economy. Food and housing were expensive and in short supply.[1] In June 1946, Italy became a Republic, a general election was called and a new constitution set up a parliamentary democracy. An incredible 92 per cent of the electorate voted. Twenty-one women (and 537 men) were elected to the new Parliament under a system of proportional representation. These women, along with their male parliamentarians, were faced with clearing up the mess left by twenty years of fascism. They were tasked with creating Italy's first full democratic Parliament.

Half of the first women parliamentarians had served in the Resistance against Fascism. They had raised money for the resistance, nursed the sick, cooked for the fighters, printed and distributed anti-Fascist literature, hidden partisans and helped Jewish people flee persecution. These women represented all social classes. All had grown up under Fascism, yet a 'red thread' united them: all had taken part in the war of liberation, all were members of women's associations, some had even been the founders. For the most part, these first female lawmakers promoted policies such as equal rights for women. They campaigned for family rights and educational reforms. Together these women gradually reconstructed civil and social society, a society which had been destroyed by the regime of Mussolini.[2]

Angelina (Lina) Merlin, one of the first women elected, had been a staffette (courier), one of the most dangerous jobs in the Resistance.[3] On one occasion, she boarded a tram in Milan and sat down with the other passengers. She looked respectable, well-dressed and attractive, a young bourgeois woman shopping for her family. Her appearance concealed her intentions.

In her bag was a stick of dynamite to be delivered to resistance fighters. Suddenly two German soldiers came on to the train and searched the passengers. Lina, terrified she was about to be murdered, tried as best as she could to keep calm. She knew the dangers. She smiled at the officers, aware that one female courier had been beaten, her fingernails ripped off, her face disfigured and her eyes gouged out before she was shot. Women couriers faced death if they were caught – 623 were killed, 4,653 were arrested and tortured and 2,750 deported to Germany and never seen again.[4] Fortunately, Angelina's bag was not searched. The dynamite was safely delivered.

Angelina was born on 15 October 1887 in Pozzonovo, Padua to middle-class liberal Roman Catholic parents. She was the eldest of nine children. Her father Fruttuoso Merlin was a municipal officer and her mother, Giustina Poli, a teacher. Angelina was well-educated. On leaving her convent school she went on to train as a teacher, before completing her formal education at the University of Padua with a degree in French. Angelina followed her mother into teaching and, even though qualified as a French teacher, chose to work in primary schools.

In 1919, Angelina joined the Italian Socialist Party where she helped set up a women's section. For the next few years, she wrote articles for the socialist weekly *L'Eco dei lavatory* and other left-wing periodicals. These revealed her overriding concerns: the right to vote, equality for women both sexually and professionally and, even more controversially, the rights of prostituted women. In her view, prostitution occurred because of female inequality both in the home and at work.[5] In an article, entitled 'Maddalene' which was published in the *Workers' Echo*, Angelina argued that 'it is the defective socio-economic position that creates the need for prostitution ... the social phenomenon of prostitution is precisely ... that the woman is in a state of inferiority, both in the home and when employed'.[6] In her view, prostitutes were victims in need of rescuing.

There was no doubt that Angelina was becoming a committed activist, despite the dangers. In 1924 she directed the socialist election campaign in Veneto. As part of her work, she drew up a detailed report about the violence and intimidation used by the squads of black-shirted fascists and gave it to Giacomo Matteotti, a leading socialist politician. He used her report to criticise Mussolini's government – soon after, Giacomo was kidnapped and murdered.[7]

The Fascist police decided to target Angelina. In March 1926, when she refused to take an oath to Mussolini, she was dismissed from her teaching job. The Fascists were watching her closely. A few months later she was arrested and sentenced to five years imprisonment. In 1929, her sentence was reduced and she returned to Padua. Fearing re-arrest, Angelina moved to Milan where she worked privately as a French language teacher. In 1933, she married Dante Galliani, a doctor, former socialist parliamentarian and widower whom she had known for some time. When he died after just three years of marriage, Angelina became a mother to his two sons as well as adopting the daughter of a late cousin.

Despite the possibility of arrest and re-imprisonment, this widowed activist, now with three children under her care, remained committed to the anti-fascist struggle. She hosted clandestine meetings at her house, and it was here that the leading socialists opposed to the regime met and planned insurrection. Angelina was now a leading member of the Resistance, taking an active role in the Women's Defence Group (the Gruppa di difesa della donna), and doing whatever she could to help resistance fighters. In May 1943 when the Fascists questioned her as to why she was not a member of the Fascist party she responded 'Do you know the date of the origin of fascism? I do, 23 March 1919. Today is 18 May 1943. If I am not a member it is because I am not a fascist.'[8] In 1944 she co-founded the Italian Women's Union; in April 1945, when Milan was liberated from the Nazis, she was appointed Deputy

Commissioner for Public Education in the Lombardy National Liberation Committee; in June she joined the national leadership of the Socialist Party as head of the women's commission.

In June the following year, Angelina was elected to the Constituent Assembly representing the Socialist Party of Proletarian Unity. Angelina, along with the other women elected, established 'the fundamental values on which to build the new state'.[9] She was among the 75 parliamentarians charged with drafting the new constitution, serving on a subcommittee relating to Economic and Social Rights. Here she helped set up the principles on which Italy's welfare policies and citizenship were based.

Angelina was about to change the face of her country. She proposed that the constitution include the phrase 'without distinction of sex', a phrase that legally established the equality of women. In addition, she co-wrote the report for the subcommittee. In it, she argued that the state should guarantee every citizen the right to decent living conditions, health care and protection against unemployment.[10] The principle of equal rights for men and women at work 'in the company, the office, the school, the workshop and the field', she insisted, was essential for a mature nation.[11]

Angelina believed that poverty threatened family life, arguing that the Italian government had a duty to ensure that all citizens intending to start and maintain a family had enough money to do so. In her view, the family was built around the mother, and it was through the mother that the health of society was guaranteed. All too aware of the high mortality rate among pregnant women, Angelina fought for maternity care. At the time, many poor women gave birth at home, in squalid conditions which lacked the minimum requirements of hygiene and obstetric care. A few hours after giving birth, many women got up to do housework or even to work in the fields. Angelina advocated delivery rooms within hospitals, with pregnant women cared for by specialists, rather than less qualified midwives. It was, she argued, the duty of the state to guarantee every pregnant woman the safety of her life at the time of childbirth, and the right to deliver healthy children free of injuries or malformations. For this reason, she advocated both pre- and post-natal leave, paid for in full. Another particularly thorny issue emerged around the legal status of so-called illegitimate children. She wanted the state to stop differentiating between legitimate and illegitimate children. 'Illegitimate' children, she argued, should enjoy the same social and legal rights as those considered 'legitimate'.

Such was her reputation that in April 1948, Angelina was elected to the Senate, one of four women in the upper house. It was here that she made her biggest contribution to legal reform. On 6 August 1948 she presented a bill for the abolition of the regulation of prostitution in Italy and the abolition of the 'houses of tolerance' (case di tolleranza). The case de tolleranza were state-regulated brothels and the women who worked in them were subjected to compulsory health examinations. No men suffered this indignity. In addition, police had the power to register women they thought were prostitutes. It was a system, Angelina argued, open to abuse, largely because it was a weapon of blackmail and extortion. The women who ended up in the police net were the poorest (often the ones who could not afford the police bribe) and the ones exposed to the worst harassment. The old law was, in her view, 'a regime that allows countless abuses against any woman suspected of prostitution, . . . (and an) iniquitous and ineffective system of public health protection', in that the men who used prostitutes were never examined. It was, she argued, 'an intolerable violation of the laws of humanity'.[12] Women who had endured this exploitation or who were arrested wrongly were generally frightened to speak about it. Under this code, women prostitutes were punished for offences 'against modesty and sexual honour', – the men who used them were never charged. Angelina proposed an amendment to the Criminal Code, the closing of the state-regulated 'houses of tolerance', the end to compulsory examination of prostitutes and the elimination of prostitution. Angelina Merlin assumed that it would be an easy victory for women's rights. Most people believed that the state system of regulation was wrong and that the women trapped in state brothels, who were subjected to forced examinations, should be freed.[13] In her speeches she argued against this 'trade in human beings' and drew attention to the United Nations, which had recently drawn up an international convention against the exploitation of prostitution. She told her colleagues that the US incarcerated those who sold women's bodies whereas France had closed its brothels. She believed that there was a cause-effect relationship between the presence of brothels and the trafficking of women both at a national and international level. In all countries, traffickers had collaborators, correspondents, informants, secret hideouts, manufacturers of false passports and identity cards, special bankers and even 'exchanges' where female victims were the object of transactions.[14]

Experience showed that punishing prostitutes was completely ineffective. Instead, she argued, prostitution could be stopped if the men organising the illicit trade were punished. Undoubtedly, Angelina was more sympathetic to women. Her proposal insisted that women who occasionally worked as prostitutes should not be targeted with special repressive measures. She was convinced that women who had just entered prostitution had hopes of redemption. Angelina wanted the morality police to be disbanded and a special women's police force to take its place. She hoped – and expected – that women's groups would take care of and rehabilitate former prostitutes.

Angelina, a former resistance fighter, political activist and fearless champion, was insulted and continuously verbally attacked. Much of this debate was conducted in closed sessions because it was considered unseemly to have a discussion on prostitution in front of the press and the public. The parliamentary bill she proposed took an extraordinarily ten long years to become law, in the process changing as it proceeded. Her original Bill had specified that prostitutes were victims of men who exploited them whereas the final Bill construed women as the culprits. After ten years of battling Parliament, Law 75, 20 February 1958, known as the 'Merlin Law', was passed. The law abolished the 560 brothels which were state regulated. It also abolished the records of prostituted women, freeing them from stigma and giving them the opportunity to leave prostitution.

Throughout her life, Angelina fought for the underprivileged. She advocated prison reform, the elimination of 'NN' ('*nomen nescio*', father unknown) which was put on the birth certificates of children without a named father and for the transfer of pregnant women convicts to hospitals when giving birth. She was also a good constituency MP. In 1951, aged 64, Angelina was not afraid to get her feet wet when her district suffered from flooding: she was found in the muddy valleys, 'a little woman tucked in rubber boots among the rescue men', all the while criticising those responsible for the lack of bulldozers, trucks and sandbags.[15]

Angelina Merlin retired at the age of 77 and, urged on by Elena, her adopted daughter, began writing her memoirs. On 10 August 1979, she died, aged 92. Her memoirs were published in 1989, ten years after her death.

France: Eugénie Éboué Tell (1891–1972)

The French Revolution of 1789 proclaimed Liberty, Equality and Fraternity. The cry for brotherhood meant what it said: it took France 156 years to include women. On 21 October 1945, in the first election in which women could vote and stand for election, thirty-three women joined the Constituent Assembly, a Parliament set up to draft a new constitution for what would become the Fourth Republic. France was reinventing itself as

Image 7 Eugénie and Felix Éboué Tell.
Source: Musée de la Libération de Paris.

a democratic nation, rewarding those who had held steadfast in the fight against Nazism. Twenty-six of the women were former resistance fighters, many of whom had been arrested, imprisoned, and sent to concentration camps like Ravensbrück, Saarbrucken and Auschwitz. Some had witnessed the murder of their partners or male relatives. All the women, apart from one, were white.

Looks can be deceiving. Who would expect that the pretty woman shown, in full wedding regalia, would turn out to be the first black woman to be elected to a French parliament? How did this happen? France was keen to hold on to its colonies by awarding them (limited) political rights. Eugénie Éboué Tell was the first woman of African descent, and the first woman from the colonies to be elected to the National Assembly. She was elected to both Chambers: in 1945 she took her seat in the National Assembly at the Palais Bourbon on the banks of the Seine and in 1946 she joined the Senate at the Palais Luxembourg. This strong-willed, passionate woman was one of the most influential voices of black feminism, citizenship and decolonisation in the twentieth century, committed to forging France and its former Empire into a new union based on equality.[16]

Born in 1891 in Cayenne, French Guiana, she was the daughter of Joséphine and Herménégilde Tell. Her father was the first black director of the prison Saint-Laurent-du-Maroni in French Guiana, a remarkable achievement for someone with slave ancestors.[17] His father, Eugénie's grandfather, Hippolyte Tell, was a former slave, set free in 1848 at the age of ten. By the early stages of the twentieth century, Eugénie's parents were wealthy enough to send her to a girls' high school, the Lycée pour jeunes filles in Montauban, France, where she was trained as a primary school teacher, returning in 1911 to teach in her home country.

In 1921/2 Eugénie married Félix Éboué, a colonial official who was about to climb high up the administrative ladder.

In 1936 he was appointed Governor General of Guadeloupe and worked his way up to become governor of French Equatorial Africa. He was the first man of African descent to be appointed to such a senior position. Dutifully, Eugénie followed her husband around his diplomatic posts, helping him fulfil his role as colonial governor. They became viewed as a power couple. Eugénie was a trained teacher, thus competent to help her husband with his research. Sometimes her knowledge surprised everyone. For example, Eugénie helped her husband understand the Drum-and-Whistle speech of two of the Central African Republic tribes. The local populations were both amazed and thrilled that anyone should understand their language and Felix's authority was boosted by his wife's intervention.

During their stay in Chad, France was invaded by Germany and a puppet state led by Vichy was set up. Most colonial administrators supported the Vichy regime but the Éboués were an exception. The couple publicly backed Charles de Gaulle at a time when it was neither popular nor safe to do so. Indeed, Felix was the first colonial governor to reject the Vichy regime by championing de Gaulle's London-based Free French movement and opening Equatorial Africa as a base for the resistance army. Encouraged by the Éboués, de Gaulle set up the Empire Defense Council to fight against the Nazis throughout the colonies – the couple remained close to de Gaulle all their lives. Both Éboués were also members of the SFIO, the French section of the Workers' International. A committed socialist as well as a Francophile Gaullist, Eugénie defies easy categorisation but her main aim throughout her life was to further the rights of colonial citizens.

Eugénie joined the Free French Women's Forces and worked as a nurse in the military hospital in Brazzaville, capital of French Equatorial Africa. As a trusted wife of the most senior administrator, she was privy to the movements of African troops committed to defending France. Seen as enemies of

Vichy France, the Éboués' Parisian home was confiscated, the couple were condemned to death in absentia and three of their children held as hostages. Two of their sons were incarcerated in German prisoner-of-war camps and their daughter banned from attending school. In the end, all three escaped from France using passports issued in Britain.

Brazzaville, where the couple lived, served as the capital of Free France; its radio station, Radio Brazzaville, was the voice of Free France. In 1944 the city hosted a meeting between the French resistance and colonial administrators in which the relationship between France and its African colonies was redefined. General de Gaulle presided. All the participants, save two, were white. The Brazzaville Declaration, as it was known, recommended that all residents – regardless of birthplace – would be French citizens with equal rights. Consequently, all those adults, whether born in France or her colonies, would have the right to vote in the National Assembly. The meeting also proposed that the French Empire would disband in favour of a French Union which would integrate the colonies into a united France. Madame Éboué wanted greater autonomy for her country and other French colonies. She agreed with the decision by the French government to rename its colonies 'overseas territories' with the assumption that this implied. It was a last attempt of the French to keep its colonial powers.

In 1944 Eugenie, now the mother of four children, was widowed when her husband unexpectedly died of pneumonia while visiting Egypt.[18] She was now not just the head of the family but heir to her husband's political legacy.[19] General de Gaulle had promised to include people from the overseas territories in his government. He kept his word and helped Eugénie Éboué Tell to be elected first to the Assembly and then to the Senate.

In 1945, Eugénie represented Guadeloupe in the Constituent National Assembly, helping to draft the constitution of the new French Fourth Republic. She and the other policy makers passed legislation which shaped the newly reconstituted France. Now a socialist, she fought to gain equality for those born and living in French colonies, spending her political life insisting on equal rights for France's overseas subjects. For the first time, millions of former colonial subjects became citizens of France, theoretically defining it as a multi-racial and multi-cultural country.

In 1946, after new elections, Eugénie was elected to the Senate. It was a breakthrough Parliament: the President of the Senate was the grandson of former slaves, and more than a hundred senators were from African, Asian or Arabic descent, a situation that has never been replicated in France's governing bodies. Here, Eugenié joined forces with another woman of African heritage, Jane Vialle, and the two pushed for further rights for France's overseas citizens. In 1952, when she retired from the Senate, Eugénie was elected vice-president of the French Union, a consultative body established by the new Republic and headed by the French President. The new Union combined metropolitan France and its overseas territories to create a unified France consisting of the mother country and all its colonies. In 1965, Eugénie was again elected, this time for a district in France. It was a big geographical break. The family at the time lived in a suburb of Paris and never visited French Guiana again and only twice travelled to Guadeloupe. By this time, Eugenie identified as a Parisian.

Undoubtedly, Madame Eugénie Éboué Tell was an important force in the post-war French and Afro-diasporic politics, one of the most powerful black women in France, constantly arguing in Parliament for a range of economic reforms and government investment in overseas territories. Eugénie died, aged 82, on 20 November 1972. By the time she died, she had been awarded twenty-six medals including three of France's highest honours: the Croix de Guerre, the Resistance medal, and a Commander of the Legion of Honour.

Japan: Shidzué Katö (1897–2001)

On 6 August 1945 the United States employed their newest weapon: the atomic bomb. On that fateful day, American pilots dropped an atomic bomb on the Japanese city of Hiroshima, causing the most appalling devastation. Three days later they dropped another, this time on the city of Nagasaki. Those killed were mostly civilians; those who suffered the lasting effects of radiation were mostly civilians. Japan surrendered. It was the first and last time atomic bombs were used.

Eight months after the end of the war, Japan held its first election. The victorious allies, keen to rebuild Japan into a modern state, forced parliamentary democracy on the country. The American General MacArthur, in overall charge of reconstruction, placed 'the emancipation of women through enfranchisement' at the top of his list of Five Reforms.[20] On 10 April 1946, women went to the ballot box and women stood for the Diet, the Japanese Parliament. The thirty-nine women elected, from across the political spectrum, all worked to make democracy palatable to their country.[21] They were regarded as the 'stars of democratisation'.[22] Shidzué was among the women elected to the Diet.[23] Shortly after, she was promoted to the upper house of councillors. She remained in Parliament until 1974.

Shidzué was born into an affluent samurai family, the eldest daughter of six. Her father Ritaro Hirota, a mechanical engineer, and her mother brought Shidzué up as a Sōdōshū, a member of this branch of Zen Buddhism. Both parents wore kimonos at home but when her father went to work, he changed and wore a Western suit.[24] Ritaro travelled frequently to the West, and brought back gifts and clothes for his wife and children. As a young girl, Shidzué wore Western clothes, climbed trees, walked on home-made bamboo stilts and fished tadpoles in ponds on the family estate. It was a pampered childhood. As she grew older, her mother, keen to ensure that her daughter followed Japanese tradition, dressed her in a kimono, employed tutors for flower arranging and tea-making and instilled in her the duties expected of a good wife. Shidzué was sent to the Peeresses' school, a prestigious girls' school founded for the children of aristocrats. It was a school which reinforced the need for subservience, chastity and domesticity, essential components of her mother's teachings of how to be a 'good wife and wise mother'.

Marriage was the preferred destiny for Japanese girls. Some parents betrothed their children as soon as they were born, and sometimes even when the woman was pregnant. Marriage was for life and wives were expected to subordinate themselves to the wishes of their husband and his family. By this time, polygamy had been abolished in Japan but rich aristocratic men employed ladies-in-waiting to serve themselves and their wives. There were two classes of ladies-in-waiting: the 'Honourable Pure' and the 'Honourable Impure'. The former remained virginal whereas the latter were 'honourably touched' by their employer. By law, authority resided with men; wives were expected to obey.

On 3 December 1914, aged eighteen, Shidzué married Baron Keikichi Ishimoto, an engineer, Christian humanist . . . and control freak. It was an arranged marriage. The bride dressed in white, the colour worn at funerals, to signify that she was dead to her parents. Her trousseau was split into two sections: one contained furniture such as several chests, a dinner table and a bookcase; the other contained bedding and clothes. An eleven-page catalogue listed her trousseau, which ranged from a platinum ring set with six diamonds and a sapphire, through to over 100 beautifully embroidered kimonos, all reflecting the wealth of her family. And three boxes of books. These bridal goods were carried by four two-ton trucks to her new home. A Japanese bride did not bring money; her trousseau was deemed sufficient. When she married, Shidzué lost all rights to this property. All of it belonged to her new family. The newly married Baroness Shidzué Ishimoto was forbidden to leave the home without permission, and expected to be submissive and obsequious to her husband and mother-in-law. Each day her mother-in-law chose which kimono she should wear.

After marriage, the couple moved to Kyushu, a major Japanese coalfield, where Ishimoto, keen to live life among working people, was employed as a mining engineer. Here they lived among the coal workers and for the first time in her young life, Shidzué was exposed to human suffering. As she commented in her autobiography, she had been 'trained only in love, beauty, poetry'[25] and always lived in elegantly appointed surroundings. Now, here in Kyushu, Shidzué was shocked by their own living situation. The young marrieds lived in a dirty, dilapidated house in an industrial area, a stark contrast from her parental home. Rats ran about freely, there was no bathroom, and when it rained buckets were placed around the house to catch the water which cascaded through the leaky roof. The newly married Shidzué was equally appalled by the working conditions. When she visited the mine, she was shocked to see men working naked in the pit, crawling on their knees along low shafts to dig out coal. Women and children, she wrote, 'had to creep into passages like wriggling worms to pull baskets of coal out to the place where the wagons stood'.[26] No day passed without an accident and every few days a miner died. Pregnant women worked until the last moment, giving birth in the dark mine. Women were weighed down by constant pregnancy and the early deaths of their children. Infant mortality was high.

In 1919, Keikichi moved to America, where Shidzué later joined him, leaving her two children at home with his family. Her Westernised husband wanted his new wife to become modern and independent: he insisted that Shidzué enrol on a secretarial course in New York. He continued to be perverse and cruel, forcing his aristocratic wife to live in a tenement block; asking her, a woman who had previously all her thoughts and actions dictated by others, to think for herself; and insisting that Shidzué, who had never worked for money, become a thoroughly modern American woman and find a job. Yet, like the submissive Japanese wife she had been reared to become, she obeyed. Almost immediately, the Baron left to work in Washington, leaving his wife to struggle with the English language, adapt to a new secretarial school and find a decent place to live that was not a slum.

Before he left, the Baron introduced her to Agnes Smedley, who in turn arranged a meeting with Margaret Sanger. Shidzué's life was about to take a dramatic turn. Listening to Margaret Sanger's account of the birth-control movement, Shidzué's experiences in the mining community came vividly to mind. She had witnessed first-hand the constant grind of pregnancy, of women worn out by work and child-rearing. Japanese women, she believed, would welcome birth control methods. In her view, uncontrolled pregnancy robbed the mother of health and increased infant mortality. These beliefs, like those of Margaret Sanger, were linked to eugenics, a set of beliefs aimed at improving the genetic quality of a given population. Shidzué came to believe that the uncontrolled fertility of poor Japanese women weakened the nation, weakened the health of children, and weakened women who bore all those babies. She began to argue for voluntary motherhood, for women to choose pregnancy rather than have it forced upon them. In effect, she became a eugenic feminist, someone who wanted women to give birth to healthy children, thereby strengthening the Japanese race. These ideas, and the way they were later used to forcibly sterilise women in Nazi Germany, are – quite rightly – seen as abhorrent, racist and are now discredited.

Shidzué carried the banner for birth control to her native country. In 1922, now back in Japan, she helped Margaret Sanger organise her first tour promoting birth control, and later accompanied her on all her seven trips. Shidzué set up the Women's Association for Birth Control, translated

Sanger's pamphlets, wrote her own and published a periodical entitled *Small Family*. She devoted the rest of her life to helping women gain control over their bodies by providing knowledge and advice on how to stop unwanted pregnancies. In so doing, Shidzué was pilloried in the press, hissed at in the street and regarded as a betrayer of both her class and gender. Birth control was not a subject to be discussed in polite society, especially by a woman who should know better.

In 1936, Shidzué set up Japan's first birth control clinic in Tokyo, where she supplied women with advice on how to limit their families. In so doing, she challenged Japanese beliefs about class and gender norms. Shidzué's views were abhorrent to those who believed that Japanese women should be subservient and not engage in politics. The military regime was hostile, banned contraceptives and made it illegal to provide advice on family planning. In 1937 she was arrested, detained in prison for two weeks, forced to close her birth control clinic and banned from promoting family planning. By now, her husband no longer wanted an independent wife but someone who was submissive to his beliefs. The couple separated and later divorced. It was not easy because, as aristocrats, they needed permission from the Imperial Household Agency. After her divorce, Shidzué supported her family by writing, lecturing and opening a shop which sold sewing materials. In 1944 she remarried. Her new husband, Kanjo Katö, was a leading socialist and a year later Shidzué, now aged 48, gave birth to a daughter.

In 1946, Shidzué Katö was elected to the Japanese Diet. Here she not only encountered male hostility but sexual harassment and ridicule. She was excluded from meetings. Shidzué may have been hurt by this behaviour but she remained adamant. Her past experiences had made her resilient. She was not afraid to face the opposition of male parliamentarians and continued to push for birth control and the abolition of the feudal family code. In 1950 she was elected to the Upper House. She was one of six women on the 72-member subcommittee to decide on Japan's new constitution. She asked that equality for men and women and the abolition of the Japanese patriarchal system be embedded in the Constitution. In 1975 she was awarded the First Order of the Sacred Treasure. In 1999 Japan approved the birth control pill. Two years later Shidzué died aged 104, after a life devoted to promoting women's equality.

Pakistan: Shaista Suhrawardy Ikramullah (1915–2000)

Like Shidzué, Shaista Suhrawardy Ikramullah was an aristocrat. In 1947, Shaista was one of two women elected to the first Constituent Assembly of the newly formed Pakistan.[27] A year earlier, Shaista had been elected to the Constituent Assembly of India, but, like Constance Markievicz before her, refused to take her seat because she did not recognise the Indian Parliament: Shaista believed in independence for Pakistan. Her presence in Pakistan's first assembly was a bold statement, a statement that Pakistan was embracing modernity in an era when women's participation was minimal worldwide. The Western press condescendingly remarked that Begum Ikramullah 'is at once exotic and modern. She wears the traditional dress of that part of the world, the flowing sari, and yet, she is typical of the new women of the Moslem countries.'[28]

On 22 July 1915, when the victorious nations of the First World War were reformulating Europe and India was part of the British Empire, Shaista Suhrawardy was born in Calcutta (now Kolkata). Her father, Sir Hassan, was a district medical officer, while her mother, Shaherbano, came from an aristocratic land-holding family in Bengal. Her grandfather, Nawab Abdul Latif, had followed conventional Islamic traditions and her mother Shaherbano was brought up in purdah. In contrast, Shaista's early life was formed by both Western and Muslim culture. Her anglophile father hired English governesses, and insisted his children wore Western clothes; her mother, steeped in Islamic culture, ensured her children were fully aware of Muslim traditions. Shaista was taught Urdu and Persian, introduced to Islamic literature and instructed in the Quran. In addition, her mother observed the zenana lifestyle, remained in strict purdah and insisted that Shaista observed this from the age of nine. As Shaista wrote in her autobiography, she 'spent [her] childhood and early girlhood between the Arabian Nights world of [her] mother's family and [her] ultra-Westernised home'.[29] It could have led to a cultural schizophrenia, but Shaista remained unworried by this dual existence, insisting that she 'used to slip easily from one to another'.

In 1933, the eighteen-year-old Shaista married Mohammed Ikramullah, an Indian civil servant. It was an arranged marriage. She was now Begum Ikramullah. She dedicated her book *From Purdah to Parliament* like this: 'To my husband who took me out of purdah and has regretted it ever since.' It was a light-hearted dedication as the two were happily married. Indeed, Shaista's husband was sympathetic from the outset to his wife's political beliefs, replying to critics 'My wife is an intelligent woman . . . I will not and cannot control her.'[30] When her father insisted that his daughter complete her BA in English Literature at Calcutta University before the wedding, his future son-in-law agreed. Soon after the wedding the couple moved to New Delhi where Ikram, as he was known, was appointed a colonial administrator, the only Muslim administrator in the city. Here, Shaista was expected to accompany her husband on his official duties. She was nervous, not just because of the travel, but because she would have to come out of purdah. She commented, 'I did not enjoy my first experience of being out of purdah at all. I felt embarrassed at being looked at by hundreds of men.'[31] She was one of the first Indian Muslim women to show her unveiled face in public.

In 1936 Ikram was transferred to London. Shaista and their young three-year-old son joined him. Two daughters were

later born in England. The care of three young children did
not curb Shaista's life, possibly because her wealth and position allowed her to pay for someone to cook, clean and look
after the children. Shaista felt freer in London than she had
in India, regularly visited the theatre and ballet, read as much
as she liked and studied for a PhD at the School of Oriental
and African Studies, University of London. She became
Dr Begum Ikramullah, the first Muslim woman to be awarded
a doctorate by the university.

The couple returned to Delhi in 1939. Here she met
Mohammad Ali Jinnah, the charismatic leader of the Muslim
League, and his sister Fatima, both of whom encouraged her
involvement in Muslim politics. Shaista joined the Muslim
League, helped set up the Muslim Women's Students
Federation, and joined the Muslim League Women's Sub-
Committee, all organisations committed to an independent
Pakistan. Soon she became a major figure within the Muslim
League.

In 1947, Britain declared it was leaving India. In August
1947, after horrific violence, Pakistan became independent.
In September, Shaista, with her family and her newly born
daughter, moved to Karachi, the capital of the newly formed
Pakistan, 'the land of promise, the land of hope, the land for
which thousands had sacrificed their lives . . . we were now a
nation and a state'.[32] In the first few weeks of Pakistan, Shaista,
who had helped to bring it to fruition, recognised that she
and her colleagues were facing a momentous challenge: how
to feed, clothe and find accommodation for the five million
refugees fleeing from India. In addition, there was a desperate
need to comfort those whose families had been murdered and
whose wives and daughters had been raped.

Between 1947 and 1954 Shaista was a member of the
Constituent Assembly. Here she backed three causes: the unity
of East and West Pakistan, the rights of religious minorities and
the rights of women. With the other female member, Jahanara,

she worked hard to enshrine the rights of women into the constitution. The two women championed the 'Muslim Personal Law of Shariat', a law which guaranteed women full rights to inherit property, and guaranteed women equality of status, equal opportunities and equal pay, all within Islamic law. The two women faced fierce resistance from their male colleagues but won their case and in 1951 the law became effective.

Meanwhile, in 1948, as a measure of her success, Shaista was appointed a member of Pakistan's delegation to the United Nations, where she helped draft the Universal Declaration of Human Rights in a committee chaired by Eleanor Roosevelt, the wife of the American President. The Declaration of Human Rights in 1948 marked a pivotal moment in world history. In the aftermath of their victory against Fascism and Nazism, nations across the globe sought to prevent a recurrence of the Holocaust. The rights that were included form the basis of international law, laws which the United Nations still works to promote. Shaista Ikramulla, a delegate from newly established Pakistan, helped draft its constitution, particularly Article 16 on equal rights in marriage, child marriage and forced marriage. Shaista, who had spent a large part of her life in purdah, or sex segregation, secluded from public eye, was now at the epicentre of decision making in an international organisation.

She was also a member of the committee on the 'Convention on the Prevention and Punishment of the Crime of Genocide'. The subject was a very emotive one as thousands of Muslims had been killed and their homes destroyed during the partition of India and Pakistan. On 9 December 1949, the Convention was adopted. Years later, although Shaista lamented that there was abuse of human rights across the world, she held the Declaration 'as a goal, to which those who believe in the freedom of the human spirit can try to reach'.[33]

Her husband was a high-flying diplomat serving as High Commissioner in Canada between 1952 and 1954, Ambassador to France 1954 and High Commissioner to the UK between

1955 and 1959. Shaista, still a dutiful wife as well as a politician, accompanied him. When the couple returned to Pakistan in 1959, they found it changed. A new military regime had overthrown the civilian government. At first the couple supported the new regime. Ikram was appointed Foreign Secretary and Shaista helped draft an important piece of legislation – Muslim Family Laws Ordnance – giving women more rights by requiring all marriage to be registered, curtailing polygamy, preventing male-instigated divorce and guaranteeing maintenance payments for abandoned wives. In 1961, as military rule consolidated further, the couple moved back to London, where Ikram died.

In 1964 Shaista was appointed Pakistan's emissary to Morocco, the first woman in that post, where she developed an increasing interest in the Arab world. In 1967 she was distressed by the Arab-Israeli war, lamenting 'the sufferings of our Arab brethren as a result of the iniquitous establishment of the State of Israel . . . a dagger plunged into their heart'.[34]

Shaista, was not only a wife and politician but an established author. She wrote articles for Urdu women's magazines and English-language newspapers, and books, including *From Purdah to Parliament* and *Beyond the Veil*. Shaista bridged the gap between the old and the new. She was born just before the disappearance of the Mughal Empire, and lived her early life under the British Empire, witnessed its demise and played a part in creating a new state, 'a state born out of the dreams and desires of one hundred million people'.[35] She died on 11 December 2000, and was posthumously awarded Pakistan's highest honour: Nishan-i-Imtiaz.

Israel: Golda Meir (1898–1978)[36]

On 14 May 1948, Golda Meir was one of two women who signed the declaration for Israeli independence. A year earlier, amid growing unrest and violence, the United Nations had recommended a partition of Palestine into separate Jewish and Arab states. Israel established its own Parliament, the Knesset, and introduced proportional representation. In the first election eleven women – all from Russia – won a seat in the Knesset. Golda was one of them. She trailblazed through Israel, forging ahead in uncharted territory: as Ambassador to Russia, as Minister of Labour, as Foreign Minister and as Israel's first and only female head of government.

Golda, known as Goldie, was born in Kyiv, then part of the Russian Empire, to Ukrainian-Jewish parents. She was one of three living children, five of her siblings had died at birth or in infancy. Her mother, Blume, and her carpenter father, Moshe Mabovitch, lived in fear of the vicious anti-semitic attacks by Cossacks, marked by looting, destruction of property and physical violence, sometimes rape, often murder. The Mabovitches, like many Jews in their town, regularly boarded up the door of their family home. It was here that Golda's lifelong Jewish identity, and her need to protect Jews, took shape.

Life was tough enough without the fear of pogroms. The family often went hungry; housing was pitiable and there was never enough money for new clothes or extravagances. Not surprisingly, large numbers of Jewish people emigrated. In 1903, Moshe moved to the USA, found work and saved enough money to bring his family over to Milwaukee, Wisconsin. It was impossible to leave Russia legally, so Mrs Mabovitch bought forged passports and used smugglers to help the family escape across the border to Austria before leaving for the USA. Members of the family who remained in Austria were murdered in the Holocaust.

From the age of eight, Golda worked in her mother's newly established grocery store. Two years older, her strong commitment to social justice became clear. Golda was brought up in a Yiddish-speaking Eastern European Jewish area, living in the same kind of squalor and poverty her mother thought they had left behind. Some families were desperately impoverished. At the age of ten, Golda set up the American Young Sisters Society to buy textbooks for students who could not afford them. Her future life as a fund-raiser was being laid. She continued to work part-time in the shop while at High School, resisting her mother's attempts to leave school and get married to a man twice her age.

By the age of fifteen, Golda's tenacity was evident. When supposed fast asleep and dreaming, she quietly slid open her bedroom window and, careful not to make a sound, climbed out and ran away from home. Golda wanted to study, not marry. She escaped to live with her married sister in Denver, Colorado. At first, it was fun living with her sister and husband, attending high school and joining in their evening meetings discussing Zionism, feminism, trade unionism and other topical issues. It was the start of her political education, a beginning to her life as a Zionist socialist. About a year later, her parents persuaded their daughter to return home by allowing Golda to attend high school and graduate. She joined the Labor Zionist youth and, after a spell at a teachers' training college, taught at a Yiddish-speaking school. In 1917 she married Morris Mayerson, a man she loved.

In November 1917, the British issued the Balfour Declaration, which expressed a commitment to the 'establishment in Palestine of a National Home for the Jewish people'. Immediately Golda began planning to emigrate to Mandatory Palestine. While waiting to leave, she raised funds for Poale Zion (workers of Zion), a Zionist-Marxist-Jewish group committed to founding a Jewish state. Golda's Judaism was not orthodox: she was an atheist, drove and worked on Saturdays, ate non-kosher food, and had love affairs with Zionist leaders like Aaron Remez and Zalman Shahzar. Nonetheless, her unshakable identity as a Jewish Zionist was to consume her life.

In 1921 Golda and Morris moved to Palestine, then still part of the British Mandate, and worked on one of the earliest kibbutzes, picking almonds, planting trees, feeding and breeding chickens. Soon Golda was elected as the kibbutz's representative on the Histadrut, a labour organisation committed to workers' rights, and slowly climbed her way up to become the head of its Political Department. She loved walking down the streets in Tel Aviv, happy to be in the 'only all-Jewish town in the world'.[37] By 1928, Golda had two children and a broken marriage. Now a single mother, Golda was 'always rushing from one place to another – to work, home, to a meeting, to a music lesson, to keep a doctor's appointment, to shop, to cook, to work and back home again'.[38] When she kissed her children goodbye in the morning, she feared she might not return home 'that my car might be ambushed, that I might be shot by an Arab sniper or stoned to death by an Arab mob'.[39]

By 1938, it was clear that European Jews were at risk: German Jews, after five years of the erosion of their human rights, faced terror during 'Crystal Night'. When Germany annexed Austria it immediately implemented antisemitic laws. Jewish émigrés fleeing these pogroms sought help from Europe and North and South America. In July 1938, at Evian-les-Bains in France, delegates from 32 countries and representing 24 charities or voluntary organisations attended an American initiated conference to discuss the persecuted German and Austrian Jewish refugees who wished to flee their homeland. In theory, Golda represented British Mandatory Palestine. In practice she was not allowed to speak. Years later, Walter Mondale, Vice-President of the USA, commented that 'the decency and self-respect of the civilised world' had been at stake. If each country had agreed to take in 17,000 Jews, then the Holocaust would not have happened. There was little decency or self-respect: the only country to accept large numbers of refugees was the Dominican Republic. Even Golda could not have predicted that two out of three European Jewish people would be murdered.

In 1939, just before the outbreak of the Second World War, the British government revoked its support for the Balfour Declaration and limited the number of new Jewish immigrants to Palestine. During the Second World War, Golda worked for the World Zionist Organisation and the Jewish Agency (JA). When the British arrested all the male leadership for illegally smuggling Jewish refugees escaping from the Holocaust to safety in Israel, Golda took over the agency. In 1946, after the war, she became acting head of JA, responsible for negotiating between the Palestinian Jews and the British Mandatory authorities.

In May 1948, Golda was one of the 24 signatories to Israel's declaration of independence. By now, she was Israel's most prominent woman. Immediately, the newly formed state was invaded by five neighbouring countries, Egypt, Jordan, Syria, Lebanon and Iraq, who were opposed to Israel taking over Palestinian land. Almost immediately Golda visited America to garner support for Israel, touring the big cities and fund raising. Two fundraising trips alone raised around 125 million dollars, money which was critical to the success of Israel. The war increased Israeli territory and led to the displacement of hundreds of thousands of Palestinians. Golda disapproved and likened it to what had befallen Jews in Germany. To silence her, Golda was sent to Russia as Israeli Ambassador. Later, her remarks were less sympathetic, notoriously arguing that the Palestinian people did not exist and endorsing Israeli annexation of the West Bank, the Gaza Strip and the Golan Heights.

The first elections in January 1949 brought Golda into the first Israeli Parliament. Meanwhile, male activists organised a provisional government, excluding Golda from it. David Ben Gurion, the Prime Minister, protested and insisted that it was a moral and political necessity to include at least one woman. Ben Gurion insisted she adopt a Hebrew name. She changed her last name from Myerson to Meir. Ben Gurion appointed her Minister of Labour, 'seven beautiful years' for

Golda in which she became one of Israel's most powerful politicians. It was her era of success, building houses, settling immigrants, finding work and drafting new legislation for the state of Israel. A thousand immigrants, people from displaced person camps in Germany, the entire Yemenite Jewish community, and almost the entire Jewish communities of Bulgaria and Yugoslavia were settled. Some had fled pogroms in Syria, Lebanon, Egypt, Turkey and Iran. The population of Israel doubled as around 800,000 immigrants arrived in under eight years. Some called for restrictions on immigration: Ben Gurion and Golda thought otherwise. In 1950 the Law of Return granted every Jew the right to immigrate to Israel.

In 1956 Golda was promoted to foreign minister, the only female foreign minister in the world. Here she served ten years, becoming the voice of Israel in world politics. In her first few months of her post, the Suez Crisis erupted when Israel, Britain and France invaded Egypt to depose President Nasser and take control over the canal, a major shipping route. Golda had planned the incursion with the two other countries. The United Nations, the USA and Russia declared the war illegal. For Golda, it was a disastrous failure, and an international humiliation.

In March 1969, Golda, now in her early seventies and retired, was elected Prime Minister of Israel, serving until 1974. There were several flashpoints. In 1972, eleven Israeli athletes were massacred at the Munich Olympics by Palestinian terrorists. When the world looked away, Golda took decisive action and ordered Mossad to find the assassinators and eliminate them. Her greatest test was the Yom Kippur war, on the Day of Atonement, the holiest day in Judaism which began on 6 October 1973 when Egypt and Syria launched a surprise attack. Two thousand and seven hundred Israelis were killed. At considerable risk to himself, the King of Jordan had secretly warned Golda that Israel was to be attacked. Her Generals persuaded her Israel was safe, thus leaving the country unprepared.

In March 1974, with Israel victorious, Prime Minister Golda Meir stood in Israel's military cemetery looking at rows and rows of graves as the Kaddish, the prayer for the dead was intoned. A month later she resigned.

On 12 December 1978, Golda Meir died. For more than fifty years, she was at the centre of Israeli political life, shaping its destiny, a destiny that resulted in the oppression of Palestinians. In June 2024, the United Nations Human Rights Council released a report accusing both Israel and Hamas of 'violations of international human rights law, international humanitarian law and possible international crimes'. The report was in response to Hamas's horrific attack on Israel and Israel's equally horrific response.

The political careers of all the women in this chapter took place in turbulent, yet generally optimistic, times. Nazism – though not Iberian Fascism – was defeated, the Allied Powers were victorious, the Holocaust was over and the widening of various forms of democracy continued briskly outside communist-controlled countries. The two new nations of Israel and Pakistan, emerged from the tumultuous aftermath of the Second World War and the dismantling of one of the British colonial empires. Both newly created countries introduced a form of democracy which included women. Others such as Italy, France and Japan, were forced to reexamine their political structures.[40] In all the latter three countries, women benefitted when democracy was either established or expanded.

The five countries in this chapter – Italy, France, Japan, Pakistan and Israel – were in different geographical regions, its peoples worshipped different religions and held different ideologies, but they shared common features. Each was profoundly affected by the Second World War, each embraced – if somewhat reluctantly and sometimes partially – the democratic principles embodied in the post-war consensus. In 1945, in a concerted attempt to address mass global inequalities, much of the world broke with its past. Progressives wanted to create a new, more equal society. There was a global shift to give women some power. In 1947, the United Nations Commission on the Status of Women was established. The newly elected women from Albania through to Vietnam, all looked forward to their future with confidence. Democracy had triumphed. And with it, women's equality. It was the beginning of the end of history – or so it was believed.[41]

Chapter Five

New Horizons, 1950–1960:
Argentina, Indonesia, Egypt, Greece,
Ethiopia, India

Millions of people all over the world can sing along to the ballad 'Don't Cry for Me Argentina' from the hit musical, *Evita*. The musical is based on the life of Eva Duarte Perón, whose political power, personal charisma and ruthlessness continues to attract and repel in equal measure. In 1946, her husband Juan Perón was elected President of Argentina. He gave his wife the job of promoting women's rights: the two presented a women's suffrage bill to Congress, 'requesting' it be passed. In 1947 women gained the right to vote.

Elsewhere in the world, colonialism, which did not sit well with the post-war democratic ideals of freedom, liberty and self-determination, was threatened by independence movements. Countries such as Indonesia, India and Egypt which had recently freed themselves from colonial yokes wrote new constitutions. Both Greece and Ethiopia, which were occupied during the war, reformed their political systems. This new world order, with its emphasis on self-determination, created opportunities for women's political participation.

Argentina: Delia Delfina Degliuomini de Parodi (1913–1991)

In 1952, 23 women were elected to the Argentinian Chamber of Deputies. Every single one was a Peronist party representative, all helped into power by Eva Perón, the First Lady of Argentina and President of the Female Peronist Party (Partido Peronista Feminista) set up to encourage women to engage in politics. Delia Delfina Degliuomini de Parodi was one of the first women to be elected.[1]

Delia's life story, with its rise from poverty to power, perfectly embodied the Peronist dream. Delia was born in Ingeniero Luiggi, a small town in Pampas province in the middle of the country, into a poor Italian immigrant family. She was one of five, the youngest child of Carlos and Clothilde Degliuomini from Lombardy, Italy. Money problems forced the family to move to a tenement in Abasto, a poor area of Buenos Aires, where her father worked as an odd-job man. When Carlos died, Delia's mother worked as a seamstress to support her young family. As a little girl, Delia went with her mother to pick up and deliver garments to the homes of her clients. Despite these disadvantages, she finished junior high school, attended secretarial college and began full-time work.

Delia became a dedicated Peronist, attracted by its pro-gramme for the redistribution of wealth, educational reform, social welfare and the rights of workers. Peronists targeted marginalised people like her own family who were attracted by its commitment to the poor, its close links with the trade unions, its commitment to nationalising key industries and its efforts to promote equality. It was a populist movement centred on the charismatic personalities of Juan and Eva Perón. Delia started work in the Peronist administration as a secretary. It was here that she met Juan Carlos Parodi, her future husband. Delia was beautiful, always dressed impeccably, was correct in her behaviour and had great organisational ability – qualities which were attractive to the ambitious Juan Carlos. In 1942, the couple married. Her husband's brother-in-law was General Vargas Delmonte, friend of Juan Perón. Delia was catapulted into a new family. She was now part of an influential group of politicians, all of which entrenched her loyalty to Peronism.

The Peronists believed in educating aspiring would-be poli-ticians. Delia was chosen to attend the Peronist High School, an elite political school for future leaders of the Peronist party. Students were taught political leadership by General Perón, the history of Peronism by Eva Perón, and economy and ethics by a range of other lecturers. Delia, who had never attended university, was being groomed for a political life within what was to become a centralised authoritarian government which stifled dissent and undermined democratic institutions. Peronism is accused of fostering a culture of political patronage, of using state resources to build loyalty and dependence. It was a patronage from which Delia benefitted.

When Perón became President, he instigated the first national census for 37 years. He needed accurate data on population, demography, income levels and living conditions if he was to achieve his aim of transforming Argentina into a more equitable country. Eva Perón selected census enumerators, choosing only those who were loyal Peronists. She chose her protégée, Delia. Delia worked in Belgrano, a Buenos Aires neighbourhood. Each morning she set out with a purpose, moving from door to door uncovering the needs of the neighbourhood, resolving problems and recruiting women to the Peronist cause. In her view, it was important 'to listen without getting angry'. Delia believed in 'politics as the main tool to promote and implement the changes that are needed to transform people's lives' and to achieve that collectively.[2]

For her second political assignment Delia was moved to the Province of San Luis, one of the poorest provinces in the country, where people lived in caves because they could not afford a house. Here diseases like tuberculosis were rampant and hunger endemic. It was fertile ground for promoting the social work of the Peronists. Delia was put in charge of the entire party organisation in the province, again using the census as a cover for politics. She was an excellent organiser. 'We first introduced ourselves, who we were, what we represented . . . and then we commented that the country needed women to be integrated into political life, not in a passive way or through the husband's thinking or the son's thinking, but in a good way.'[3] The group's main target was working-class women, focusing on adult female literacy and numeracy but offering other activities, ranging from teaching English and French to teaching secretarial skills such as shorthand.

Travelling in a jeep across the most isolated places of the territory, Delia established doctor's surgeries, built houses for the cave dwellers, improved working conditions, and initiated social assistance for those in need. In one year, she launched 350 women's units, appointing women teachers, inspectors and headmistresses to organise them. Delia listened carefully to the women she met and taught them how to cast their newly won vote, using mock ballot boxes as practice. Newly enfranchised women had no history of voting; for many politics was a male preserve, a sphere historically reserved for men. Delia's mission was not just to persuade women to cast their vote but to use their latent political power. She encouraged women to join the party and trained them in Peronist politics, thus consolidating loyalty to the regime. At women-only meetings they discussed political and social problems, the problems of Argentina, what the country needed, what concerns the women had. Delia was a charismatic speaker, an attractive married woman unafraid to break boundaries. There is no doubt that Delia encouraged thousands to enter national politics.

In July 1951 the Partido Peronista Femenino (Female Peronist Party), a woman-only party, was set up by Eva Perón. Delia was on the all-women committee targeted to recruit or persuade women to vote for Juan Perón candidates in the forthcoming election. She told crowds that 'we know many roads lead to Rome, but all roads lead to Perón'.[4] Delia headed the list of candidates for national deputies in a Buenos Aires constituency. It was Peronist policy not to campaign in one's own constituency. As a result, Delia led the electoral campaign in San Luis, visiting hundreds of houses and ranches, making sure that women were ready to vote. It was an outstanding success: 72.8 per cent of women in her campaign area voted for a Peronist candidate. The national average was 63.7 per cent. Her efforts, and the efforts of others, in targeting women voters had worked. The women of Argentina had been crucial to Peron's success.

Delia was elected. On 7 May 1952, days after taking office, she became the first Argentinian woman to speak in the Chamber of Deputies. Here she put forward several new laws: laws to protect domestic servants from abuse; laws to give rights to children born out of wedlock; a law to confirm equality in divorce; and laws to regulate the price of basic goods. A year later year she was elected First Vice-President of the Chamber of Deputies, the first woman to occupy that role. In that same year (1953) she was part of the Argentinian delegation to the Inter-Parliamentary Union held in Vienna, where she confirmed her stature at an international level. Delia fought hard to persuade women to enter Parliament: in the next election women won one third of the seats.

By now, she was a trusted close friend of Eva Perón. In 1952, the death of her patron and protector brought new challenges. She was lucky. General Perón believed Delia when she assured him that it was her firm intention to maintain the memory of his late wife and continue Eva's work in the party. Soon after, General Perón appointed Delia as Interim National Director of the party. She was now expected to 'replace the irreplaceable', acting as a substitute for a charismatic popular figure and finding a new way of running the organisation. She regularly resorted to praising her late friend as a 'lady of suffering', 'miracle made flesh' and insisting that she was merely enacting the wishes of Eva Perón. In fact, Delia appointed leaders without consulting the General, prioritising loyalty not just to the movement but to herself personally. Moreover, Delia ensured that women loyalists were represented in the civil service, in the Party, in international organisations. The Peronist Party maintained control at every level: Peronist Catholics were even asked to spy on their priests, to go to confession and try to find if the priest advocated measures against the government. It became a politics of fear. One directive consisted of 'silencing by all means the person or persons who allow Perón or Eva Perón to be attacked'.

On 22 September 1955, Juan Perón was overthrown in a military coup. He went into exile. Delia was at home, ill, and in bed. The new regime took its revenge quickly and without compassion. Delia was arrested and held for 42 days in solitary confinement at the Humberto Women's Prison, charged with crimes of illicit association, illicit enrichment and treason. The new junta took everything from her house and burnt it.

After serving her time, she was transferred to the custody of the Good Shepherd nuns and forced to endure its suffocating regime for political prisoners. The nuns were the opposite of Christians – because they hated Peronists they imposed subhuman conditions. Food was little better than pig swill, lights were turned off at 9 p.m., cell doors were locked and a petty regulatory regime was enforced. On 7 March 1958 she was paroled. She was exhausted, and severely weakened. She weighed a mere thirty kilos when she left the convent.

When she was released, she kept a low profile but covertly promoted the Peronist cause. Delia travelled to Spain several times to meet General Perón, who was living in Madrid, liaising between him and his supporters in Argentina. For this political action, Delia was expelled from Spain, imprisoned by Interpol in France and returned to Argentina. Shortly afterwards, her husband died of a heart attack. She attended his funeral in a blonde wig, nervous that she would once again be arrested and returned to prison. Despite these threats, Delia continued her political activity quietly and surreptitiously, rebuilding the party's base to enable Perón's political comeback. When Perón finally returned to Argentina after 18 years of exile, Delia Parodi played a key role in his successful return. In 1973 he was once again elected President.

By this time, Delia's health was deteriorating. She was diagnosed with an incurable disease which slowly progressed. On 13 May 1991 she died aged 78.

Indonesia: Umi Sardjono (1923–2011)

Women in Muslim countries, as in other jurisdictions, were discriminated against, were denied rights and excluded from government. All too often, in the Islamic world the rights of women were limited: women were excluded from the vote, excluded from Parliament, expected to remain in purdah, and forbidden to speak freely. Human rights violations were widespread. However, just as Christian countries across the world behave differently, Muslim countries differed too. In some countries, women were making feminist waves.

Indonesia is the fourth most densely populated country in the world and the one with the largest Muslim community. In 1945, after a four-year struggle for freedom, a struggle in which women played a crucial role, Indonesia freed itself from the Dutch Empire and declared its independence. Ten years later, elections were held in which seventeen women were elected to the Constituent Assembly, the governing body of the country.

One of the first was Umi Sardjono, an atheist, anti-fascist, feminist and communist who had fought for Indonesian independence.[5] One of the country's most prominent political activists, Umi witnessed seismic changes: the end of Dutch colonial rule, Japanese occupation, an independence war and a brutal militaristic regime. Her political activism was rewarded by her election to Parliament. Unfortunately, politics is brutal. Politicians climb up its ladder slowly but fall off all too quickly. Umi's fall was precipitous. In October 1965, she was arrested and imprisoned without trial for fourteen years. Here she was physically, sexually and psychologically tortured by the functionaries of the regime.

Umi was born Suharti Sumodiwirdjo on 24 December 1923 in Central Java, then part of the Dutch Empire, to parents who were part of the Javanese elite. She was the second child of Ruslan Sumodiwirdjo, a civil servant, and his wife. Both were enlightened parents and sent their daughter to a Dutch

primary school which educated children from the upper
classes. Encouraged by her father, she studied at the Academy
of Social Politics. Umi joined several nationalist organisations,
one of which was the Anti-Fascist Indonesian Peoples Freedom
Forces. This was an underground party which fought against
Japanese occupation of their country. It was here that she met
and married a leading communist, Sukisman Sardjono. When
the Japanese invaded in the Second World War, the couple
ran a food stall which catered for Japanese soldiers. It seemed
an innocent occupation but the stall acted as a message centre
for the underground resistance movement. The two managed
to discover important information about Japanese manoeu-
vres until both were arrested, imprisoned and tortured. In a
later interview, Umi spoke of being beaten while upside down,
deprived of food and water and forced to drink her own urine.

Umi was a communist who drew inspiration from
Clara Zetkin, later describing her heroine as a 'socialist female
warrior'.[6] Like Clara, Umi believed that only an end to capitalism and a total transformation of society into a socialist
state would ensure justice and equality. In 1948 she organised Indonesia's first International Women's Day. Two years
later, she co-founded Gerakan Wanita Sadar (Movement for
Politically Aware Women) which morphed into the Indonesian
Women's Movement known as Gerwani, an independent
group which was sympathetic to communism. Umi became
its President. One of its policies was to establish schools and
daycare centres which were free of charge. It also sought to
increase women's wages, obtain menstrual leave for women
workers, and reform agrarian law to give the land-workers
more control. The group hoped to become a mass movement
committed to the rights of women. Its members could see that
women were not just economically discriminated against but
had few rights as workers, and even fewer rights in marriage.
By the 1960s, Gerwani had approximately 1.5 million members
with branches in almost all regions.

Image 8   Umi Sardjono, 1956,
courtesy of the Indonesian National Archive.

In 1952, Umi was elected as a member of the Indonesian Communist Party (PKI) to the House of Representatives. Here she tried to end forced marriage, polygamy and child marriage. She successfully removed a law which insisted that women be accompanied by a male family member if they went abroad. She also tried to introduce equal marital legislation. By 1954 a draft general marriage law, a draft Islamic marriage law and a draft Christian marriage law were in place. However, only the Islamic draft was taken seriously. Umi spoke against the inclusion of polygamy, arguing it was an anti-modern force which lowered the status of women. Her ideas received an antagonistic response from Islamic groups, a problem because they represented most of the population. Yet, despite opposition, Umi fought hard for the rights of women: she set up kindergartens, schools and literary courses for adults.

In 1965 a failed coup d'etat, which killed six army Generals, and one aide-de-camp, changed the political landscape of Indonesia. The coup was blamed on the Indonesian Communist Party, then the third largest communist party in the world ... and Gerwani. The Indonesian army under the control of Major General Suharto seized power and carried out a genocidal campaign against communists and their supporters. Women in Gerwani were accused of dancing naked in front of the soldiers, gouging out eyes and mutilating the genitals of the officers. These accusations had no substance. Misogynistic rumours about the alleged sexual depravity of Gerwani women circulated, feeding into a narrative that they wanted to undermine the values and identity of the recently created Indonesian Muslim state. In March 1966, Suharto made Gerwani an illegal organisation. Its members were tortured and murdered. Torture was sexualised. Many women were raped, orally, vaginally and anally. Others were tortured by being immersed in a bath, submerged in a tank of faeces, burnt with cigarettes or given electric shocks to their breast and their reproductive organs. Women were beaten to death or executed along with their entire family.

After her own release from a cruel prison experience, Umi lived in fear, crippled by what she had endured, believing she was under constant surveillance and was in danger of being re-arrested. It was a justifiable paranoia as former political prisoners had their identity cards stamped with 'ET' (the acronym for political prisoner), were not allowed to vote, not allowed to work in government posts and denied freedom of movement. In one interview, Umi described herself as being 'killed' by the repressive regime.

This newly established authoritarian militaristic regime, a regime which lasted until 1998, murdered half a million people and imprisoned a further one million. It called itself the New Order. In 2015, the International People's Tribunal found the Indonesian government responsible for mass murder, wrongful imprisonment, enslavement, torture, exile, sexual violence, false propaganda and genocide. Umi was not alive to witness this. On 11 March 2011, Umi Sardjono died, aged 87, at home, in poverty and in pain.

Egypt: Rawya Shams al-Din Attia Rawiya Ateya (Atiyya) (1926–1997)

On 14 July 1957 Rawiya Ateya became the first woman to take her seat in the Egyptian National Assembly. She was the first woman elected to the Egyptian Parliament, and the first to be elected in the Arab world.[7] She was the only woman in a House of 350 men. Her election was viewed as a milestone for Arab women's rights.[8] Egypt had just experienced seismic changes. On 23 July 1952, King Farouk of Egypt was toppled in a coup d'etat led by a group of army officers who wanted to abolish the monarchy, establish a Republic and end the British occupation of their country. In 1954, one of them, Lieutenant Colonel Gamal Abdel Nasser, became Egypt's second President and drafted a new Constitution of Egypt which set up a one-party state, established a National Assembly and set a date for the election. The new constitution granted votes for women and their right to stand for election.

Rawiya's family prepared her for politics. She was born on 19 April 1926 in Giza Governorate. Her father, Shams al-Din Attia, was secretary-general of the liberal nationalistic Wafd party in Gharbiyya. At the age of ten, Rawya went to the prestigious Princess Fawzi Secondary School. Unusually for Egyptian girls at the time, she went on to study at Cairo University. In 1947 she gained a diploma in education and psychology followed by a diploma in Islamic studies and an MA in journalism. For fifteen years, Rawiya worked as a teacher, and a journalist.

Rawiya was steeped in politics at a young age. We just have tantalising glimpses of this. When her father was imprisoned for his beliefs, she visited him in prison. In 1939, now aged thirteen and still at school, she led a demonstration of her school students against British colonialism. While taking part, she was wounded by a stray bullet and taken by Huda Shaarawi, the pioneer of the Egyptian women's movement, to the headquarters of the General Women's Union (the Huda Shaarawi Society) for medical treatment. It was Huda Shaarawi and her colleagues who strengthened Rawya's political beliefs.

In July 1956, Nasser announced the nationalisation of the Suez canal. At the time it was British-controlled and Britain benefitted from its profits: Nasser argued that the Egyptian people had a right to sovereignty over the waterway. In response to this, Britain, France and Israel joined forces and invaded Egypt to gain control over the canal and topple Nasser. It was a fiasco and a failure. The American President General Eisenhower condemned the invasion, forcing Britain, France and Israel to withdraw and seek peace. The support of the USA fortified Rawiya's pro-Americanism at a time of intense Arab nationalism and anti-imperialism.

Rawiya, now thirty years old, played an active role in the Suez war. She was the first woman to be commissioned to the rank of Captain in the Liberation Army. In this post she trained 4,000 or so women in first aid and nursing. In 1957 she founded the Society of Women Mobilised for Social Service to take care of the families of men serving in the armed forces. She was called the 'mother of fighters and martyrs'. For her service to the country she loved, Rawiya was awarded several military honours: the badge of the Third Army and the Medallion of 6 October.

On 14 July 1957, Rawiya took her seat in the National Assembly as a member of the National Democratic Party. She was one of sixteen women standing for election; the other 1,980 candidates were men. According to opinion polls, seventy per cent of Egyptian men were opposed to women standing for Parliament. Rawiya spoke of being 'met with resentment for being a woman. Yet I talked to them and reminded them of the prophet's wives and families until they changed their opinion.'[9] Rawiya Ateya pushed hard for women's rights, often against a very conservative male opposition. Cleverly, she used religion, focusing on the Prophet's wives, to bolster her argument for equality. She succeeded in persuading Parliament to pass an Act which awarded two-months maternity leave for working women. In July 1958 she presented a Bill to abolish polygamy. It failed. Two years later she left Parliament.

Rawiya remained politically active. During the 1973 war between Israel and a coalition of Arab states led by Egypt and Syria she continued to chair the Society of Martyrs and Soldiers. Each day she visited soldiers on the front-line. She also served on the board of the Red Crescent, which like its sister organisation, the Red Cross, was founded to protect human life and health, to respect all humans regardless of race or religion, and to prevent human suffering.

In 1984, Rawiya returned to formal politics when she was elected to the People's Assembly for the National Democratic Party, a party which emerged from the Arab Socialist Union. As a parliamentarian she raised the question of family guidance, marriage counselling and birth control. In 1993, she was elected President of the National Council of Family and Population, a position she held until she died. Meanwhile, in 1990, when Saddam Hussein invaded and annexed Kuwait, Rawiya again sprang into action. She organised ambulances, nursing staff and civil defence courses for Kuwaiti women refugees and she sent gifts to Kuwaiti soldiers. After a life of political activity, Rawiya died aged 71 on 9 May 1997.

Greece: Elena Skoura (1896–1991)

In Greece, the birthplace of democracy, it took thousands of years for women to vote and enter government. In 1952, women eventually gained the right to vote and with it the right to be elected. No woman won a seat in the first general election. In January 1953 Elena Skoura won a by-election for the Hellenic Synaerymos (Greek Rally) party in Thessaloniki. She was the first woman to be a member of the Greek Parliament.

Elena Skoura was an example of yet another woman written out of history. I began, as usual, with enquiries to the Greek Embassy, who responded with enthusiasm and gave me an introduction to the Library on Gender and Equality. From here, I was kindly provided with PDFs of Elena's speeches in Parliament and was recommended a book to read. All in Greek. The book, of course, was not online but I traced it to a second-hand book seller in Athens. Unfortunately, they only shipped to the EU. Happily, I have family in Hungary who duly took possession of the book and brought it over when they visited.

Elena is another example of a woman with an encouraging father. She was born in Volos, Greece, on 21 December 1896.[10] She bridged the centuries. Her birth occurred in the twilight of the nineteenth century and she lived through almost all the twentieth. Her mother, Sofia, was a noblewoman, her father, Athanasios Papachristou, owned three shops. There were no girls' secondary schools in the town and as soon as she finished primary school Eleni was expected to sit at home crocheting lace. Eleni's father thought differently. He wanted his daughter to be educated and persuaded the Minister of Education to allow her to attend the Greek School for Boys. Ten other girls joined her. Eleni's passion was singing. She had a beautiful voice. In 1915, after two of the family shops burnt down, the family moved to Thessaloniki where she studied vocal music at the state conservatory. Her teachers were so impressed by her voice that the young teenage Eleni performed with the symphony orchestra at a concert in front of the Prime Minister and other politicians.

Elena's father hoped that his talented daughter would leave Greece to study elsewhere in Europe but before that happened Elena fell in love. In 1919 she met the handsome, well-educated and highly desirable Dimitris Skouras, at the time the youngest prosecution lawyer in the city. In October the two married at the Agios Minas. It was a social event with all the elite of the city present. At first, Elena was a conventional wife, cooking, cleaning and taking care of her husband but her life was about to change. The First World War had ended but Greece was embroiled in a war against the crumbling Ottoman Empire, trying to reclaim land in Anatolia where large numbers of Greeks lived. In 1922, the Turkish army defeated the Greeks, forcing more than a million ethnic Greeks to leave the country. Refugees made their way 'home', to a country already battered by war, by the collapse of the currency, and economic turmoil. Elena stepped in to help. She joined the local council where fund-raising and helping refugees, particularly orphans took up a fair share of her time. Soon she was fully committed. She joined XEN (the Greek YWCA) and helped establish a Working Girls' Shelter for homeless young women. Gradually, Elena became politicised. Ten years later, she despaired that refugees were still suffering, that poverty and misery were everywhere, that exploitation and unemployment were rampant, and that not one politician was willing to help. In 1936, Ioannis Metaxas established a dictatorship and he asked Elena to move to Athens to set up a new women's organisation which replaced XEN. Elena was torn: she disagreed with the dictatorship but was persuaded by her husband that she could work for the good of young women. Her work was to be interrupted by events even more hazardous than being employed by a dictator.

At 3 a.m., on 28 October 1940, Greece received an ulti-matum from the Italian fascists. In 1940 Greece entered the

Second World War on the side of the Allies. Soon the country was invaded by the Italians, the Bulgarians and the Germans. Brutally, the Nazis armed forces bombed the country and murdered its inhabitants. They reduced the Greek population to starvation in a deliberate Nazi strategy to wipe out the population. More than 300,000 Athenians died from starvation. A broad resistance movement flourished and Elena joined it, actively opposed to the war-time Nazi occupation of her country. She was appointed President of the girls' shelter, Falangitissa House, and a wartime charity, the Shirt of the Soldier, set up by Princess Frederiki to provide support for soldiers and their families.

Elena soon became responsible for resistance work in Thessaloniki. She characterised Fascism as the 'curse and shame for the human race'.[11] In early summer of 1942, she was arrested along with her husband and brother and imprisoned by the Germans. Fortunately, Elena had destroyed all incriminating documents before she was arrested. After her release, Elena enrolled in the School of Law at Aristotle University.

When the war ended and when other countries were working to rebuild their damaged lands, Greece was embattled in a fratricidal conflict which nearly destroyed the nation. It was a war caused by a communist rebellion against the established government. During this period, Elena was a 'lady volunteer assistant' of the Queen's Fund.[12] This Fund, established in July 1947 by Queen Fredericka, mobilised women to rescue Greek children who had been made homeless or orphaned. Between 340,000 and 375,000 Greek children lost one or both parents. The Queen's Fund founded 53 'Child Towns' in which around 18,000 children were housed and cared for.

Meanwhile, Elena took the lead in establishing the 'National Association of Greek Women', the first women's organisation in the country. In 1951, she took over the women's section of the Hellenic Synagerimos in Thessaloniki. Two years later, on 20 January 1953, Elena Skoura stepped into the Greek

Parliament as an MP, the only woman among 299 men. Predictably newspapers commented that a 'cute, serious lady' dressed in an all-black top appeared in Parliament.[13] 'I am' she declared 'deeply touched by this victory, achieved after a hard fight. . . . I know that as the first and only woman in the House I have a great responsibility and many duties. We have a lot to do for Greek women.'[14] The male MPs greeted her warmly, standing and applauding her as she first entered the Chamber. They later confessed that they had expected a woman wearing boots, who smoked and who drank ouzo.

Elena was only in Parliament for three years. During her time in office, she fought for women and children, devoting herself to social causes and fighting against inequalities. One of her achievements was changing the age of marriage for police officers. At the time, policemen had to be 45 years old to marry, which, according to Eleni, created immorality. She succeeded in changing the law so that police officers could marry at 25. For years after this, she was sent flowers by grateful married couples.

In July 1964 democracy was overthrown by a military coup d'etat which eroded human rights, suppressed opposition and tortured those who disagreed. There were no women in this 'government'. Elena's life and liberty were in danger. Her previous work as a lawyer, a resistance fighter and equal rights advocate was abhorrent to the new regime. But once, when a police officer came to her house to arrest her, he recognised her as the MP who had lowered the age of marriage for him and his colleagues. Grateful for her mediation, he told her not to open the door to anyone, go away and hide and he would pretend she was not at home.[15] She was safe. She was soon to be alone. In 1965, her husband Dimitris died. She told a friend, never 'did I feel so alone . . . There were no frictions between us. We loved each other so much.'[16]

In July 1974, the 78-year-old Elena witnessed the restoration of Greek democracy when the Junta was overthrown. The state honoured her with the Military Medal for Extraordinary Accomplishments and the Order of Beneficence. There is a bust of her outside the Town Hall in Volos, the town in which she was born. When her husband died, she was promised an honorary pension. It was an empty pledge. Elena never received any money from the government and died in poverty. Moreover, she was forced to sell her medals to fund her stay in a nursing home. She died, aged 95, in the Home.

Ethiopia: Senedu Gebru (1916–2009)

Change was also happening in another traditional Christian country. In 1957, Senedu Gebru, a feminist resistance fighter, was elected to the Chamber of Deputies, the lower house of the Ethiopian Parliament. In 1955, the Emperor, Haile Selassie, had enacted a new constitution giving votes to all those over 21 who were born in Ethiopia. There were no political parties. Individuals had to fund their own campaign and own either land or goods in the area they wished to represent. Only the wealthy could afford to run for office. Independents won 210 out of 210 seats.

The only woman to succeed, Senedu Gebru, was part of Ethiopian aristocratic life, expected to conform to the patriarchal values of society and only to exercise political influence indirectly, if at all. What led her to break with this tradition? Senedu was born on 13 January 1916 in Addis Alem, a small town in central Ethiopia a short distance from the capital Addis Ababa. She was the eldest of two daughters and a son born to Weyzero Kasaye Yelamtu, an Orthodox Christian, and her husband Gebru Desta, a well-known intellectual and European-educated writer. He was a high-ranking politician, once representing Empress Zewditu and her son Ras Teferi (the future Emperor Haile Selassie) in Britain and the USA. Her mother taught Senedu about Christianity, while her father, who was an enlightened and progressive man, encouraged his daughter's education more widely. Senedu often accompanied her father on his official visits to the imperial palace and other institutions, all the time gaining knowledge of how these places worked.

Senedu and her sister were both European-educated, first at the Swedish Mission school in the city, then in 1928 in Switzerland and in France. Senedu was fluent in many languages: Italian, German, French, English. In 1933, aged seventeen, she returned to Ethiopia. She worked as a language teacher and an interpreter for foreign journalists. One year later, her parents arranged a marriage to French-educated Lorenzo Taezaz, a man sixteen years older who was a well-established, high-ranking diplomat.

In October 1935 Fascist Italian troops, spurred on by Mussolini's warped vision of a new Roman Empire, invaded and then occupied Ethiopia. It was a one-sided fight. Ethiopians had few weapons and munitions. The West would not sell them to the country. In contrast, the Italians were replete with arms, air power, munitions, numerical strength. The Emperor fled and Lorenzo accompanied him into exile. Senedu stayed in Ethiopia, ended her marriage and moved to the town of Goré where the provisional government had relocated.

Here Senedu fought to liberate her country from foreign invaders. She joined the Red Cross, focusing her efforts in looking after wounded soldiers and civilians. She also joined the Holleta Military Academy, trained to fight and learned how to use a machine gun. In Goré she was the first woman to join the Tiqur Anbassa (Black Lions), a resistance group formed by army officers. For three years she acted under the protection of the Red Cross, and wearing the Red Cross uniform she was able to pass information back to the resistance about Italian troop movements. Most of the resistance fighters, including her younger brother, were murdered by the Italians. The occupation was murderous, particularly after a failed assassination attempt of the Italian viceroy. Thousands were shot, pregnant women were disembowelled, houses were set on fire with their occupants trapped inside. One eyewitness reported that 'the streets were strewn with dead bodies . . . the method consisted of setting fire and massacring them . . . scourging naked women to death'.[17] Senedu escaped with her life. Captured and interrogated by Italian forces, Senedu was interned for two years on Asinara, an island off the coast of Sardinia, for refusing to divulge the secrets of the Ethiopian resistance.[18] Fortunately, Senedu had friends all over the world: the pro-Ethiopian Sylvia Pankhurst helped disseminate Senedu's articles about the invasion to an international audience.[19]

In 1941, after Ethiopia's liberation, Senedu returned to teaching. In 1945 she was appointed headmistress of the Empress Etege School for Girls, founded by the Empress Menen, Queen Consort. It was the first girls' school in the country. Here she wrote and staged plays, which often focused on anti-fascism and the heroism of Ethiopians as well as more conventional topics like love and marriage. As well as a political education, Senedu aimed to instil confidence in public speaking and social awareness in her female students. She was a prolific poet and novelist. By the end of her life, she had written about eighty published and unpublished works.

Senedu was a successful teacher, but she was also a political activist. She ran for Parliament as a former resistance fighter. On 22 November 1957, soon after she was elected, Senedu became vice-president of the Chamber of Deputies. Here she served for four years, working hard for equality between men and women.

In 1960 Haile Selassie appointed Senedu Vice President of the Senate. She was an unconventional choice: a three-time married and twice-divorced woman who had the first of her three children when she was 38 years old, quite unlike a traditional Ethiopian woman of her class. In 1966 she was appointed General Secretary of the Ministry of Social Affairs.

After her time in Parliament, Senedu became President of the Ethiopian Red Cross. A year later, concerned as ever about the most vulnerable, she helped establish a Rehabilitation Training Centre in Addis Ababa for the destitute and severely handicapped which provided handicraft skills and on-the-job training. Within two years, the centre helped 375 people who were either blind, physically disabled or homeless.

When her third husband, Colonel Assefa Lema, was appointed Ambassador to Germany, she followed him as Education attaché. In 1974, when the Marxist-Leninist revolution deposed the Emperor, she returned to Ethiopia while her husband moved to the USA with their children. Her life in formal politics over, Senedu Gebru lived quietly in her villa next to a golf course in Addis Ababa, writing poetry and plays. One of her poems, *Yetikur Anbessa Tigil Bemirab*, was about the struggle of the resistance group, the Black Lions.[20] Towards the end of her life, she was considered a 'standard bearer for Ethiopia's freedom and progress, . . . an inspiration to all Ethiopians struggling for gender equality'. She was named a 'lady for all seasons': a playwright, resistance fighter, feminist, diplomat, philanthropist and educator.[21] On 19 April 2009, aged 94, she died in her own bed at home.

India: Anna (Annie) Mascarene (1902–1963)

Anna Mascarene was a Dalit, an 'untouchable', at the very bottom of the caste hierarchy, yet she managed to enter Parliament. How did this happen? It was a combination of personal integrity, incredible courage and a change in the political situation. In 1947 India gained its independence from Britain, and three years later after widespread violence and the displacement of people, India and Pakistan split. On 26 January 1950 India adopted its own constitution as a socialist, secular and democratic republic. The first elections, held between

1951 and 1952 returned Anna Mascarene to the Lok Sabha, the House of the People. She was among the first women to be elected. Jawaharlai Nehru became the first President.[22] For women, it was the culmination of a century-long struggle for both the right to vote and the right to stand for Parliament.

Anna was born on 6 June in Thiruvananthapuram, Kerala, the southernmost state of India, into a Roman Catholic family. She was the sixth in a family of eight. The family were Dalits, a group of people who were historically marginalised and oppressed within the Indian caste system. The family were Christians. Conversion to Christianity sometimes offered Dalits like Anna's family better opportunities for education and work. Her father, Gabriel, became a minor government official and encouraged his daughter's education. She was considered a brilliant student, gaining admission into the prestigious Trivandrum Maharaja's College, where only the very brightest students were enrolled. In 1925, aged 23, she graduated with an MA in both History and Economics. In 1927, when the Maharaja allowed women to take legal degrees, Anna began studying law at her same college. When she graduated, Anna taught law at the college and started practising law in Trivandrum, eager to use her knowledge in the national independence movement, which was gaining support.

In 1938 she was one of the first women to join the Travancore State Congress, a newly formed party, which was critical of the princely, governing body and its policy of remaining part of the British Empire. Violence against women politicians, particularly those who challenge patriarchal norms, is a recurring theme in this book. Anna was no exception. There were repeated attacks on her life and property. On 28 April 1938, after returning from a canvassing tour, her house was broken into when she was asleep. All her possessions, save her travelling bag next to her bed, were stolen. She woke up when the thieves entered her bedroom and noticed that one carried an axe, possibly intended to murder her. She reported it to the police. The next day while she was walking along a road she was hit in the back by a policeman on a bicycle. Police harassment, the abolition of free speech and assembly, assaults on State Congress leaders continued. Annie disregarded these abuses of human rights, and went on holding meetings. At midnight on 13 November 1938, Anna was arrested, tried and sentenced to eighteen months' imprisonment for making seditious speeches. She served three years. It was her first prison experience, but it was not to be her last.

In November 1941, Anna visited Mahatma Gandhi. She stayed with Gandhi for several months and here met a number of national leaders including Nehru. In 1942, in the middle of the Second World War, Mahatma Gandhi launched his Quit India Movement, demanded an end to British rule in India and launched a mass protest. Annie joined it. This was the start of the biggest non-violent protest ever seen in India. The country 'became one vast rebel camp': thousands poured onto the streets; workers went on strike; students refused to attend universities and colleges.[23] Tens of thousands were arrested, including Gandhi, who spent the war in prison. On 30 August 1942 Annie was arrested for delivering 'an inflammatory speech' and sentenced to two years in prison. In 1945, she was again arrested, sentenced and put in prison; on 20 November 1946 she served another six months for incitement. In fact, she had written a report on a communist-inspired uprising in Travancore which was brutally squashed by the police. In her report, she condemned the indiscriminate violence of the officers who had used machine guns to suppress an uprising of unarmed people. Those who ran away from the guns were chased and killed. The bodies of men, women and children were piled up on the side of the road and burned. The authorities deemed her report a further incitement to violence.

By 1946 it was clear that India would be independent. Anna was one of fifteen women and 284 men elected to the Constituent Assembly of India set up to draft a new constitution. She served on a select committee set up to frame a uniform civil code, realised that their suggestions would shape the new nation, and ensured that the 'rudimentary principles of democracy' were for the 'days to come, for generations, for the nation'.[24] Indeed, the future – and now independent – Parliament codified their suggestions into law: the Hindu Marriage Act, the Hindu Succession Act, Hindu Minority and Guardianship Act, Hindu Adoptions and Maintenance Act. During this time, Anna was also appointed Minister in Charge of Health and Power in the Parur T K Narayana Pillai Ministry. She was the first woman minister in the newly independent India.

In May 1952, the outspoken, charismatic Anna Mascarene stepped into the Indian Parliament. She was independent, and had run as an Independent. Her independence, one newspaper reported, showed itself in 'the things she says, in the way she says them; in her trick of tossing her head to emphasise a point . . . and in her very stance' as she drew herself up to the mere five feet of her sturdy figure.[25] On her first day in Parliament, Annie raised concerns about the lack of women in government. During her parliamentary tenure, she spoke against the Preventive Detention Act, a former colonial law that empowered the police to arrest anyone they thought might commit a crime in future. In her speech, she argued that 'if I am familiar with anything in life it is detention, detenus, detention camps and lock-up'. We have, she maintained 'a law based on equity, justice and good conscience . . . this Detention Act violates all these rules of equity, conscience, justice and obedience to law'.[26] No changes were made and the Act remained in force until 1969. Anna only served one term. In 1957 she lost her seat, never to return to government.

On 19 July 1963 Anna Mascarene died in the General Hospital in Trivandrum. She was 62 years old. She was alive to witness the election of Nehru's daughter, Indira Gandhi in 1959 but had died before Gandhi became India's first female Prime Minister.

Some women in this chapter rose to power through family connection, some had supportive fathers who encouraged their daughters, some were merely talented individuals who succeeded even when the political odds were stacked against them. At first, it seems as if very little, either in terms of religion, geography, politics or culture, seemed to unite them. However, whether from Argentina or Indonesia, all these women lived, breathed and worked in a violent male world. Far too many experienced defamation, repression, torture, and imprisonment. All had broken the bonds of a toxic femininity that held them tight, a femininity which encouraged them to conform and discouraged them from developing as full human beings.

These Argentinian, Indonesian, Egyptian, Greek, Ethiopian and Indian women were all committed to some form of feminist politics, often forged in nationalism, or in independence and resistance movements. They were politicians who, along with the women from many other countries which elected women for the first time, were part of a tsunami of women surging forward to take their rightful place in their respective parliaments.[27] The world was indeed changing. It seemed that one form of democracy or another was spreading across the world, giving women unparalleled opportunities.

Chapter Six

Decolonisation and Beyond, 1960–1970: Afghanistan, Bahamas, Cyprus, Iran, Zambia

The image of an Afghan woman is someone in a burqa, her body and face completely covered. It is a crime to show any bit of skin in public. In 1996, a fundamentalist Islamic group, the Taliban, took control of Afghanistan. Immediately they denied women basic rights: girls and women were not allowed to attend school or work; they were forbidden to leave the house without a chaperone; and not allowed to access health care provided by men, which essentially made it inaccessible. In effect, women were imprisoned in their home, completely controlled by their male relatives who were free to injure or kill them. Forced marriage reappeared. In their first year of rule, the Taliban cut off the thumb of a woman for wearing nail polish. The Taliban were overturned in 2001, only to return with a vengeance in 2021, setting up the misogynistic Ministry for the Propagation of Virtue and the Prevention of Vice.

Afghan women were not always oppressed. Before the Taliban seized power, women played a significant role in Afghan life. In 1964, as part of King Zahir Shah's political reforms, a new constitution gave women the right to vote and to stand for election. In Iran, Mohamad Reza Pahlavi, the Shah of Iran, aimed to modernise his country by expanding democracy, granting women's suffrage and the right to stand for office. Both monarchs were overthrown, one by a coup, the other by the Islamic revolution. Consequently, women's freedom disappeared but not before they had made an impact.

Afghanistan: Anahita Ratebzad (1931–2014)

In 1965, six women were elected to the House of the People, the Afghan Parliament.[1] One of them was short, slim, dark-haired Anahita Ratebzad, who won a Kabul seat representing the People's Democratic Party of Afghanistan, a recently formed Marxist-Leninist group which took a pro-Soviet approach to politics.[2]

Anahita, named after the goddess of water, fertility and healing – a life-giving force – was born on 1 November 1931 in Guldara in the Province of Kabul to a Pashtun father and Tajik mother. She was well connected: her father was a cousin of Queen Soraya. Violence was endemic in Afghanistan. Soon after she was born her father was taken away, forced to exile to Iran and later murdered for his political beliefs. Her mother was left alone to take care of Anahita and a son, who was born after her husband was killed. The family became impoverished. Her upper-class mother was compelled to work as a nursemaid to save the family from starvation. In 1946, aged fifteen, Anahita was forced to marry the surgeon Dr Karamuddin Kakar, with whom she later had a daughter and two sons. When the couple moved to the United States, Anahita studied English before enrolling at the University of Michigan school of nursing where she gained a nursing degree. When she returned to Kabul she worked as director in the women's hospital, then as a tutor of student nurses. Now with three children, she left her job and enrolled in medical school. In 1963 Anahita qualified as a medical doctor in Kabul, the first female physician in Afghanistan.

As she gained confidence, Anahita became political. She separated from her husband. And threw away her veil. In Afghanistan veiling was voluntary but commonplace. In 1957, concerned that women were disadvantaged by this tradition, she led a group of unveiled women nurses to help at a male hospital, challenging the conservative mores of Kabul society.

It was a brave decision, one which drew disapproving comments from those who wished to keep women hidden.

Anahita's courage became known outside of Afghanistan. In 1958, aged 27, she was part of an Afghan women's delegation to the Afro-Asian Conference on Women held at the Grand Oriental Hotel, in Colombo, Ceylon (Sri Lanka).[3] This prestigious conference, organised by five national women's organisations, marked the rise of women's rights campaigns in Asia and Africa. It was a high-profile conference held in a beautiful hall full of women leaders. The Prime Minister of Ceylon opened the conference and Lakshmi Menon, India's deputy foreign minister, shared the platform with other women political leaders.[4] Conference concerns centred upon women's welfare, women in the workforce, and the illegal trafficking of women and children.

At the second plenary session, Anahita stepped nervously on to the stage. Speaking in front of such a distinguished audience of women leaders from around the world was undoubtedly intimidating.[5] She spoke about what she knew: the health problems affecting women and children. Her report, *Training of Health Personnel*, given in English, was a well-organised, well-structured speech. She began with a short history: in 1932 a Nursing School was opened in Kabul at the Female Hospital; in 1949 a midwifery school; in 1955 courses for auxiliary nurse midwives; in 1957 a Faculty of Medicine for women. In Afghanistan there were four categories of female medical personnel: nurses; midwives; auxiliary nurse-midwives; and a handful of doctors. She pointed out the difficulties of looking after a population of around 12 million, many living in remote areas where the majority were illiterate. She ended 'although the principles of Islam give equal opportunities of education to men and women, the historic-social "purdah system" and the consequent separation of males and females has stood in the way of progress. . . . Endeavours are being made to promote the teaching of the real principles of Islam as regards the status of women, principles which are in favour of women's rights.'⁶ Her conference speech was well received in Ceylon but back home she was criticised by more traditional Afghans who feared the expansion of women's rights.

Anahita faced enormous challenges, challenges that might have frightened others. Medical facilities were only available in the capital and a few other cities. The life expectancy of Afghans was 38 years. Infant mortality was dire: fifty per cent of children died before the age of five. One doctor served 3,000 people. Anahita began to realise that medicine and health care alone could not solve the problems of poverty, living conditions, poor education and general lack of rights. She turned to politics.

In 1965 Anahita co-founded the Soviet-backed People's Democratic Party of Afghanistan and the Democratic Organisation of Afghan Women (DOAW). She was not frightened to speak out against inequalities or challenge traditional social norms. On 8 March 1965, she led a march celebrating International Women's Day. It was the first time Afghan women had commemorated the day, the day initiated by Clara Zetkin more than fifty years earlier. Women all over the world were gaining courage from each other.

In the same year Anahita stood for election to the House of the People. She handled her election campaign with consummate skill, helped by DOAW, whose members encouraged women to vote. Her election was a breakthrough moment. Not only did it open a political space for women but it allowed her to promote women's rights in Parliament. Anahita pushed for legal reforms to improve women's lives, focusing particularly on health care and education.

Afghan politics was volatile, turbulent and uncompromising. The country was devastated by decades of civil war, invasions, widespread corruption and incompetent governments. One day, a politician was in power; the next day in prison. In 1978, and now a republican, Anahita played a crucial role in the revolution which overthrew the monarchy. In the days before the uprising, she was arrested and imprisoned; two years later she was Minister of Social Affairs.

Between 1980 and 1985 she served as Deputy Head of State, the equivalent of vice-president of Afghanistan. In this post she was partly responsible for Article 38 of the Constitution which stated that all citizens 'both men and women, have equal rights and duties before the law, irrespective of their national, racial, linguistic, tribal, educational and social status, religion, creed, political conviction, occupation, kinship, wealth and residence'.[7] America, fearful of the spread of Russian influence, undermined the Afghan revolution by arming the Mujahideen. These were disparate groups of men, largely motivated by conservative Islamic beliefs, who wanted to overthrow the socialist-inclined government. They succeeded. And some of their sections morphed into the Taliban.

In 1992, after the collapse of her government, Anahita fled to escape the Mujahideen. Her socialist and feminist politics were anathema to this misogynistic regime. She left first for India, then moved to Bulgaria and finally to Germany where she was granted political asylum. In 2014 Anahita died, aged 82, in Dortmund of kidney failure. Her remains were taken back to Afghanistan and buried in Kabul.

Bahamas: Doris Sands Johnson (1921–1983)

In the 1960s the British Empire continued to shrink. As countries gained independence, they adopted full democracy, enabling women to vote and to stand for election. In countries as far apart as the Bahamas, Cyprus and Zambia, women formed part of governing bodies. Increasingly it seemed as if Francis Fukuyama's prophecy of liberal democracy's triumph over absolute monarchy, fascism and communism was to be fulfilled.[8] Women, previously absent from high politics, took the opportunity democracy afforded, voted, stood for election and won.

Not all women were fiery revolutionaries but instead blazed their trail in quieter, slower ways. In the Bahamas, Dame Dr Doris Sands Johnson achieved several firsts: she was the first woman to stand for Parliament, the first to be a government minister, the first to serve in the Cabinet, the first to be President of the Senate, the first to serve as Acting Governor General of the Bahamas.[9] In 1979, Queen Elizabeth II awarded her an OBE. These remarkable achievements were the result of her profound and lasting commitment to equality and her refusal to be cowed by Bahamian male chauvinists like those in the *Nassau Guardian* who commented that her 'tread is firm, the smile serene and the torso buxom'.[10]

Doris was born on 19 June 1921 in St Agnes, in the Bahamas, the third in a family of ten children belonging to Sarah and John Sands. She left school at 15 and began work as a pupil-teacher at Eastern Secondary School. Doris worked while continuing her education: first graduating with a BA from Virginia Union University, USA, then an MA at McGill University, Canada, and in 1962 a doctorate from New York University. Meanwhile, on 3 January 1943 Doris married Ratal (Carl) Johnson at the Zion Baptist Church in Nassau. The couple had one son, Gerald. Doris was a fervent Baptist, worshipping at the Bethel Baptist Church. It was a place which took Christ's Sermon on the Mount – a message of serving the poor and marginalised – as a central tenet of its faith. Members of the church provided schooling, took stands on social justice and promoted political equality.

Back then, the Bahamas was a Crown Colony, under the jurisdiction of the British government. It was a two-party state, split along racial lines. The Progressive Liberal Party (PLP) represented the Black community; the United Bahamian Party (UBP) represented the white. Only property-owning men – which in effect generally meant white men – were allowed to vote; all women were disenfranchised. Doris became a suffragist activist. In 1958, she joined the Women's Suffrage Movement and energised it with her passion and oratory. A year later, all adult males were given the right to vote; all women were excluded.

On 19 January 1959, Doris led a demonstration to the Bahamian Parliament. In a scene unique in Bahamian history, she gave an impassioned speech to the most powerful men in the country, the Members of Parliament. Being a woman, she was not allowed to speak in Parliament and so addressed her audience in the Magistrate's Court. The male MPs, all in full morning dress, packed tightly into the spectators' gallery and even the prisoners' dock of the Magistrate's Court to hear Doris speak on the moral right of women to vote. 'We women', she insisted 'press this demand and ask such enactment on the basis of not who is right, but what is right for our country. ... We women ask only that you gentlemen move now to secure the rights of 54 thousand women.'[11] She put forward the reasons that women had used across the centuries, arguing that we 'have accepted and paid all the taxes which are imposed on us by a Government in which we now have no representation. Since we are powerless to limit these taxes, we are forced to bring charges of tyranny and despotism against our Government.'[12] Little notice was taken. Doris, who was determined to remedy this injustice, took her petition to the mother of Parliament: the House of Commons, London.

In November 1960, Doris and a colleague were sponsored by Bahamian suffrage societies to visit Britain and present a petition asking for votes for women. They met Ian McLeod, the Secretary of State for the Colonies, two sympathetic women MPs, Joan Vickers and Eirene White, and members of the International Alliance of Women. In January 1961, a Select Committee of the Bahamas Parliament advocated votes for women: the PLP and Independents opposed it. A further appeal was made to the British Parliament. In February, no doubt pressurised by Britain, Bahamian women were given the vote and the right to stand for Parliament.

In 1967, when the PLP won a majority of seats, a win that marked the end of white minority rule, Doris Johnson was appointed to the Senate, a groundbreaking moment for women in Bahamian politics. Her political career took off. She used her position to push social welfare, better access to educa-tion especially for the underprivileged, and improvements in health care.

On 10 July 1973, the Bahamas finally gained independence and Doris was elected President of the Senate. In 1979 she was appointed acting governor general and made a Dame Commander of the Order of the British Empire. On 21 June 1983 Doris Sands Johnson died. She was aged 62.

Cyprus: Kadriye Hacibulgur (1905–1988) and Constantia Varda (1916–1993)

In the Mediterranean, on the island of Cyprus, women were also making their mark. Cyprus had been part of the Ottoman Empire before being annexed by Britain during the First World War. In 1925 it was transformed into a British Crown Colony. At the time, Cyprus consisted of eighty per cent Greek Christians and Greek Orthodox and seventeen per cent Turkish Muslims. The Turkish Cypriots wanted union with Turkey; the Greek Cypriots union with Greece. The Greek National Union of Cypriot Fighters (EOKA) waged a campaign of terror against British rule to force the government to concede independence and for the country to be part of Greece. The Turkish set up their own nationalist movement: the Turkish Resistance Organisation. There was no liaison between the two, no common anti-colonial struggle, no agree-ment to launch a joint armed insurrection. Ethnic identities were constantly reinforced through education, the media and cultural institutions.

In 1960, Cyprus finally gained independence from Britain. Two Communal Chambers were created: one for the Greek Cypriots; one for the Turkish Cypriots. Kadriye Hacibulgur was the first woman to be elected to the Turkish Chamber; Constantia Varda was the first woman to be elected to the Greek Chamber. Two feminists, two national identities, one island, one government. Would it work?

Researching this book was challenging, informative and often great fun. People across the globe were willing to share information about the great women in their country with me. I had great help when researching Kadriye Hacibulgur. The Turkish Cypriot Consulate put me in touch with Esra Emin, who furnished internet sources that I would have been unable to find without knowing Turkish. She also told me about a conference paper published by Eastern Mediterranean University, *Iz Birakmiş Kibrish Turkler*, which had a section on Kadriye. The university kindly sent me a copy. Now I could begin.

Kadriye Ahmed Hulusi Hacibulgur, the second eldest of seven children, was born in Nicosia on the cold night of 7 November 1905. The night she was born was K'adir night, hence her name.[13] She had two brothers and four sisters. Their parents, Ismet and Ahmet Hulusi Hacibulgur, were both Turkish nationalists who saw Turkey as their homeland. Her father owned the newspaper *Birlik*, a paper dedicated to publishing news from Turkey and raising the consciousness of Turkish Cypriots. His aim was to consolidate the national identity of Turkish Cypriots to their mother country.[14] Kadriye later contributed articles to the family newspaper, one of the first women to write for the press. She could have lost her job as public servants were forbidden to write and publish. The family were all followers of the moderniser and future first president of Turkey Kemal Atatürk – Kadriye's father was one of the first men to remove his fez and wear a hat.

Both parents agreed with Atatürk's commitment to female equality. Kadriye studied at the Victoria Islamic Inas Industrial School, a secondary school founded in 1901 by the British authorities to educate Turkish Cypriot girls. Until then there had been no secondary school for Turkish Cypriot girls. Subjects included the Holy Quran, Tajwit, Turkish reading, Sarf, Concise Geography, History of the Ottoman Empire, Calculus and – typically for a girls' school – embroidery, crocheting and sewing. Great importance was attached to studying English. The school was an educational institution where enlightened parents, like the Hacibulgurs, sent their daughters. Kadriye wore a yellow, white and sandy coloured uniform with a coat of arms embroidered on her jacket. She graduated in 1920 and was appointed a teacher at the Ortaköy Primary School. All the teachers working at the school initially wore veils and burqas until 1925 when a newly appointed headteacher from Turkey encouraged them to abandon this dress code. Soon students like Kadriye and staff came to school without veils and burqas.

On 29 October 1923, the day on which Mustafa Kemal Atatürk proclaimed the Turkish Republic, a great festival was held in Cyprus. Houses, schools and mosques were decorated with the Turkish flag. The British authorities squashed this outbreak of nationalism, banning students and teachers from mentioning Atatürk. Nonetheless, Kadriye, now a young teacher, encouraged her students to draw Atatürk's picture on the black board and repeat the words 'Long Live Gazi Mustafa Kemal' together before each lesson. The British authorities tried to scare her with threats of exile.

Kadriye collected money for the Red Crescent for the reconstruction of Turkey after its war of independence. At one meeting, she made a fiery speech, pulled off her veil and threw it into the crowd. Kadriye's actions, as one former student noted, was the mark of a tireless, strong woman, a woman with style and charisma, unafraid to challenge authority. Her action spread across Turkish Cyprus, starting the struggle for women to throw off their head coverings.

Kadriye progressed up the educational ladder, becoming one of the country's most respected teachers. In 1959 she retired from her post as Headmistress of the girls' section in the Atatürk Primary School in Nicosia, where 500 girls were enrolled. Kadriye had been a teacher for about forty years.

In 1960, shortly after her retirement and now aged 55, Kadriye was elected as a member of the Cyprus Turkish National Union to the Turkish Communal Chamber. She remained in office until 1970. As the first woman MP from the Turkish community, she had a lot to prove: she travelled from village to village, asking people their problems and trying to solve them. Everyone, according to one niece, loved her: many would come and just hug her hands. She was seen to be highly effective. One of her achievements was gaining equal pay for high school and primary school teachers. She died in 1988, aged 83. For the last three years of her life, she had Alzheimer's, and could remember little about either her past or present.

Kadriye's colleague, Constantia Varda, was a Greek Cypriot, born in Larnaca. She studied at the Pancypriot Commercial High School, leaving in 1933. She was a dynamic and active student, a member of the school's hockey team, dance group, theatre group and Larnaca Hiking Club. After school she began work as a secretary at the Militiadis Oikonomakis law firm where the owner encouraged her to study law. In 1944 she married Militiadis Varda, a businessman who worked next door to the solicitor's office. Constantia took a correspondence course at the Middle Temple; in 1957 she graduated as a barrister. The 42-year-old Constantia was the first woman barrister to be appointed in Larnaca, where she spent her working life fighting for women's rights. In addition, Constantia defended EOKA fighters, a guerilla group which fought for independence from Britain and for 'Enosis', that is, union with Greece. However, Constantia was a communist and did not agree with

EOKA's violence or its methods of intimidation, yet as a lawyer defended them in court.

In 1960, Constantia stood for the Community Assembly and was elected as a member of the Progressive Party of Working People (AKEL), a Marxist-Leninist communist party. AKEL had been formed in 1941 from the collapse of the Soviet communist party, which had disintegrated because of the Nazi-Soviet pact. Immediately, disaffected communists like Constantia joined the anti-fascist resistance movement. It was a party which aimed to unite all the Cypriot working-class, Greek Cypriots and Turkish, and was opposed to the violence of EOKA. In 1985, Constantia Varda became President of the Larnaca Bar Association, holding that position until she died. She died in 1993, aged 77.

I can find no evidence that these two women ever met, but it is difficult to believe that they did not. The two must have discussed, and perhaps vehemently disagreed about, the situation in Cyprus. In 1963, three years after independence, fighting broke out between the Greek and Turkish Cypriots. In 1974, Greek Cypriot nationalists staged a coup d'etat to unite the island with Greece; five days later the island was invaded by Turkish troops. In 1983, a separate Turkish Cypriot state was established in the north. The island is still divided, despite efforts to unite it.

Iran: Farrokhroo Parsa (1922–1980)

At dawn on 8 May 1980, a 58-year-old Iranian woman, Farrokhroo Parsa, was bundled head to toe into a potato sack, wrapped in ropes which would be used to hang her and dragged to the gallows. Her death was painful. The ropes broke, she regained consciousness, and she was taken to the gallows to be hanged once more. Eventually she was executed by a firing squad, the first woman to be judicially murdered by the newly established Islamic Republic.[15] The new regime wanted to crush women like Farrokhroo, who had been one of the first women to take her seat in the Iranian Parliament and the first female Cabinet Minister.

Farrokhroo was born on 24 March 1922 in Qom to a Zoroastrian family. Her mother, Fakhr Afagh Parsa, was a women's rights activist, and her father, Farrokhdin, a civil servant who worked at the Ministry of Commerce. At the time of her birth, Farrokhroo's mother was under house arrest for her outspokenness on women's rights: she was editor of *Jahān-eZan* (*Women's World*), publishing articles on the necessity of girls' education and reform of the marriage laws. Not surprisingly, Farrokhroo grew up a feminist, committed to women's equality. Certainly, her radical and unconventional upbringing provided the courage to speak up for women's rights.

Farrokhroo's parents ensured that their daughter was well-educated: a first degree in biology was followed in 1950 by a medical degree from the University of Tehran. For most of her life, Farrokhroo worked as a teacher. She began teaching biology at a high school before climbing up the educational ladder. In 1957 she was appointed Principal of Noorbakshsh High School; in 1960 she was appointed Secretary-General of the newly established National University of Iran. Meanwhile she married Ahmad Shirinsekhan, with whom she had three children. Farrokhroo mixed in elite circles. One of her former school students, Farah Diba, later became the third wife of the Shah, Mohammad Reza Shah Pahlavi.

In 1963, Reza Pahlavi, in a bid to modernise Iran along Western lines, launched his 'White Revolution', a series of reforms which included the distribution of land from large landowners to peasants, educational reforms, industrial expansion and political reforms. The Shah's policies on women's rights were transformative: women were granted the right to vote and stand for Parliament. Ayatollah Komeini, later to become Iran's Supreme Leader, declared that giving women the vote was tantamount to prostitution and issued a fatwa against it.

In 1963 Farrokhroo Parsa was among the first eight women to be elected to the Iranian Parliament, the Majlis.[16] In 1965, she was promoted to Deputy Minister of Education and two years later to Minister of Education, the first time a woman had held a Cabinet post. During her time in Parliament, Farrokhroo worked hard to improve the lives of women. The number of girls attending elementary school increased dramatically, from 80,020 to 1,508,387; by 1978, women composed 33 per cent of university students; the age of marriage was raised from thirteen to eighteen; polygamy was restricted; abortion was made legal; birth control became accessible; special courts were established to handle family conflict; and more women entered the professions. School textbooks were revised to portray girls and women as workers, not only as mothers cooking and cleaning the house. Many of these initiatives marked a significant break from traditional Islamic law, putting Iran far ahead in the region in terms of gender equality.

In 1971 Farrokhroo Parsa lost her seat. She opened her own medical practice and worked for free at a children's clinic. In January 1979, the Shah was forced to leave Iran; in February Ayatollah Khomeini returned to Iran after fifteen years in exile. Farrokhroo was in London. She was warned not to return to Iran. Ayatollah Khomeini, Supreme Leader of the Revolution, was now in power, and within a few months reversed the social reforms of the Shah. Women were forced to wear the hijab and follow strict dress codes. Khomeini stated that it was 'an obligation of the female to cover her head because women's hair exudes vibrations which arouse, mislead and corrupt men'.[17]

Despite the risks, Farrokhroo went back home. Immediately she was arrested, tried by hooded judges in the misogynistic, murderous Islamic Revolutionary Court and sentenced to death on trumped-up charges for 'wasting and plundering public properties, propagating corruption and prostitution . . .

appointing pervert individuals to important ministry positions, organising mixed outdoor camps and violating Islamic morality'. She was not allowed a defence lawyer and had been declared guilty before her trial. Her judicial murder took place in the red-light district of Tehran, a miserable attempt to damage Farrokhroo's reputation and re-enforce the Supreme Court's message of subservience to the religious authorities. Farrokhroo Parsa was the first woman to die for political offences since the revolution. Her death marked the start of an horrific repression. The following years were ones of terror, marked by human rights abuses like arbitrary arrest, torture and mass executions.

In her last letter to her children, written in prison, Farrokhroo wrote 'I am a doctor so I have no fear of death. . . . I am prepared to receive death with open arms rather than live in shame by being forced to be veiled. I am not going to bow to those who expect me to express regret for 50 years of efforts for equality between men and women. I am not prepared to wear the chador and step back in history.'

Farrokhroo Parsa's body was buried in a Tehran cemetery. Almost immediately her grave was bulldozed over. When a replacement gravestone was inscribed, it was again razed to the ground. Her family could not find where her body was buried. In making her body disappear the regime hoped to crush what she represented. Childcare centres were closed, abortion became illegal, adultery was punished by stoning. Repression continued. Executions were common. In 1983 women were given 74 lashes for not adhering to strict hijab; in 1984 a special patrol was established to deal with violations including showing of hair and wearing lipstick. In 2019, Nasrin Sotoudeh was sentenced to 38 years in prison and 148 lashes, simply for protesting against the hijab laws. In 2025, Iranian women endure widespread human rights abuses under a political system that legally discriminates against them. They are still being raped, lashed, tortured, executed and stoned simply for challenging Iranian mullahs.

Zambia: Gwendoline Konie (1938–2009)

In south-east Africa, a distinguished writer ignited change. Gwendoline Chomba Konie, the first woman to be appointed to government in both Northern Rhodesia and Zambia, was a poet whose verses resound across the centuries and across national boundaries.[18] Her book *In the Fist of Your Hand* denounced male arrogance and violence. It is a poem included in the *Penguin Book of Modern African Poetry*.

> Like a worm I write in your tight fist
> As you try to smother my voice
> And my mind with your brutal grip . . .
> For I will not let fear swallow
> My breath, my dreams, and my hopes!
> My hidden courage will saw off your fist.

In 1962, shortly before independence, Dr Gwendoline Noreen Chomba Konie was appointed a member of the Legislative Council of Northern Rhodesia by the British Governor General, Sir Evelyn Dennison Hone. She was the first woman ever to be in government. In 1964, when Northern Rhodesia broke away from British colonial rule and became Zambia, African women over the age of 21 gained the vote, and the right to stand for Parliament. Gwendoline was one of two women elected to the 125-member National Assembly.

On 9 October 1938 Gwendoline Konie was born in Lusaka, the capital city of what was then Northern Rhodesia, now Zambia. She was a member of the Bemba clan, Bantu-speaking people. Both parents were teachers in different parts of the country; her father, William Bernard Konie, was the first black person to teach at Lusaka's prestigious High School. At the age of eight Gwendoline was sent to a Methodist boarding school. The school, an all-girls school with women teachers, was strict. She was forced to fend for herself, yet it was here that she learned early leadership skills as a class captain, a house captain and then a school captain. At home, she was encouraged by her parents, who believed in treating all their children equally. There was, as she noted later, 'no special work for boys and special work for girls. Everybody cleaned and cooked. I therefore did not grow up with an awe of men.'[19]

Gwendoline travelled overseas for higher education. Her father had impressed on her that when Zambia became independent, the country would need well-educated people to help in the administration. She had wanted to study Music, but took her father's advice and read social science at Swansea University, Wales. She later read law and international studies at the American University in Washington, USA. Knowledge, she believed, was power.

A year and a half before Zambia became independent, Gwendolin returned to her country. She had qualified as a social worker but the racist colonial politics of the day meant that, as a black African woman, she was not allowed to work as one. It was to be her first challenge against discrimination, and she took the issue right up to the Chief Secretary. Gwendoline's determination soon reached the ears of the Governor. He was impressed and he asked her to serve in the Legislative Council. After consulting with Kenneth Kaunda, then leader of the coalition government, she accepted the post, thus becoming the first woman and the youngest member of the Council. Here, as she said later, she was 'catapulted into the world of men – professionally, politically and socially'.[20]

In 1964, Zambia became independent. In 1972 a new constitution established one-party rule by the United National Independence Party with a President as Head of State and a Prime Minister who headed government. Legislative power was held by the 125-member elected National Assembly. A central committee, consisting of 25 members, held executive power over the National Assembly. Gwendoline was picked to train for the Foreign Service and later appointed to the

Ministry of Foreign Affairs. Once again, she was the only woman. In 1972, Gwendoline was appointed to the Presidential Office. President Kenneth Kaunda recognised her talents and made her Zambian Ambassador to several Scandinavian countries. Between 1974 and 1977, Gwendoline was Zambian Ambassador to Sweden, Denmark, Norway and Finland. In 1977 she was appointed Zambian's Permanent Representative to the United Nations, the First Zambian and the first African woman to hold that post. In 1979, she left the Foreign Office to become Permanent Secretary in the newly created Ministry of Tourism. When Kaunda was replaced by Frederick Chiluba, she was appointed Ambassador to Germany.

In the 1980s, Gwendoline founded the *Women's Exclusive*, a magazine which focused on women's issues. In 1983 she offered suggestions on how to involve women in politics. It is advice that resonates today. Firstly, she argued, political parties should give women a quota of posts; secondly governments should set aside a number of places for women on commissions, committees and other bodies; thirdly, steps should be taken to select women as project managers, advisors and experts; fourthly, governments should research what factors impede women in politics; fifthly, women's organisations need to encourage women to take up politics; sixthly, governments should provide training for women along with support for childcare and household management; seventhly, special efforts should be made to encourage women to take up policy-making posts; and lastly, governments should create programmes to help women into mainstream national politics.[21] Gwendoline Konie was well aware that women could not become politicians overnight. Her advice is a blueprint for how it might happen.

In 1978, Gwendoline helped found the Zambian Alliance of Women (ZAW), a non-governmental organisation to promote equality, development and peace. By now, Gwendoline was an internationally acclaimed politician. In 1984, the American activist, Robin Morgan, and the French philosopher,

Simone de Beauvoir, founded the Sisterhood is Global Institute, an international feminist think-tank which grew out of their edited book *Sisterhood is Global*, to which Gwendoline contributed.

In 2001 Gwendoline stood for the Zambian Presidency, 'because I believe the first country in Africa to tackle poverty, hunger and disease, coupled with the policy of bringing more women into decision making, will develop . . . in 1997, if you had asked me whether I would stand for presidency, I would have said "you are crazy". But as I kept coming from Germany to Zambia and seeing the economic decline and poverty I began to think more.'[22] She had recently formed a new party – the Social Democratic Party – to promote her ideas of poverty alleviation and gender equality. Women, she argued, brought a certain dimension to politics that men could not. Women, she said, 'persevere, they have ingenuity because they can make something out of nothing and work hard and always believe they must do well'. Tackling poverty and gender equality, she believed, was fundamental to development. Her vision of eliminating poverty was not shared: she found it difficult to raise funds, or garner support from key individuals. As she commented, 'we live in a traditional society so . . . there are different expectations of women than of men'. And Gwendoline Konie was breaking all of them. In the presidential election she won only 0.59 per cent of the vote, receiving a mere 10,253 votes out of more than a million votes cast.

In 2005 she left national politics. She became President of Light on Africa, a non-governmental organisation which focused on helping women with AIDS/HIV and poverty. She remained an important figure in Zambian politics. When she died Gwendoline Konie was given a state funeral. On 22 March 2009, Dr Kenneth Kaunda, former President of Zambia, gave a eulogy to the recently deceased politician. In his oration, he paid tribute to her as a builder of Zambia, as a fighter for women's rights, and as an ambassador for the country.[23] 'Gwen, my dear Sister, you were part of this wonderful revolution. You were part of this fight against British colonialism in Zambia.'

Many of the women in this chapter have not just disappeared from history but have never been in it. None, as far as I can gather, have had full-length biographies written about them. Their courage, as with so many other women in this book, was breathtaking. Anahita Ratebzad, for instance, fled her home in Afghanistan, fearing that if she remained she would meet the same fate as brave Farrokhroo Parsa, who was murdered by Iranian fundamentalists.

For me, the experiences of these women raise more general questions, largely around gender and power. Progress is generally regarded as a positive step in the right direction, involving positive change and development. Certainly, the end of colonialism marked a significant step forward in advancing the rights and status of women in the Bahamas, Cyprus and Zambia. Elsewhere in the world too, a new, and usually democratic, dawn broke as women joined their governing bodies for the first time.[24]

However, what one person views as progress may, for another, be experienced as a setback, a shift into a less favourable, even oppressive reality. It is difficult, in the twenty-first century, to feel much sympathy for colonial powers which saw their loss of dominance in newly independent countries as a decline, when in fact it marked the dismantling of unjust privilege. Yet history is rarely simple or straightforward. The fall of monarchies in countries like Afghanistan and Iran was widely hailed as progress. Yet in both countries, women lost hard-won rights when those monarchies were replaced by authoritarian and religious regimes – regimes that oppressed, silenced and in some cases murdered women. . . Democracy, which gained significant momentum during the twentieth century, now faced new threats. And as democracy was challenged, so too were the rights of women, often the first to feel the impact when freedoms slip away.

Chapter Seven

Global Challenges, 1970–1980: Switzerland, Mozambique, Pitcairn Islands[1]

The men of Switzerland, a land-locked European country known for its mountains, chocolates, cheese and cuckoo clocks, were reluctant to allow women to take part in government. Military service was compulsory for men, and the vote – as it once was in Britain – was associated with the defence of the realm. In 1848 the Swiss Parliament was established. It took 123 years for women to be allowed to sit in it. In 1971, after a national referendum, and a century-long campaign, women gained the vote and the right to stand for the National Council, the Swiss Parliament. In the first election, twelve women won seats.[2] Flowers were put on each of their seats. It was a mixed message of welcome, a gesture of chivalry, but a reminder that women parliamentarians were unusual.[3]

In contrast, newly independent nations like Mozambique did not delay in granting women the right to vote or run for office. In their view, parliamentary democracy was for everyone, not just the male elite. The Pitcairn Islands present an unusual and troubling example of women in government where life in a tight-knit, isolated community led women to take part in one of century's the most shocking scandals.

Switzerland: Elizabeth Blunschy (1922–2015) and Tilo Frey (1923–2008)

One of the first women was Elizabeth Blunschy, elected as a member of the right-wing Christian Democratic People's Party, a Roman Catholic Party. Her home Canton of Schwyz was a Conservative district which had voted against women's right to vote;[4] the other was Tilo Frey, elected as a member of the more left-wing Free Democratic Party. She was the first person of African descent to be elected to the Swiss National Council. The two women were different in so many ways, yet they shared one common goal: to improve the lives of women. Their biographies need to be written; most of their lives still hidden in Swiss archives. Neither were firebrands, 'trouble-makers' who challenged the status quo; on the contrary they were both quiet reformers who carefully, steadily tried to improve the lives of their Swiss constituents.

Elizabeth, neé Steiner, was born on 13 July 1922 in a house on Hauptplatz, Kollegiumstrasse in Schwyz, a German-speaking, mainly Roman Catholic Canton in Switzerland. She was from an old established family. Her parents, Dora and Hans Steiner, and her three sisters all lived together in her grandmother's house where generations of the family had lived for 200 years. Built in the seventeenth century, it was one of the most beauti-ful town houses in the main square. Her father, Hans, was a lawyer, a former member of the National Council, a municipal councillor and a Federal judge of the Supreme Court. Her mother, Dora Schuler came from an old Schwyz family too; her ancestors were merchants, trading in wine, food and cloth with Italy.

Elizabeth's first memories, aged two-and-a-half, were of gunshots fired to celebrate her father's election as a Federal judge. As a result of his promotion, the family moved to Lausanne, the French-speaking part of Switzerland, where the family and two servants lived in a spacious eight-room apart-ment. Elizabeth grew up bilingual. According to Elizabeth, she and her sisters were over-protected, lacking carefree contact with children the same age. They were all very obedient, well brought up, conventional young girls. A nanny accompanied them to their private Catholic primary school located on the other side of the city – most other pupils walked on their own. By the time Elizabeth was five she could already read, and for the rest of her life education was effortless. She completed her school education at the girls' grammar school run by the Menzing sisters, an order of Catholic nuns. The girls were not spoilt. Their mother had control of the home finances. She was a woman who guarded every Swiss franc and sent her daughters to sewing classes to learn to sew all their own clothes, clothes that were comfortable and made to last.

For two semesters, Elizabeth studied law at the French-speaking University of Lausanne. She lived at home under her mother's supervision. Her mother was a 'helicopter' parent who 'knew my lecture timetable by heart, and if I came home twenty minutes later than usual, she registered it immediately'.[5] She transferred to the German-speaking University of Freiburg, finally independent and able to speak her mother tongue. It was here, free from parental control, that she met Alfred Blunschy, who was also studying law. The couple soon became inseparable, hiking in the mountains, dancing at balls, and attending every student event. On 15 July 1947, the two were married in Einsiedeln. Elizabeth's marriage was a great liberation for her: she was free from the suffocating embrace of an over-anxious mother. Alfred was the love of her life, though there were warning signs that it would not be a long one. Alfred suffered from asthma as a child and later, when the two were a couple, a shadow was found on his lung. It was the dreaded, and at that time incurable, tuberculosis, caught before vaccinations and penicillin were available.

Meanwhile Elizabeth completed her law degree and went on to gain a doctorate. The couple moved back to Schwyz where they set up a joint law firm: Elizabeth was the first woman to be admitted to the bar in her Canton. The couple lived in her parents' old house in Schwyz, temporarily unoccupied while her parents were in Lausanne. Elizabeth expected to be her husband's helpmeet in the firm but Alfred's illness set them on a different course. Shortly after they married, Alfred suffered a relapse and Elizabeth ran the law practice, driving to visit her husband at the weekends where he was recuperating in the sanatorium in Davos. It was to be a constant refrain: Alfred working, getting ill, Elizabeth running the law firm and visiting him in hospital. There was an added burden. When her parents retired, they reclaimed their old house. Elizabeth and Alfred set about commissioning a new house for themselves. In the autumn of 1951, they moved into their new home.

The couple had three children: Isabelle in 1952, Toni in 1954 and Felix in 1958. In these years, Elizabeth played a sympathetic wifely role. Her husband was active in local and cantonal politics, but because women were without the vote, Elizabeth could only support him rather than stand for election herself. Nonetheless, she maintained that politics was in her blood. She was the daughter of a Federal judge, had trained as a lawyer and married a political activist. The couple discussed politics constantly. Elizabeth supported Alfred when he became an active member of the Christian Social Party. She helped him when he was elected its President, when he became a municipal councillor, when he became municipal president and lastly a cantonal councillor. 'It was a matter of course', she said 'that I supported my husband in his law practice and in his political work. I shared his interest in politics.'6

The two were committed Roman Catholics, their religious beliefs informing all their work. For six years, Elizabeth and Alfred embarked on a theology course for Catholic laypeople, passing sixteen exams to be awarded the 'Missio Canonica', a formal qualification which allowed them to teach religion. Elizabeth later said that the theology course was a 'great personal enrichment', opening new ways of seeing the world. All her life she remained deeply religious, attending church services regularly. Her faith, she believed, helped her cope with, if not overcome, her future challenges.

Elizabeth was very aware of the problems of the socially disadvantaged and it was this that contributed to her political activism. She worked for several women's organisations, charitable, religious and cultural. Women, she maintained, were sympathetic to the weak because they experienced first-hand what it meant to be considered inferior. In 1957, she was asked to be President of the Swiss Catholic Women's Association. The organisation wanted a female lawyer who could represent them in their struggle for votes for women. She was 35 years old with no experience of organising. The presidency marked her political coming of age. It was here that Elizabeth became aware of the limitations placed on women, on their lack of educational and work experiences. She learned how to stand in front of a large audience, to speak in public, to organise and chair board meetings and how to negotiate a consensus with the many disparate individuals in the Catholic group. She was President until 1961, becoming the symbolic figurehead of Catholic women's suffrage. When the Catholic Women's Association voted in favour of women's suffrage, they were opposed by the powerful association of Bishops, who voted against. It was to be a rocky road towards equality.

There were other injustices besides the parliamentary vote. Even before she became a member of Parliament, Elizabeth worked on various commissions, all of which drew upon her legal expertise. At the end of the 1960s, despite being a mother with three children, Elizabeth regularly worked late at night to solve problems of adoption law, of marriage law, of trying to work out child allowances and social housing. Like mothers all over the world who worked for pay, it was inevitably a struggle to keep everyone satisfied.

When her husband was asked to be a parliamentary candidate, he refused and nominated his wife. In October 1971, Elizabeth was elected, one of eleven women. She voted in the national elections but was unable to do so in her municipal council because the Canton had voted against women's suffrage. This was, Elizabeth thought, 'extremely absurd'.

On election, she acerbically commented that 'there are already some who think I should be cleaning the house or weeding the garden'.[7] Alfred, proud of his wife's accomplishments, now acted in a supportive capacity, driving her to the station to catch her train to Parliament and meeting her when she returned. Elizabeth remembers that she was startled to see him after the first week, as he 'had a fever and felt very bad. When I had to travel back to Bern the following Monday, I was terrified. He was suffering from a persistent 'flu which, together with the asthma, finally damaged his already strained heart. Worrying about my husband overshadowed the joy of my new role. I remember sitting at the back of the Holy Trinity church in Bern . . . after work and seeking help and comfort in prayer.'[8] Alfred never really recovered and was admitted to hospital with angina. On 17 November 1972 he died of heart failure, after telling his wife not to worry. For the next four years, Elizabeth wore black. It was too painful to wear anything bright or colourful.

This forced Elizabeth, like many women politicians, to navigate the demands of home and work. Her eldest daughter Isabelle had just finished business school, her sons were both at secondary school. To make ends meet, Elizabeth returned to her law practice, drafting wills, helping with adoption papers, paternity payments and inheritance settlements. It was a juggling act, trying to balance her domestic life and professional commitments. She envied her male colleagues whose wives ran the household whereas the first thing she had to do 'was tie on my kitchen apron to get the household in order'.[9] She 'imagined how the gentleman colleague at home can immediately sit down at his desk, while I first had to go to the kitchen to see if there was anything else to eat at all'. All too aware of the difficulties faced by new politicians, she helped others. One colleague spoke of how Elizabeth received her graciously, and offered advice to ease her way in the 'confusing world of parliamentary business'.

On 2 May 1977, Elizabeth became the first woman to be elected President of the National Council, the equivalent of the British Speaker in the House of Commons. A big celebration took place in her home town. She travelled back from Bern in a special train, was greeted by crowds waving flags, a procession through the town and a celebratory sumptuous meal at an evening reception. Elizabeth had a lot to prove, knowing that her every move as President would be watched. She prepared carefully: 'As the first woman to hold the chair . . . I couldn't afford to make any mistakes.'[10] All this fame could have inflated her ego but Elizabeth remained down-to-earth. Even as President she answered her own doorbell, took her guests' coats and made them coffee. There was no fence outside her house, 'no guards, no doorman, no household staff, no personal secretary'.[11] She insisted on behaving like a normal citizen.

In Parliament Elizabeth focused on asylum, development aid, environment and health, marriage and child laws. Family law was close to her heart. She was determined to improve the legal position of children and women and suggested many reforms. In her view, unmarried fathers should take responsibility for their children, women should retain the citizenship of their birth when they married, and matrimonial property law (which benefitted men) should be changed. More controversially, she called for the unconditional protection of life. As a Roman Catholic, Elizabeth was anti-abortion. There should, she argued, be sufficient child allowances, maternity insurance and creches to help support mothers. Her pro-life stance was reflected in other areas. She was in favour of a ban on the export of arms, particularly to developing countries, rejecting the argument that it would harm the Swiss economy. In her view, nuclear weapons, biological and chemical weapons and anti-personnel mines were catastrophic instruments of destruction and devastation. No God-fearing country, she insisted, should have anything to do with them.

Between 1977 and 1987 Elizabeth was President of Caritas, a German-founded Catholic organisation named after the Latin word meaning love and compassion. It is committed to end world poverty. Elizabeth wanted to create a humane asylum law. She insisted that refugees should only be sent back to their home country if it was safe to do so. In her view, one of the major tasks of the world community was to invest more in conflict countries, helping people to live there in peace and security. Everyone, she insisted, should have enough to live on. Switzerland, she insisted, should be prepared 'to give up some of our prosperity to poorer countries. The disparity between rich and poor countries is too great, and if we don't manage to achieve a certain balance, we will increasingly have problems . . . we cannot live in peace . . . as long as there is inequality and underdevelopment in the world.'[12]

In 1981, the Theological Faculty of Lucerne awarded Elizabeth an honorary doctorate, the first it had ever awarded. It was in recognition of her 'commitment to justice in the service of refugees and the unborn, to peace research, and just social security, by which she has implemented essential demands of Christian social ethics . . . and thus tried to realise the spirit of the gospel for the good of our present society'.[13]

In 2010, now aged 88, Elizabeth published her autobiography, *A Life for Greater Social Justice* (*Ein Leben für mehr soziale Gerechtigkeit*). At her book launch, she surprised everyone by taking the microphone and making a spontaneous thank you speech. She died, aged 92. She had no fear of 'falling into a big, black hole. At the end of this tunnel, through which everyone has to pass, you fall into the arms of God. My husband, parents and siblings are waiting for me there. It will be more beautiful than we can imagine.'[14]

The other parliamentarian elected was an Afro-Swiss woman, pictured above. Tilo Frey was born on 2 May 1923 in Maroua, the capital of the Far North region of Cameroon, the daughter of a white father and a black mother. Her father, Paul Frey, was an engineer from Zurich who worked temporarily in the region. Her mother was Fatimatou Bibabadama, a member of the Fulani people.[15] The couple never married. Tilo

Image 9   Tilo Frey and Liselotte Spreng, both members of the FDP.
Photo © Prisma by Dukas Presseagentur GmbH/Alamy.

spent her early years with her mother before leaving at the age
of five to live in Switzerland because her father believed she
would have a better future in his home country. Meanwhile her
father married. Paul and his new wife, Katscha, adopted Tilo,
and together they made sure their daughter was well-educated.
Tilo began her studies at the Neuchâtel Canton school.

   In the 1920s Europe was turning Fascist, and Switzerland
was no exception to this racist ideology. From an early age,
Tilo suffered racist abuse. She spoke later of how her father
taught her how to defend herself, by advising her to fit in as
much as possible, and to 'act as white as a lily', meaning that
she should act like the white people around her. Dutifully, Tilo
put on her 'white mask' to navigate Swiss society. Throughout
her life, Tilo took her father's advice seriously and conformed
to rather silly formal societal rules, such as expecting men to
open doors and carrying a spare set of stockings in her hand-
bag in case they laddered. She always looked immaculate. As a
black woman in a white country, she felt it necessary to do so.

In 1938 Tilo studied at a teacher training college in Neuchâtel, and worked as a primary school teacher, then as a shorthand typist at the Ecole de Commerce, also in Neuchâtel. In 1972 she was made director of the Ecole Professionnelle of young women. Tilo joined the Free Democratic Party (FDP) of Switzerland, a liberal party which was committed to developing the welfare state. Between 1964 and 1974, she sat as an FDP member of the General Council of Neuchâtel, where she also served as Chair. Tilo was becoming increasingly interested in politics as a means of changing Switzerland.

In 1971 Tilo Frey stood as a candidate for the Free Democratic Party. Her election win was a surprise to all: Tilo left the election hall early, convinced that she would lose. She had made history, not just because she was one of the first Swiss women to be elected but because she was the first Afro-Swiss woman in Parliament. Tilo's victory was marred by unpleasantness. She endured horrendous racism and suffered racist abuse, such as being called a 'dirty n. . .'.[16] She rose above these taunts. The language used by Swiss newspapers was undoubtedly racist. Swiss feminists point out that the press both exoticised and condemned Tilo Frey. Her mother, newspapers reported, bequeathed her a marvellous tanned all-year-round complexion and black hair that owed nothing to hair dye. That, the papers argued, is why she stands out among the women in the National Assembly. Newspapers also condemned Tilo as being disrespectful to the National Council for choosing a white dress and jacket for her first days in Parliament, defying the convention that everyone wore dark colours. Tilo was as 'white as a lily', this time not to fit in, but to stand out.

In Parliament, Tilo fought passionately for gender equality, the decriminalisation of abortion and helping developing countries. She spoke on the need for family allowances. At one time, she asked for a grant of 10,000 Swiss francs for family aid organisations which supported mothers and prevented the hospitalisation of the disabled and the elderly. The grant was awarded. She also tried to amend the matrimonial law which governed cohabitation, asking for equal treatment for both married and unmarried couples. She remained in Parliament until 1975.

On 27 June 2008 Tilo Frey chose to end her own life through voluntary assisted dying. She was 85 years old and very ill. Tilo had never married, had no children, no brother or sister or any cousin or other relative. There was no family to look after her.

In 2019, Neuchâtel renamed its main square Espace Tilo Frey. It had previously been called Espace Louis-Agassiz, named after a racist racial theorist who had classified black people as inferior. It is the first and only square dedicated to a black woman, a signal that Switzerland was no longer honouring a racist white man but a black woman who had experienced racism, and who had made history of another kind.

Mozambique: Graça Simbine Machel (1945–)

In Britain, the European Song Contest is regarded with wry amusement, an event with cheesy music and over-the-top theatricality. Not everyone takes it seriously. In 1974, ABBA won in Brighton with *Waterloo*, a number which launched their pop career into the stratosphere. However, the Portuguese song which came last was much more significant. It started a revolution.[17] The ballad, *E Depois do Adeus* (*And After the Goodbye*), played at a precise time on all Portuguese radio stations, was the signal for army captains to challenge Salazar's Fascist regime. Within 24 hours the dictatorship had fallen, democracy quickly installed and its colonial empire dismantled. ABBA's win may have propelled them into stardom, but the Portuguese song (which was awarded only three points) changed the course of modern European and African history.

On 25 June 1975, after centuries of Portuguese colonial rule, the south-east African country of Mozambique, with its

9.704 million inhabitants, gained its independence. Since 1964, FRELIMO, the Front for the Liberation of Mozambique, had waged a fierce guerilla war against Portuguese occupation. The Portuguese military, aware that it was losing its fight, withdrew from Mozambique.[18] Now the hated colonial rulers were vanquished, the country was free to frame its own future.

In 1977 the first General Election was held: FRELIMO was the only party allowed to stand. It was a party that preached communism, declaring itself a Marxist-Leninist party committed to centralised planning, nationalisation of key industries and the redistribution of land. It produced a shortlist of candidates for the newly created People's Assembly. Twenty-seven women were elected, all members of FRELIMO, some of whom had fought in the liberation army.[19] One of them was Graça Simbine Machel, an outstanding woman in this book of remarkable women.[20] Graça showed herself to be an extraordinary leader not just in Mozambique, but internationally. Her fluency in several languages – English, French, Italian, Portuguese, Spanish and Xitsonga – no doubt helped.

Graça is a multi-decorated women who holds six honorary doctorates, an OBE from Britain, and a Dame Grand Cross of the Order of Isabella from Spain. She has been awarded honours across the world: in 1992, the Africa Prize for Leadership for the Sustainable End of Hunger; in 1995, the Nansen medal for her work with refugee children; in 1997, the Global Citizen Award for her work with women and children; in 1998, the North-South Prize. In 2010 she was named as one of *Time* magazine's most influential people; in 2012 she was appointed President of SOAS, London. She was the First Lady in two countries: in Mozambique when she was married to President Samora Michel and in South Africa as the wife of Nelson Mandela.

Graça Simbine was born on 17 October 1945, in Incandine in Portuguese East Africa, as Mozambique was then known, into a rural, poverty-stricken family. She was the youngest of six children, born seventeen days after her father, Filipe, a Methodist minister, died. Her mother Matilde, now a single parent, ensured that her children were well-educated, an atypical undertaking for black girls and boys in the colonial Portuguese country. At the age of six, Graça began her studies at a Methodist Mission school, before passing exams for a place at the prestigious Liceu António Enes. She had walked to the entrance exam without any shoes because her mother could not afford to buy any. She was the only black African in a class of 40 white students. 'Why is it', she said later, 'I'm made to feel strange in my own country? They're the foreigners, not me.'[21] In 1967 Graça won a scholarship, another rare achievement, to study at the University of Lisbon, where she read modern languages. Here she met other African students from a range of colonial countries and joined the secret and illegal FRELIMO. When the Portuguese secret police found out about her anti-colonial activity, she was forced to abandon her studies and leave for Switzerland.

In 1973, Graça temporarily returned to Mozambique. Later that year, she moved to Tanzania, trained in guerilla warfare, and worked as deputy directory in the FRELIMO-run secondary school in Bagamoyo, on the Indian Ocean coast. FRELIMO was committed to women's equality. It encouraged women to take part in armed struggle, thereby challenging traditional beliefs that women should stay at home. Here, working as a revolutionary guerilla, she met Samora Machel. The two were set to become a power couple in a new country, a new Mozambique.

In 1974, on her permanent return to Mozambique, Graça joined the team that negotiated the country's independence from the Portuguese government. A provisional Mozambique government was instituted. Equality between men and women was enshrined in the new constitution. Women and men, it stated, have equal rights and duties, a belief that determined governmental policy. In June 1975, aged thirty, Graça became

Mozambique's first Minister of Education and Culture, the only woman in the Cabinet. At that point, the country had one of the world's highest illiteracy rates, largely inherited from colonialism. As a former teacher, Graça was all too aware that the Portuguese legacy of mass illiteracy had done immense harm to Mozambique, and that a decently educated population would enhance the development of the country. As Minister, she worked hard to implement universal education for every child: she increased the number of pupils enrolled in both primary and secondary schools from forty per cent to over ninety per cent for boys and over 75 per cent for girls. Mozambique's school population increased from 400,000 to 1.6 million. Graça also initiated adult literacy classes, for all those who had been victimised by colonialism.

In September 1975, Graça married the recently designated President Samora Machel, a divorced man. The Zambian leader Kenneth Kaunda and the Tanzanian leader Julius Nyerere were guests at the wedding. The couple had two children together – a boy and a girl – and she helped raise five more from Samora's previous marriage. The two were a revolutionary powerhouse. Samora was President; Graça was in the Cabinet, on the FRELIMO Central Committee and on the national secretariat of the Organização da Mulher Moçambicana (Organisation of Mozambican Women). Both were committed to women's emancipation. New laws awarded pregnant women sixty days' paid leave; women workers had permission to miss two days of work a month without losing their pay; and new anti-discrimination laws protected women at work. In 1981, a progressive Family Law was put forward which established monogamous marriage, provided joint ownership of property and child maintenance. It also eliminated the distinction between children born in marriage and those born out of wedlock. In 2004, the law was passed.

The newly independent country faced serious challenges. In the 1980s Mozambique was split apart by a brutal civil war between FRELIMO and RENAMO, a foreign-created and funded army supported by apartheid South Africa and backed by the CIA. In 1986, Samora died when his Russian jet plane made a fatal wrong turn and crashed into a remote hillside just inside South Africa. Many believed it was a state-sponsored political assassination by the apartheid regime. Graça was devastated: photos show her stricken with grief. For five years, she dressed in black. She resigned as Minister of Education. In 1991, encouraged by her son, Graça Machel returned to politics.

In 1992 the civil war ended: more than one million were dead, three million had fled and over a quarter of a million children were orphaned. Graça witnessed at first hand the devastation caused by RENAMO, which had deliberately destroyed 45 per cent of primary schools and 490 health clinics. RENAMO also kidnapped young boys and girls, forcing boys to fight against the legitimate government and the girls to be sexual slaves. The whole infrastructure of the country had collapsed. More than two million landmines remained strewn around the country, killing around 40 people every month.

In 1990, during the civil war, Graça founded the Fundação para a Desenvolvimento da Comunidade (Foundation for Community Development), an organisation designed to support children. In that same year, she became President of the National Organisation of Children of Mozambique. Her main concerns were centred upon the children who had been orphaned, injured and traumatised during the civil war. She wanted to understand why 'we have societies which deliberately target children – kill them, torture them, even make them become part of the destructive process'.[22]

In 1994, Kofi Annan, Secretary-General of the United Nations, appointed Graça Machel to investigate how children were affected by violent conflict. In her excoriating, precise and emotional report, *The Impact of Armed Conflict on Children* published in 1996, Graça set the UN agenda to protect children

caught up in war. It is stark, passionate and essential reading, now available on the internet.[23] Millions of children, she
argues, are caught up in conflicts not of their making, victims
of a 'general onslaught' or 'calculated genocide'.[24] In ten years,
between 1985 and 1995, two million children were killed, three
times as many injured or disabled. All too many suffered sexual
violence or other depravations. In 1995, 30 different civil wars
were taking place, wars that were split along ethnic, religious,
political or cultural lines. All had themes in common: crops
were destroyed, schools and places of worship were bombed,
and children were slaughtered, raped, maimed, starved and
subjected to other unspeakable cruelties. 'Such unregulated
terror and violence', she maintained 'speak of deliberate vic-
timisation. There are few further depths to which humanity
can sink.' 'War', Graça argued, 'violates every right of a child –
the right to life, the right to be with family and community, the
right to health, the right to the development of the personality
and the right to be nurtured and protected.'[25] In 1997, she
persuaded African governments to sign an international treaty
banning the use of land mines.

Graça Machel's report outlined the widespread use of sex-
based violence. Rape, prostitution, sexual humiliation and
mutilation, trafficking and domestic violence, she insisted, all
functioned as a weapon of war. In 2008, the UN affirmed that
rape was a war crime. In April 2014, 276 young girls from
the Christian community in Nigeria were kidnapped by Boko
Haram, an Islamic terrorist group. Amnesty International esti-
mates that at least 2,000 girls and women have been abducted
and forced into sexual slavery. The solution, Graça advised,
was to address the root cause of violence by promoting equality and sustainable development.

On 18 July 1998, Graça Machel, the 52-year-old widow of
one revolutionary leader, married another revolutionary hero:
the 80-year-old Nelson Mandela. It was seen 'as a match made
in heaven, born from oppression forged in hell. The father of

the nation and the widow of the revolution.'[26] Stevie Wonder, Nina Simone and Michael Jackson sang; Desmond Tutu delivered the sermon; blessings were given by Muslim and Hindu religious leaders.

In 2007, Graça Machel joined Desmond Tutu, Nelson Mandela, Ban Ki-Moon, Jimmy Carter, Kofi Annan and others to form the Global Elders, a group of world leaders working to resolve the world's biggest problems. Today Graça remains a committed feminist, a committed educationalist and a committed human rights activist, often focusing on the rights and protection of children.

Pitcairn: Carol Christian (1950–)

At the beginning of the twenty-first century, people over the world were shocked by a large-scale child sexual abuse scandal. It was perpetrated by powerful men in the world's most remote island: Pitcairn. It is a British overseas territory situated in the southern Pacific Ocean roughly between New Zealand and Chile. Few people visit: there is no air strip, no harbour and no scheduled boats. The Pitcairn community of around fifty are descended from the white mutineers of HM *Bounty*: the Christians, the Warrens, the Youngs and the Browns and their unnamed Tahitian companions. The island is governed from Britain by an appointed Governor whose offices are in New Zealand. It was one of the first countries in the world to introduce universal suffrage.

On Christmas Day 1975, when people in Pitcairn traditionally vote, Carol Christian was one of the first two women to be elected to Pitcairn's chief administrative body, the Island Council. The islands were, and still are, the smallest democracy in the world. Elections were simple: there were no ballot boxes, no registrations, no scrutiny. Pitcairnese nominate a candidate and others second it. If there are no opposing names, the candidate wins.[27] However, politics and life in general in a microstate can be intense, agitated and highly personalised, borne out by the experience of the Pitcairns.

Carol was born on 3 April 1950, the daughter of Charlotta Zita Warren and Charles James Bert Christian. She was the sixth-generation descendant of *Bounty* mutineer, Fletcher Christian. In 1976 she married another descendant, Jay Warren, by whom she had two children, Darralyn and Charlene.

Pitcairn was seen as Paradise, but it held a dark secret. The island had a depraved secret culture of abuse: sexual fondling of infants, sex games with young children, an island practice of 'breaking-in' – i.e. raping – girls as young as ten years old. Some, like Carol Christian, thought it a normal practice. This cultural trait was challenged: it was child abuse on a grand scale. Pitcairn was a 'male dominated society where men were doing exactly as they pleased. . . . It's ingrained in the mentality of men in Pitcairn that this is an OK thing to do.'[28] One of the striking aspects of the affair was that Carol sympathised with the abusers rather than give support to the abused women.

In 1999, British police investigated alleged child sexual abuse when an underage girl accused two men of raping her. In 2000 Operation Unique was established: a New Zealand child abuse specialist, Karen Vaughan, led the interviews of every woman who had lived in Pitcairn since 1980.[29]

There was an international outcry. In 2001, Clare Short, then Secretary of State for International Development, cancelled the funding of a new road in Pitcairn as 'it seemed to me like the Catholic Church and the Boy Scouts . . . It had to be confronted. What's the alternative? Don't do anything so they can carry on sexually abusing young people?'[30] In 2004, seven men – a third of the adult male population – were put on trial for 31 counts of rape and other counts of sexual assault, sexual abuse of minors. It was to be the first criminal trial on the island. Pitcairn had a courthouse, with three gaol cells which were used to store life-jackets. The cases were harrowing. Young teenagers had been gang raped. Serially. One man was charged with assaulting five girls, including a five-year-old who was forced to give him oral sex. One of the accused, Steve Christian, was accused of raping a twelve-year-old girl while two other boys held her down. After the rape, he told his friends 'your turn if you want'. Another raped one girl from the age of twelve to fifteen almost weekly. 'After a while', she stated 'I stopped saying no. There was no point to saying no. So I just lay there and let him do what he had to do.'[31]

Carol Christian defended the men. One was her husband, Jay Warren. In her view, it was perfectly normal for girls to have sex, like she did at twelve years of age. 'There's never been a rape on the island', she insisted, 'I was one of them, I had sex at twelve. I went in fully knowing what I was doing and I was not forced.'[32] Underage sex, she insisted, was normal.[33] At the same time, she spoke of an unpleasant experience at the age of ten when a man tried to rape her and where she 'screamed like hell'. Thirteen women held a women's meeting at the home of Olive Christian where the trial was denounced. Two of the original accusers, Carol's daughters Darralyn and Charlene, withdrew their allegations. Reporters claimed that sources close to the case believed that the victims were pressurised to withdraw their accusations because 'they were told they'd be thrown out of the house, their fathers would commit suicide, the whole island would fold'.[34]

Six men were found guilty. The only man acquitted was Carol's husband. She told TV New Zealand that his reputation had been destroyed, as the 'whole world now sees him as a child molester'.[35] The abuse continued. In 2016, Mike Warren, a former Mayor who had led the child abuse investigation, was found guilty of possessing images of child abuse.

Meanwhile, life went on. Carol sold her wooden carvings to visiting tourists and ran a small guest house. In 2024, Carol advertised the 'ultimate Pitcairn experience'. Guests were invited to stay in their house, eat delicious home cooking, and sleep in either a queen, or king-sized bed. Guests would have 'plenty of time to enjoy everything Pitcairn can offer'. All for US$125 per night.[36]

In this decade, democracy, in one form or another, continued apace as countries either broke from the yoke of colonialism and established more equal legislatures and/or recognised that it was undemocratic to exclude half the population from their governing bodies.[37] And with the increase in democracy, came not just political rights for women but educational, social and economic opportunities. Switzerland, a partially democratic country for centuries, was the penultimate European country to appoint women to government. The collapse of the Portuguese dictatorship freed countries under its rule to determine their own future. Mozambique, along with Cape Verde, Congo, Guinea, São Tome and Principe, all elected their first women parliamentarians. There were common themes. Women's progress whether in rich, industrialised countries or poor, agricultural regions often conflicted, undermined and challenged age-old traditions of masculinity. Men, who no longer held all the power, were unable to put forward laws which discriminated against women. Pitcairn offers an unusual example which illustrates that power does not always reside in governments. Here was a country where male brutal force dominated and women were controlled, not through laws but through sheer naked force.

One country missing from this chapter is Syria, a country often in the news. I wanted to include one of the first women to take a seat in Parliament. In November 1970, Hafez al-Assad seized power in Syria. He established a People's Assembly to draft a new constitution for the country. This held that the Ba'ath party was the leading party and that only the National Council for Revolutionary Command could appoint the President. The constitution also pledged to guarantee women opportunities to participate in the political, cultural, social and economic life of the country, removing 'restrictions that prevent women's development and participation in building the socialist Arab society'.[38] In June 1973, the first women were elected to Parliament: Hana Hamwi, Boshra Kanafani, Munuar Mackluta, Salma Najeeb and Hajar Sadek. All were prominent women in the Ba'athist Party and promoted their party's programme. Assad was keen to promote a secular, modern Syria, a Syria that directly contrasted with that promoted by the Muslim Brotherhood. Only women who did not wear a hijab were allowed to run for office, serve as ambassadors or be part of any delegation. In theory, Assad promised reforms; in practice, he governed over a repressive regime where opposition was brutally crushed. Such was/is the nature of the situation in Syria that it proved (for me at least) impossible to gather any more information.

Chapter Eight

Navigating the 1980s: Liechtenstein, Turks and Caicos, Angola, Zimbabwe, Iraq, Tuvalu

By the 1980s, women around the world had made modest inroads into government. Progress was slow, often uncertain, and certainly hard-won, yet gradually, women carved out space within the political sphere. The list of countries that entirely excluded women from their legislatures dwindled. Liechtenstein, the last European country to maintain a male-only Parliament, finally relented – 124 years after its first constitution.

In 1962, the Turks and Caicos islands, a British Overseas Territory, granted women the right to stand for office. It would take another twenty-two years before the first woman entered its Parliament. Meanwhile, the continuing collapse of colonial empires opened doors for women in newly independent states. Across Africa, women secured voting rights and the right to stand for election from the outset – and many were elected, putting the older Western democracies to shame. Meanwhile, in a totalitarian Arab state – Iraq – women were given a chance to frame the country's laws. In 1978, Tuvalu, the world's smallest and least populated nation, gained its independence. Eleven years later, it elected its first female parliamentarian.

Liechtenstein: Emma Eigenmann-Schädler (1930–)

Liechtenstein is a constitutional monarchy with a parliamentary democracy. A very small landlocked country, bordered by Switzerland and Austria, Liechtenstein has under 40,000 inhabitants. It is the richest country in the world, based on its financial services, high-tech goods and tourism. It is a leading offshore financial centre, well known as a tax haven with favourable banking and corporate laws. These features made it an attractive destination for those seeking to shield assets and in 2008 the country was forced to tighten up its regulatory system.

Liechtenstein was the last European country to grant votes for women. In July 1984, after a male-only referendum, women were given the right to vote and stand for election to its then fifteen-member governmental body, the Landtag. On 16 April 1986, 56-year-old Emma Eigenmann-Schädler was sworn in to Liechtenstein's Parliament, becoming the first woman to enter the hallowed male enclave. She was elected to represent the Underland constituency as a member of the Progressive Citizen's Party, a conservative political group. Each new deputy took an oath before the Hereditary Prince Hans Adam. 'It is a particular pleasure', the Prince iterated, 'for me to able to welcome a woman to Parliament for the first time in Liechtenstein history.'[1] Emma graciously accepted his comments but 'would have preferred it if I had not been the only woman to make the leap into parliament'.[2]

There was not much literature even in German about Emma. Fortunately, I had help. The London embassy provided me with contact details. Dr Wilfried Marxer sent me information and Cornelius Goop not only sent me references but even provided me with three newspaper interviews with Emma in the local newspaper *Liechtensteiner Volksblatt*. I could make a start.

Emma was born on 30 October 1930 to Elwina Katharina Hoop and Eugen Schädler in Nendeln, a village in the north central part of Liechtenstein. She was the eldest of four girls. Her family owned a ceramic factory in the town, a factory with a shop still operating successfully today. All four daughters were expected to help in the business. Elizabeth was educated in the nearby town of Schaan at the St Elizabeth Institute. At the age of sixteen she went to the Salve Regina Institute in Switzerland where she completed an apprenticeship in ceramic painting before studying ceramics at Höhr-Grenzhausen, Germany, the centre of the ceramic industry. She was being schooled to work in the family firm.

When she returned to Liechtenstein, it was indeed to the family firm, Schädler Keramik, AG. On 4 August 1953, she married August Eigenmann, who joined her in the family's ceramics business. The couple had two children. Sadly, in 1967, her husband August died. Emma was left alone to bring up the children and run the family business. Fortunately, she was a businesswoman to the core. It was no surprise that in 1973, she became head of the family firm, leading it until 1995. Between 1979 and 1995 she was a member of the board of the Liechtenstein Chamber of Commerce and Industry, which had been set up by her father.

Emma was born into a political family. Her father had represented her Unterland constituency, one of her uncles was a member of the Landtag, her mother was the sister of the Prime Minister and her maternal grandfather had been Prime Minister. Consequently, her journey from the family house to the Landtag House was relatively smooth. When she was elected the Parliament only had 15 members so Emma did not have to navigate dangerous male territory: she knew the rest of the politicians very well. She felt safe.

Even so, Emma saw herself as being alone in the political wilderness, very aware that it would not be easy to change the thinking needed to 'accept women as partners in politics'. When her election result was announced she went home 'to hole up for a few days to digest it, I felt almost sick, I didn't want to see anyone. But then I said to myself "It's no use, now people are watching, you have to get through it." And I did.'[3] Constantly and consistently, she maintained that her role was not to be part of the battle of the sexes, that she did not 'want to just represent women's concerns or women, because I don't like to make a distinction between men and women in this way. I put partnership in the foreground, as it also takes place daily in business life.'[4] Mrs Emma Eigenmann-Schädler had

Image 10   Emma Eigenmann in conversation with
Josef Biedermann, courtesy of Liechtensteinisches
Landesarchiv, Vaduz. Photo by Klaus Schädler, Triesenberg.

run for office under the motto 'Partnership not confrontation',
with the slogan 'it's qualifications that count, not whether
you're a man or a woman'. As managing director of her family's
ceramic business, she had developed exemplary negotiating
skills. Even so, she insisted that there needed to be a change in
political style and in political debate, arguing that 'women are
different. They want a more humane style of politics.'[5] Emma
was re-elected in 1989 and served until 1993.

Emma consistently advocated the principle of equal rights,
campaigning in Parliament for further education for young
men and women so that they could take up managerial positions in local companies. She was a keen environmentalist. In
1987, she, and six colleagues, put forward a motion calling for
the legal protection of a nationwide agricultural zone. They told
Parliament that while the population was increasing, the area
of cultivated land was decreasing. They feared that it would not
be too long before the Liechtenstein valley floor was built over
and agriculture would suffer.[6] The beauty of the landscape,
with its mountains, valleys and crystal-clear rivers was under
threat, she argued, from over-development. Liechtenstein
would suffer once these natural assets had disappeared.

After leaving Parliament, Emma returned to the family's ceramic firm, involving herself in both the business side and the artistic side. She enjoyed creating new glazes for her ceramics. She continued to be a keen environmentalist. Long after her time in Parliament, she railed against lorries careering through small towns and villages on their way to industrial estates, damaging the health of the local population because of the pollution and noise they brought along.

When asked, at the age of 80, what a perfect day looked like, she replied, 'I do my household chores, and I love to sew or knit when I can. Then I do my shopping and occasionally have one of my grandchildren around. I also have three sisters. Two of them live nearby. When I have time, I also love to read or go on a short trip.'[7]

In 2025 she was 94 years old. Slowly, carefully and methodically, Emma Eigenmann-Schädler changed Liechtenstein, helping her country to be more environmentally friendly. On her 90th birthday, with a mind as sharp as ever, she looked back with pride on the mark she had left on politics and business.

Turks and Caicos: Rosita Beatrice Butterfield (1936–2015)

Turks and Caicos, two tropical islands in the Caribbean, are part of British Overseas Territory. They too made history for their financial irregularities. The islands were vulnerable to money laundering due to their offshore financial services sector and their weak legislative regime. Rosita Beatrice Butterfield, a married mother with three children, stepped into an economic and political maelstrom. In 1984 she made Turks and Caicos history by becoming the first woman to be elected to its Parliament.[8] Yet no sooner had she been elected than she was forced to defend her party leader. In 1985, the leader of the Progressive National Party and Premier (Prime Minister), was arrested for bribery. Drug dealers were involved. In 2009, the British government suspended the Turks and Caicos Assembly and imposed direct rule because there were 'clear signs of political amorality and immaturity and of general administrative incompetence'.[9] The Premier was arrested for corruption. Rosita, like Emma Eigenmann-Schädler, had a calm and unflappable temperament, well able to overcome such difficult situations.

Rosita was born on 14 November 1936, in Kew North Caicos to Savellita A Higgs and Isaiah Missick. The parents arranged home tutoring until they enrolled their daughter at Kew Elementary School, followed by the Bottle Creek Elementary School. Rosita ended her schooling at the Grand Turk Secondary School, but it was not the end of her educational journey. Here was a woman who was to be committed to lifelong learning.

Rosita began her career as a primary school teacher in her old school before switching to nursing. In 1953 she joined the staff at the Grand Turk Hospital. Here she worked and studied, qualifying as a Registered General Nurse, then later as a State Certified Midwife. Rosita was a diligent student, winning numerous awards: for the best overall student, the most efficient surgical nurse and the most vigilant nurse. She was the first woman in Turks and Caicos to operate an X-ray machine and to complete a course on psychiatric nursing. She was also awarded a certificate to practise midwifery: over the course of her life, Rosita delivered 103 babies.

At 7 p.m., on 22 March 1961, after an eight-year engagement, she married Albray V. Butterfield at the Seventh Day Adventist Church. She was now Mrs Butterfield. The couple moved to Florida but returned to the island in 1971, where they – and their three children – lived for a time in a trailer. Housing, in this tax haven paradise, was too expensive for the local population and certainly too expensive for the Butterfields. At first, Rosita was employed as a Chief Nurse, an admirable career but one which was not well paid. In 1978 she resigned her medical career to help her husband with his business, becoming Director of the Butterfield Gold Group of Companies, a company investing in industrial services like construction, fuel distribution and quarrying. The couple became rich. And moved from their trailer.

Deeply religious, Rosita Butterfield was a pastor of Faith Tabernacle Church of God. She established the Aglow International Chapter, an interdenominational Christian group, which aims both to pray and care for those in need, and the Soroptomists, a women's group committed to transforming the lives of women and girls. In addition, the couple founded the Albray and Rosita Butterfield Foundation to help those in need. Undoubtedly, Rosita was the consummate philanthropist, serving on various committees, helping with funds to build new churches, medical facilities and colleges. She also set up scholarships for underprivileged students and even paid for street lights in her home town of Kew. As a friend, she was kind and generous, giving people money to pay their mortgage, car loan or student fees. The couple knew how hard it was to balance earnings and outgoings in a country known for its high cost of living and relaxed tax laws.

In 1984, now aged 48, Rosita was the first woman to be elected to the Turks and Caicos Parliament as representative of the Progressive National Party. She donated her entire salary to her constituents, arguing that it 'was not her salary, but the taxpayer of the Turks and Caicos Islands'.[10] Two years later she was elected Deputy Speaker of the Legislative Assembly, then in 1991 Speaker of the Legislative Assembly. She was the first woman to hold these posts, and took it all very seriously, proudly wearing the ceremonial dress of a black robe and a white wig. It is said she brought order and decorum to a deeply disruptive Chamber. In 1992 she was awarded an MBE for 'public and community service' in the Turks and Caicos islands.

Rosita Beatrice Butterfield died, aged 78, on 10 January 2015. She was honoured with a state funeral and a 21-gun salute on 5 February 2015. Flags were lowered and flown at half-mast. A national holiday was given in tribute. A special mausoleum was built to house her body. The family asked that those attending wear black with red accessories, making the funeral a sea of black and red. Both the Premier and the Governor paid tribute. The Premier, described Rosa as a 'woman of excellence, a nation builder', a woman of boundless energy and outstanding work ethics, competent, influential, loyal and trustworthy. In his eulogy, the Governor altered a quote from Shakespeare's Hamlet about his father to honour Rosita. He said 'she was a lady, take her for all in all, I shall never look upon her like again'.

Angola: Maria Mambo Café (1945–2013)

On the Atlantic coast of south-west Africa lies the vast country of Angola. On 11 November 1975, the country became a sovereign state. It was the last country in sub-Saharan Africa to gain its independence. When the fascist dictatorship in Portugal was overthrown, the Angolans engaged in a hard-fought independence struggle before the country (like Mozambique) freed itself from colonial control. In 1980 the nation held its first general election. Here a fiery, uncompromising and bold woman strode into its history. Maria Mambo Café, a guerilla fighter and high-flying economist, joined eighteen women and 130 men to enter the first governing body, the People's Assembly as a representative of the Movimento Popular de Libertação de Angola (MPLA), a Marxist-Leninist group which was the biggest and most influential party. She was set to become the most powerful and high-ranking women in the country. [11]

Maria was born on 6 February 1945, in the village of Subantando in the province of Cabinda, north Angola. Her mother was Dina Chilala and her father was Zacaruas Mendes Café, an evangelical pastor. At the age of twelve, her parents moved to Luanda where she attended the Liceu Salvador Correia school. She also joined the choir at the Missão Evangélica de Luandant, beginning a lifelong love of making music.

In the early 1960s, Maria became a member of the MPLA. The cause of Angolan independence was set to consume her whole adult life. Her part in the liberation struggle, and the constant fear of arrest and imprisonment, forced her to live in exile in Leopoldville, Congo. Her nom-de-guerre was Tchiyna.[12] In 1964, to prepare her for a future leadership role, she was sent to study economics at the Patrice Lumumba University in the Soviet Union. At the time, the Soviet Union aligned itself with anti-colonial struggles across Africa, and provided funding, weapons, training, political backing and scholarships to thousands of African students. The Patrice Lumumba University trained potential leaders like Maria in Marxist-Leninist philosophy, hoping that they would return to their respective countries and spread pro-Soviet ideas. In 1968 Maria was awarded a degree in economics, and was set to put Soviet economic policy into practice.

Maria became secretary of the Organisation of Angolan Women, the Juventude do MPLA (the youth wing of the MPLA) and Cabinet Secretary to the future President Agostinho Neto, with whom she had a close relationship. Here she fell for a guerilla, José Mendes de Carvalho (his nom de guerre was Hoji Ya Henda), a legendary commander of the MPLA. Life was precarious in war-torn Angola, and her husband was killed in combat. She later met another guerilla, António França, whom she married . . . and later divorced. Maria was no obsessive revolutionary who talked only of politics. She liked to have fun. In her spare time, she was the lead singer of a group which included another future President of Angola, Eduardo dos Santos.

In 1974 she returned to Angola, and as a respected and an active member of the MPLA, took part in the negotiations which led to Angolan independence. 'Her tireless desire to work and to serve the party and the homeland', said one friendly obituary, 'led her to remain active, overcoming all of life's difficulties and setbacks, even though she was aware of the physical and health limitations she faced in recent times.'[13] She returned to a country about to be devastated by a civil war.

The country needed intelligent, committed leaders, particularly when Portugal ended its 400-year rule by walking away without establishing a new government, or taking care to ensure a transition period. When they left Angola, the Portuguese either took vital equipment with them or sabotaged it. Over three quarters of vehicles were taken and 6,250 farms abandoned. The MPLA assumed power: Maria was appointed Deputy Minister of Internal Trade. The new independent government was recognised internationally but not universally welcomed. Few countries offered help.

Between 1975 and 2002, Angola was embroiled in a civil war, one of the longest and most destructive conflicts in Africa.[14] The war involved three factions, all sustained by opposing foreign powers. The two main ones were the MPLA and the National Union for the Total Independence of Angola (UNITA). The MPLA was supported by the Soviet Union and Cuba; UNITA was supported by the USA, apartheid South Africa and some Western allies. These Cold War politics, played out in the heat of the African sun, ravaged Angola's economic, social and political stability. It devasted the country. The infrastructure crumpled with severe consequences for education, health care, housing and transport. When the agricultural sector collapsed, widespread disease and malnutrition followed. Over 500,000 were killed, tens of thousands – men, women and children – lost limbs from landmines and half the population displaced from their homes. One in four children died before they reached the age of five. The economy was destroyed. Over half of its oil revenues had been spent on military equipment. There was little money left for development.

Maria was at the heart of government, trying to balance her party's survival with trying to rebuild a newly independent country, already ruined by too many years of colonial rule. Widely regarded as highly committed, loyal and hard-working, she held several high-ranking positions in government. In 1977, Maria Café was appointed Deputy Minister of Internal Trade. In 1982 she was appointed Minister of Social Affairs, the first woman to be in the Cabinet. Here she was at the forefront of addressing social welfare and development challenges in post-colonial Angola. The following year she joined the Politburo. In 1986, Maria Café was again promoted, this time to Deputy Prime Minister and Minister of State for the Economic and Social Sector. She was a 'super minister', a key figure in shaping Angola's post-independence economic policies and the most powerful woman in government. Maria reported directly to the President.

However, her success was not too last in the ever-changing politics of Angola. On 14 December, 1987 Maria was relieved of her portfolio. She was a communist hard-liner who was opposed to the economic liberalisation favoured by the President. Her star faded. In 1988 she was sacked from her post and demoted to Secretary for Youth Affairs and briefly made Governor of Cabinda, an oil rich area which accounted for most of Angola's oil production.

As one of few women in leadership roles, Maria Café was a role model. Here was a woman at the top of government who had the power to improve the status of her sex. Maria certainly improved her own situation, living a luxurious life-style. By the end of her office, she was the 49th richest Angolan and the wealthiest woman, with assets of over $100 million dollars. Being chair of the Angola Bank of Commerce and Industry helped. Not only was she was accused of corruption but the whole government faced widespread accusations of mismanagement of the natural resources such as diamonds and oil and embezzlement of state funds.[15] Maria was criticised for managing sectors that were rife with allegations of misappropriation of money and assets. She, along with other government members, had failed to improve the living standards of ordinary Angolans despite the country's vast oil wealth. It is estimated that more than a billion dollars in oil revenue disappeared every year. Maria Café was not prosecuted. Unfortunately figures like Maria operated in an environment where patronage, nepotism and lack of accountability were systemic. At one time she received $10 million from the Bank to develop her personal projects – there was no accountability. Corruption remains a persistent problem in Angola – there are few mechanisms for holding the government to account or to stop those in high office from misappropriating funds.[16] Meanwhile, Angola had one of the world's worst maternal death-rates, only fifty per cent of the population had access to clean water, most people had no access to health care, unemployment benefits or other social welfare provisions. Only 57 per cent of women were literate.[17]

On 1 December 2013, Maria Mambo Café died in Lisbon, Portugal. She had been seriously ill with breast cancer. She was 68 years old. Her body was taken back to Angola, a mass was held at the Central Methodist Church and she was buried at the Alto das Cruzes Cemetery in Luanda. The airport in Cabinda was renamed Maria Mambo Café in her honour.

Zimbabwe: Joice Mujuru (1955–)

Joice Mujuru fought passionately to liberate her country, Zimbabwe (formerly Southern Rhodesia), from British colonial rule. One of Joice's first actions as a guerilla fighter was to shoot down a helicopter with a machine gun when it tried to attack her and her comrades. It was this incident which earned her the nom-de-guerre Tueurai Ropa (Spill Blood). An uncompromising firebrand, Joice fought hard against colonialism.

At 11 a.m., 11 November 1965, the well-known white supremacist Ian Smith had made a unilateral declaration of independence, illegally severing its links with Britain and announcing that Rhodesia was now an independent sovereign state. This seizure of power was condemned internationally. The United Nations denounced it as an illegitimate usurpation of power by a racist settler minority but the British government refused to send in the army to depose the illegal regime. Black Africans had little choice: they either succumbed to this egregious situation or fought. Joice decided on the latter, playing a significant role in the country's liberation struggle. In 1979, the regime collapsed, Ian Smith conceded defeat and on 18 April 1980, Zimbabwe was created as a newly independent country. The African National Union (ZANU) won a sweeping victory: eight women were elected.[18] One of them was Joice Mujuru, the only woman appointed to a full Cabinet post by the new President Robert Mugabe.[19]

Joice was born on 15 April 1955 in Mashonaland Central, north-eastern Zimbabwe, one of twelve children.[20] At the time, the country was a British colony called Rhodesia. Joice attended Howard High, a Salvation Army mission school, before enrolling at a school in Lusaka, Zambia, where she was the only girl student. In 1973, after two years, she left school to join the Zimbabwe African Liberation Army, which had a station in Zambia. Later, she studied for a BA, an MA and in 2014 was awarded a PhD by Robert Mugabe.

In 1974, Joice moved to Mozambique. In her early twenties, she became camp commander at Chimoio camp, where she directed guerilla actions. Here she met her future husband, the head of the army General Solomon Mujuru (whose guerilla name was Rex Nhongo). In 1976, the couple married. A year later, Joice became a member of the central committee of the

Zimbabwe African National Union and secretary for women's affairs.

Meanwhile, the white Rhodesian authorities wanted Joice Mujuru either captured or dead. In November 1977, when enemy soldiers invaded the camp, she dodged them by hiding in a lavatory; a year later, and now nine months pregnant, she fought off other attackers. The day after the second attack, the first of her four daughters was born.

In 1980, when Zimbabwe became independent, 25-year-old Joice Mujuru was appointed as Minister of Sports, Youth and Education. She was the youngest minister. And the only woman. She had several ministerial posts in Mugabe's government: as Minister of State in the Prime Ministers' Office; Minister of Community Development, Co-operatives and Women's affairs; governor of Mashonaland Central; Minister of Information, Posts and Telecommunications; Minister of Rural Resources and Water Development. In 2004, she became Vice-President of the party and of the country. Joice Mujuru was seen as Mugabe's natural successor.

By the end of the twentieth century, Zimbabwe was struggling. Its economy had shrunk and foreigners were reluctant to invest because of questions about its political honesty. As Minister of Telecommunications, Joice effectively prevented a rival from establishing his mobile network, and instead awarded the contract to a firm belonging to her husband and the nephew of Mugabe. Critics accused her of corruption. The local media reported that she received thousands of dollars in bribes from prospective investors in her duty-free shops and in the mining industry. She was accused of continually abusing the power of her office.

Joice was making enemies. Her main adversary was Grace Mugabe, jealous of Joice Mujuru's powerful position in ZANU and the Zimbabwean government and who eyed the presidency for herself. Robert Mugabe was ageing and his health was declining – the question of who would succeed him as

President loomed larger. Grace Mugabe instigated a campaign to get rid of her rival to the presidential throne by orchestrating a series of 'meet the people' rallies where she accused her rival of unsubstantiated crimes. Meanwhile, in 2011 after 35 years of marriage, Joice's husband Solomon died in a house fire. Some say it was an arson attack, brought on by his campaign to promote his wife as the successor to succeed Robert Mugabe.

Joice was also in danger. In 2014, at the age of 59, she was accused of 'demanding ten per cent bribes, illicit dealings in diamonds and gold, attempting to defeat the course of justice, extorting investors, and undermining the authority of President Mugabe'.[21] She was even accused of trying to assassinate the President. At a politburo meeting, the President accused Joice of bringing the party into disrepute: she lost her post as vice-president; her house 'accidentally' caught fire and burnt down; and she was expelled from the party.

Joice Mujuru was a streetfighter, unwilling to accept the political humiliation being heaped upon her. In a press statement, she claimed, 'I regret that certain persons have elected to make false, unsubstantiated, malicious, defamatory and irresponsible statements about me', and defended her record in government. No longer Robert Mugabe's chosen successor, she challenged his leadership by launching her own political party: Zimbabwe People First. By this time, the economy was in free fall, relationships with the West at rock bottom and infighting within the political leadership was undermining the governance of the country. Joice Mujuru promised to fix it all.

On 15 November 2017, the army seized power and placed Robert Mugabe under house arrest. The support for President Mugabe ebbed away like a reverse tsunami. When he was forced to resign, Grace Mugabe was expelled from the party and Emmerson Mnangagwa became President in his place. In 2018, Joice Mujuru ran for President under the banner of the People's Rainbow Coalition, a group formed by four of the opposition parties. Zimbabweans, she insisted, must focus on healing. 'We are a decimated nation. We are an injured nation. We are an angry nation, angry about ourselves, angry about everything . . . we all have to work together to build the nation we want.'[22] Mujuru came seventh, receiving 12,823 votes; the winner, Mnangagwa, received 2,456,010.

In 2019, Robert Mugabe died. Joice Mujuru said she no longer had any political ambitions and was concentrating on farming and raising her family.

Iraq: Huda Salih Mahdi Ammash (1953–2016)

Meanwhile, change was happening in an Arab nation. In 1980, elections took place under Saddam Hussein, Iraq's new President. Sixteen women were elected to the Iraqi 250-member National Council. One of them was Huda Ammash. The Americans later argued that she was the world's most dangerous woman, nicknaming her Mrs Anthrax and Chemical Sally. She certainly appeared ruthless. In 1981, while at a government meeting, Huda's father heard Saddam Hussein read out the names of those who were to be shot. Huda's father's name was on the list.[23] I could find no record of her response.

Under Saddam Hussein's secular government, Iraqi women were the among the most educated in the region, 'part of the labour force and visible and active on almost all levels of state institutions and bureaucracy'.[24] The Ba'athist regime, a regime allegedly based on a mixture of nationalism and socialism, enshrined equal rights in its constitution. Female literacy rates were the highest in the region, labour laws guaranteed equal rights and equal pay at work, and women were given six months' maternity leave.[25] In 1982, Iraq was awarded the UNESCO award for eradicating illiteracy.

Into this new social and economic climate stepped Huda Ammash, one of the few women in Saddam Hussein's inner circle. Some of her colleagues considered her 'a lioness ready to pounce on her prey; others call her a fox'.[26] Certainly, she needed to have the qualities of both strength and shrewdness to negotiate the dictatorial regime. Huda was born on 29 October 1953 in Baghdad into a family of Iraqi leaders. Her father, Salih Mahdi Ammash, was a high-level figure in the Ba'ath party, who had been a Defence Minister, deputy Prime Minister and Iraqi ambassador. For a time, the family lived in America. One neighbour remembers Huda singing and dancing by herself in the street, singing the same song repeatedly. The family returned to Iraq.

Ammash was well versed in politics. She had an excellent education: an undergraduate degree from the University of Baghdad; a Master of Science degree from Texas Women's University; and a doctorate in microbiology awarded by the University of Missouri. In 1996, now a mother of four, Ammash was appointed Head of the Microbiology Society in Iraq. She was later accused of helping rebuild Iraq's biological weapons programme after the Gulf War.

Shortly after the attack on the USA on 11 September 2001, when Americans were seeking revenge, the Iraqi government was deemed to be part of the 'axis of evil'. Accusations were levelled against Iraq of violating human rights. It was accused of silencing all opposition, beheading women who violated conservative sexual norms, and torturing and raping others. And of holding weapons of mass destruction. This was all part of an American propaganda campaign to legitimise their invasion: some accusations were true, some were 'alternative facts'. In March 2003, the United States and Britain led a war against Iraq under Saddam Hussein. They justified the decision by alleging that Iraq possessed weapons of mass destruction which posed a threat to global peace. Baghdad fell in April and Saddam Hussein's regime collapsed. No weapons were found. Hundreds of Iraqis were killed. Saddam Hussein was hanged for war crimes. The war destabilised Iraq, and contributed to the rise of ISIS.

Huda was spuriously accused of developing biological weapons. The Americans nicknamed her Mrs Anthrax and placed on her the most-wanted list. She was regularly described in the American press as being behind Saddam Hussein's development of biological weapons. There were wild allegations that Huda tested anthrax and other deadly viruses on prisoners. In 2003 she surrendered to the coalition forces and was imprisoned, only to be released two years later without charge because of lack of evidence. In fact, Huda had been examining the after-effects of uranium contamination caused by US attacks in the Gulf War.

The so-called liberation of Iraq from Saddam Hussein did not augur well for women. Iraqi women lost out.[27] In 2003, the Supreme Islamic Council repealed a law which gave women equality in inheritance, divorce and the guardianship of children. In addition, they introduced a new law legalising marriage for girls as young as nine. It had previously been 18. The demise of women's rights since Saddam Hussein was deposed and executed is terrifying. Today, women fear leaving their homes in case they are raped, beaten up and harassed by men.

In 2016, Huda, who was now an exile in Jordan, was sentenced to fifteen years in prison for embezzling government money. A representative from the Iraqi Organisation of Women's Freedom insists that President George Bush was responsible for empowering the extreme religious parties who clamped down on women like Huda. This, she argues, is Bush's American legacy.[28] Huda Ammash died, probably of cancer, on 13 November 2016 in Jordan. She was 63 years old.

Tuvalu: Naama Maheu Latasi (?–2012)

Throughout the twentieth century, countries have had their borders redrawn, have sometimes disappeared, have sometimes been newly created. Tuvalu is one of the smallest and most remote countries in the world, and is about to be washed away. In 1978, this group of Pacific islands, which lies about midway between Australia and Hawaii, became an independent state within the British Commonwealth. The country, consisting of four low-lying coral islands and five atolls, is one of the most vulnerable to global warming. The 26 square kilometres of Tuvalu is sinking, swallowed by sea rise and coastal erosion. The United Nations warns that the country, at its highest only 4.5m above sea level, is one of the most likely to disappear. Australia has offered to resettle Tuvaluans affected by this catastrophic climate change. For their part, the Tuvaluans have announced the construction of a digital replica of the islands to preserve their cultural heritage.

In 1989 Naama Maheu Latasi, married with four children, became the first woman to be elected to the Parliament of Tuvalu.[29] Fourteen other MPs were elected, all as a representative of one of the eight islands. There were no political parties in Tuvalu, which meant that Naama was elected directly by her constituents in Nanumea. The new Prime Minister immediately promoted her to Minister of Health, Education and Community. She was one of four ministers and part of her brief was to help improve the position of women.

Naama came from a political family. She was the daughter of a prominent Nanumea government official who encouraged his daughter to take part in the island's community life. This was a radical break-away from the social and cultural norms of this patriarchal Polynesian society. Women were traditionally confined to the home, cleaning, cooking and looking after their family. Only men were allowed to speak and make decisions in the Faleakaupule or Maneapea, the traditional meeting halls where policy was formed; women were allowed in to serve food and listen.

Naama was a member of the both the Nanumea and the Kiribati Women's Association, groups that were organised around the Ekalesia Kelisiano, the local churches. She had also become the vice-president of the Tuvalu National Council of Women (TNCW). The TNCW had been set up in the 1970s as a formal link between the government and women to help direct women's affairs in post-independence Tuvalu. The projects which Naama helped set up include a Women's Handicraft Centre, numerous small income-generating projects for women and training programmes for women in business, government, family health and international development. In addition, she was a Girl Guides Commissioner. Naama was committed to helping women. In 1987 she attended a three-month course in Sydney, Australia, on the development of women and took part in many conferences relating to improving the lives of women living in the Pacific islands. Fortunately, Naama's supportive husband, Sir Kamata Latasi insisted that he 'gladly performed all the domestic chores including cooking for and feeding the children' when she was away.[30] In her opinion, her husband set a good example for the men of Tuvalu to follow.

In 1993 Naama was awarded an OBE for her public and community services, particularly for her work promoting women's equality such as setting up the Girl Guides Association and working for the National Council of Women. In 2007, Mrs Latasi became Lady Latasi when her husband, Kamata (1936–), was made a knight.

Naama Maheu Latasi was the first woman, and maybe the last, to serve in the Tuvalu Parliament. She died on 16 March 2012. In February 2024 giant waves flooded Funafuti, the capital city, home to most of the population and the country's political, administrative and economic centre. Elevated sea levels contaminated freshwater resources and arable land. Tuvaluans called for urgent action on climate change, urging wealthy nations to reduce greenhouse gas emissions before their country, like the mythical Atlantis, disappeared.

As the decade drew to its close, the percentages of women in parliaments across the world remained low but there was a growing awareness about the importance of gender equality in politics. Countries – ranging from older established limited democracies through to newly created former colonised nations – embraced a form of democracy which included women. Liechtenstein women surfed a democratic wave as the tide of history swept away masculine strongholds. Newly independent countries in Africa, keen to embrace the future, immediately incorporated women's equality in their constitutions.

In the 1980s, serious discussions began about gender quotas. Politicians sought a way to increase women's participation in politics. In 1985, Kenya hosted the World Conference on Women, which called for increased political participation of women globally. By the end of the 1980s, most countries across the globe had enfranchised women and permitted us to enter government.[31] A few, however, were about to retreat into chaos and/or fundamentalism. Women's rights are not set in political tablets of stone. They need constant defending.

Chapter Nine

The Journey's End? 1990–2000:
South Africa, Ukraine, Croatia, Bahrain

In 1994, democracy eventually arrived in South Africa when the system of institutionalised racism designed to maintain white minority supremacy ended. Apartheid, an Afrikaans word for apartness, was set up by the white government in 1948 and classified South Africans into racial groups: white, black, 'coloured' and Indian. Everything was segregated by race: housing, education, hospitals, parks, transport. Black South Africans, to whom the country originally belonged, were forcibly re-located to less attractive parts of the country and employed in low-paying menial work. Only whites, and then in 1984 'coloureds' and Indians, were enfranchised. This iniquitous system of apartheid was finally overthrown after years of struggle by the African National Congress (ANC). The newly created South African constitution stated that the government 'may not unfairly discriminate directly or indirectly against anyone on one or more grounds, including race, gender, sex, pregnancy, marital status, ethnic or social origin, colour, sexual orientation, age, disability, religious, conscience, belief, culture, language and birth'. It remains the most inclusive constitution in the world. Parliament was made more woman-friendly by reorganising the parliamentary calendar to match school terms, by ending debates in the early evening and by providing a creche. Laws were passed to extend abortion rights, to stop domestic violence and guarantee employment equality.

South Africa: Winnie Madikizela-Mandela (1936–2018)

In the first election women occupied 26 per cent of the seats in the National Assembly, partly because of the African National Congress's (ANC) insistence on a quota for female candidates. One of the first women to be elected was Winnie Mandela, the wife of the first Black President, Nelson Mandela.[1] Her husband promoted her to his Cabinet. Winnie was born Nomzamo Winifred Zanyiwe Madikizela on 26 September 1936 in a traditional Xhosa hut made of clay in the village of Mbongweni, a beautiful part of the Eastern Cape. She was the fifth of nine children born to red-haired blue-eyed Gertrude, a bi-racial domestic science teacher from white English and Xhosa heritage, and Columbus, a history teacher and later head-master of a mission school. The family were fervent Methodists, prayed together daily, and each Sunday attended church services. As she grew up, Winnie became all too aware of the hardship, inequalities and blatant racism faced by her black community within the apartheid system. She was inspired by her father's stories of past Xhosa heroes who had fought the white people who invaded the country and stole the land from its inhabitants.

Her father was a strict disciplinarian, expecting his children to stand up when he entered a room. The only time he touched his children was to beat them. As a young child, Winnie was expected to help in the house and on the family farm. Before school, she milked the cows, looked after the sheep and carried out general farmyard chores. After school, she assisted with the housework, the cooking and the weeding of their maize fields. Fortunately, her parents respected education. At the age of six, Winnie accompanied her older siblings to her father's school.

Winnie was nine years old when her mother died after a long illness. This unexpected death forced her to take on a mothering role, taking care of her three-month-old brother, washing and ironing her father's threadbare clothes and looking after the family's cattle. Recognising that Winnie was clever, her father sent his daughter to Shawsbury, a Methodist mission school, at Qumbu. The school was 200 kilometres away from home but well known for educating the children of black African professionals. At secondary school she joined the Society of Young Africa. After school, Winnie was awarded a scholarship to the Johannesburg Jan H. Hofmeyr School of Social Work where she gained her degree in social work and became the first black social worker at the Baragwanath Hospital in Johannesburg. At the same time, she became active in the African National Congress.

Meanwhile, Winnie met Nelson Mandela. He was a tall, handsome, well-known political figure, nearly forty and recently divorced; she was 23, strikingly beautiful and employed as a social worker. This good-looking black couple became the epitome of glamour, the epitome of black power. They married within a year of meeting. In 1958, Winnie, newly pregnant, married Nelson Mandela in the Methodist Church in Bizana. It was a Christian ceremony with hymns in Xhosa. Following Xhosa tradition Nelson paid an (undisclosed) bride price to her father.

In October 1958, Winnie was arrested, along with 1,200 other women, for protesting against the notorious Pass Laws. The arrested women were cramped together in squalid cells without beds, chairs or sanitation. Winnie started to bleed from her pregnancy, on the brink of a miscarriage, which was averted thanks to another political activist prisoner, and trained midwife, Albertina Sisulu. After two weeks in gaol, the women were found guilty and sentenced to prison or pay a fine. The ANC paid the fine. Winnie's imprisonment resulted in the loss of her job at Baragwaneth hospital. From then on, she struggled to balance family outgoings – her paltry income barely covered costs.

Image 11   Winnie and Nelson Mandela.
Photo © Trinity Mirror/Mirrorpix/Alamy.

The newly marrieds had two short years together. On
21 March 1960, when thousands of black South Africans
gathered in Sharpeville, a township near Johannesburg, to
protest against the pass laws, the police opened fire on the

demonstrators. Sixty-nine people were killed and over 180 injured. The massacre brought international condemnation. In response, the white authorities declared a state of emergency, banned anti-apartheid organisations like the African National Congress and intensified its crackdown on any opposition. Nelson Mandela persuaded the now illegal ANC to take up arms, and went into hiding. He was called the 'Black Pimpernel'. Eventually Nelson's luck ran out. On 5 August 1962, he was captured. In November he was sentenced to five years in prison. In June 1964, while still in prison, Nelson was put on trial for treason. Found guilty, he remained in gaol for twenty-seven years. Winnie was allowed to visit every six months. But they could not touch.

After his arrest, Winnie, now in practice a single mother with two young daughters, became Nelson Mandela's spokesperson, keeping his memory alive and his politics in the public sphere. For twenty-seven years, Winnie defied the apartheid state, spoke at rallies and encouraged open revolt against this iniquitous regime. During this time, Winnie experienced daily police harassment, was banned from holding meetings, and banished to a place far away from her hometown of Soweto.

On 12 May 1969, just before dawn, police broke into Winnie's home, arrested her under the Terrorism Act and took her to Pretoria Central Prison, leaving her two daughters, now aged nine and ten, alone in the house. She was imprisoned without trial for 491 days, most of the time in solitary confinement, a punishment which was 'meant to kill you alive'.[2] The authorities humiliated this beautiful, elegant, fastidious woman in every way. At times she was left completely naked. Her cell contained two sisal mats, four blankets and the floor for her bed. She was given a 'filthy plastic bottle' for her water, a sanitary bucket, a metal mug and carbolic soap. Her clothes were 'savagely thrown on the floor' and trampled upon. The light in the cell was permanently switched on. More terrifyingly, her cell was next to the 'assault chamber' where she heard the screams of prisoners being beaten mercilessly.[3] Her physical and mental health suffered. She spoke of how she would 'black-out although I would be lying flat and slightly propped up. I then felt completely numb, the whole body – I lose complete control over my muscles and struggle to breathe and have an irregular heartbeat. The body then jerks into functioning in a very painful spasm. I then breathe very fast.'[4] She grew afraid to sleep. Her other physical problems, like menstrual difficulties and an inability to pass urine, remained untreated. She suffered from nightmares and woke up screaming. At one time, Winnie decided on a slow suicide by not eating or taking her medicine. In September 1970, Winnie Mandela was released without charge. Her confinement had damaged her not just physically but psychologically, turning 'her from a warm-hearted person into a mad creature'.[5]

Throughout the 1970s and 1980s, Winnie Mandela was subjected to a disgraceful cycle of arrests, mock trials, imprisonments, banishments and constant surveillance. She was placed under house arrest, forced to stay at home from 6 p.m. to 6 a.m. during the week and between 2 p.m. and 6 a.m. at weekends; only her children were allowed to visit her. Winnie was constantly harassed, detained, charged on a range of pretexts and again imprisoned. The backdrop of her life was constant repression and violence. Her courage was legendary and she was called the 'Mother of the Nation'. She became a feminist icon, the subject of Nadine Gordimer's novel *Burger's Daughter*.

During Nelson Mandela's 27-year imprisonment, Winnie was a symbol of resistance and defiance against the regime, facing harassment, arrest and even torture, all the while remaining steadfast in her commitment to the liberation struggle. However, she became a polarising figure when it all seemed to go horribly wrong. Winnie fell from grace. She was accused of kidnapping and assaulting young people whom she suspected of complicity with the apartheid regime. Her life was referred to as a Greek tragedy. Another nickname was added: Lady Macbeth. In 1985 she declared that 'together, hand in hand, with our boxes of matches and our necklaces we shall liberate this country'. She was referring to a way of murdering suspected informants by placing a tyre around their neck filled with petrol and setting it alight.[6] She was also implicated in encouraging a reign of terror, including murder, arson, abduction and rape by members of the Mandela United Football Club, a group of about thirty young men who lived in her house. They were called 'Winnie's boys', and they called her mother. Winnie was implicated in the death of at least sixteen youngsters.

She defended her approach by saying 'I will speak to you of violence . . . I will tell you why we are violent. It is because those who oppress us are violent. The Afrikaner knows only one language: the language of violence. The white man will not hand over power in talks around a table . . . Therefore, all that is left to us is this painful process of violence.'[7] In 1989, 'her boys' violently killed a fourteen-year-old boy, Stompie Moetketsi. They sadistically kicked him hard, threw him repeatedly up in the air and allowed him to drop on to the floor, before cutting his throat with shears. The doctor who examined his dead body was shot dead. The ANC distanced itself from its most famous female activist and Winnie was put on trial. She was sentenced to six years in prison but on appeal this was reduced to a fine and a two-year suspended sentence. In 1992, Nelson Mandela publicly separated from Winnie. In 1996 they divorced and Winnie was dismissed from her position as a deputy minister.

In December 1997, Winnie, now aged 63, was brought before the Truth and Reconciliation Committee. Desmond Tutu, who led the Court, tried to bring about a reconciliation between Winnie and her accusers. Tutu begged her to apologise. Winnie Mandela was intransigent and blamed the apartheid era for any violation of human rights. In 2004, Winnie lived with her ten grandchildren and three great grandchildren, four generations of her family, in her house in Soweto, situated behind a high stone and razor-wire wall.

On 2 April 2018 Winnie died. She was 81 years old. Undoubtedly, whatever her flaws, Winnie Madikizela-Mandela played a key role in ending apartheid and in shaping the new South Africa. She was an international symbol of resistance, a woman who led the fight against one of the most heinous racist regimes in the world and its unspeakable brutalities. On 4 April 2018, in Addis Ababa, Ethiopia, the African Union Commission Deputy Chairperson paid a tribute to a 'woman of incredible strength, pride, love, determination and a woman who was able to keep alive the torch of freedom despite years of torture, harassment and hardship'.[8] Winnie Mandela remains a controversial figure. On the one hand, she is remembered for her unwavering commitment to the struggle against apartheid and her resilience in the face of adversity. On the other hand, she is remembered for heading a reign of terror in her home township.

Ukraine: Nina Karpachova (1957–)

On 5 December 1991, shortly after the fall of the Berlin Wall and the collapse of the Soviet Union, Ukraine once more became independent. In Spring 1994, Ukrainians went to the polls to elect their new Parliament. It was the first free and democratic election since 1917. In March 1994, eleven women were elected out of 450 members to the Verkhovna Rada, the Ukraine Parliament.[9] It had had a troubled history and was about to have a troubled future.

One of the women elected was Nina Karpachova, an Independent member, representing Alushta, a significant city on the Black Sea coast, part of the Autonomous Republic of Crimea.[10] She was born on 12 August 1957 in Ceadîr Lunga, Moldova, where her parents worked as lawyers. Nina followed their path. She studied law at the Taras Shevchenko National University of Kyiv, graduating with honours. In 1988, she began postgraduate studies at the Academy of Social Sciences in Moscow. Her dissertation was *Women's Political Rights: Problems of Theory and Modern Practice*, reflecting a commitment to women' rights that would dominate her life. She was invited to various American universities to talk about this subject.

When the Soviet Union collapsed, Nina returned to Ukraine where she worked as a legal advisor, taught at the university and began her career in politics. She moved to Alushta, Crimea, where she was elected deputy of the City Council and chair of the Commission on Education and Culture. In 1990 she organised the first conference in Alushta on women's rights and in 1991 founded Nadezhda (Centre for the Protection of Women's and Children's Rights.) In addition to her professional and political work, she established a Law Faculty at the Vernadsky Simferopol State University in Alushta. In 1994, trade unions nominated her as a parliamentary candidate. She confidently won the election with seventy per cent of the vote.

Nina got to work quickly as a parliamentarian. In her first year, as Deputy Chair of the Committee on Human Rights, Nina coordinated preparations for the ratification of the European Convention for the Protection of Human Rights and Fundamental Freedoms in Ukraine. Human rights, she insisted, have no borders. In 1995 she headed Ukraine's implementation of the UN Convention on the Elimination of all Forms of Discrimination against Women. She authored several important parliamentary Bills: on human trafficking, on human rights, on the adoption of orphans.

In 1998, Nina was elected the first Ombudsman of the newly created Institution of the Ukrainian Parliamentary Commissioner for Human Rights, responsible for defending and promoting human rights across the country. The creation of the Institute was resisted by those who were reluctant to have a human rights watchdog looking over their political shoulder. She fought for the rights of the disadvantaged, especially orphans, single mothers, the disabled, pensioners, miners, prisoners, migrant workers, and sailors captured by pirates and sold into slavery. In addition, Nina focused on issues around human trafficking, domestic violence, the rights of people affected by the Chernobyl disaster, those with HIV/ AIDS, and the rights of ethnic minorities such as the Crimean Tartars and migrant workers. She fought to ensure the right to a fair trial, freedom of speech, and advocated better treatment and conditions for prisoners, condemning the torture which many had endured.

Nina believed that if you saved one life, you saved the world. She helped many prisoners escape a death sentence and helped those tortured or treated badly in gaol. Ukrainians began to hear about her work and reached out to her for help. Nina received approximately 12,000 letters from citizens who complained about being tortured in prison. She knew the value of publicity in fighting for human rights. In a television interview, she claimed that most of these crimes went unpunished because the police and the judiciary worked too closely together. Detainees were beaten with rubber batons, hung upside down and doused with ice-cold water. Judges were unwilling to prosecute, arguing that they wanted to protect 'officers' dignity'.[11] Nina challenged this cosy relationship. It is no surprise that she was dubbed 'Lawyer of Millions' and 'Lady Justice'.

For Nina, poverty was an abrogation of human rights. She was the first parliamentarian to raise the issue of systemic poverty, arguing that the fight against it should be a priority of the government. Her inviolable principle was that 'human rights begin with the rights of the child', and she always paid particular attention to the protection of children. She focused on orphans and children with disabilities, and introduced special programmes for those with cerebral palsy and polio. She worked closely with the Kyiv Heart Centre to finance heart procedures for orphans and children from poorer countries.

In late 2004, Ukraine was shaken by the Orange Revolution. A series of mass protests took place in Maidan Square, Kyiv between November 2004 and January 2005 against the election of the pro-Russian President Viktor Yanukovych. Demonstrators wore the orange colours of the Nasha Ukrainia (Our Ukraine) party, whose leader was the pro-Western Viktor Yushenko (who was mysteriously poisoned during the campaign and left severely disfigured). The protestors called the election fraudulent, claiming voter fraud, widespread ballot stuffing and voter intimidation, particularly in the Eastern regions. They demanded that the election be annulled and new ones take place. The rallies caused a political crisis. Yanukovych was supported by Russia and Eastern Ukraine; Yushenko was supported by the West and Western and Central Ukraine. Nina Karpachova walked into this political maelstrom and tried to calm the waters. In 2004, she offered her services as peace-maker between the two Viktors, Yushenko and Yanukovych. She failed. In the end, because of the large-scale demonstra-tions and international pressure, the Supreme Court ordered a re-run of the elections. This time Viktor Yushenko won.

Ukraine's political landscape remained volatile. In 2010, the hard-line communist Viktor Yanukovych was re-elected President, this time defeating Yulia Tymoshenko, another pro-Westerner and ally of Yushenko. A year later, the President unjustly imprisoned his political rival. Nina leaped into action, putting her belief in human rights into practice. She helped the world to learn that Yulia Tymoshenko, who had been convicted on charges related to an abuse of power and imprisoned by the government, had been physically tortured while detained in Kachanivska prison. Nina visited her in prison, made public statements about Tymoshenko and released compromising photographs which showed evidence of torture. In 2011 she spoke out against a court hearing proposed for Tymoshenko to be heard in her prison cell. Nina stated it was a blatant breach of the European Convention of Human Rights and a 'breach of the right to defence'.[12] In 2012, just after she had resigned as Ombudsman, Nina Karpachova once again spoke out against the physical abuse that Tymoshenko had suffered. On a prison visit, she witnessed the bruises on Yulia's stomach, arms, shoulder and elbows. Nina demanded that prosecutors open a criminal case against those responsible for the torture. The health authorities denied any harm had been inflicted. Human rights organisations considered the imprisonment to be politically motivated. Nina Karpachova's position as Ombudsman was not renewed, a move widely interpreted as politically motivated. Yulia Tymoshenko was not the only one unjustly accused. Throughout this period, Nina found her workload increasing as political oppression and protest surged. She was courageous, bravely confronting the new repressive regime. In May 2012, Nina was forced to flee Ukraine.

In 2013, President Yanukovych suspended plans to move closer to the European Union and opted for closer ties with Russia. Western Ukrainians disliked this approach, seeing European integration as a way towards a better democracy and economic prosperity. Protests began in November 2013 and escalated each month. This Euromaidan protest was met with harsh police crackdowns. On 18 February 2014, Nina pleaded with President Viktor Yanukovych to 'urgently give command to stop the armed assault on the peaceful protest at the Maidan, discontinue the use of water cannons, stun grenades, laser glare and throwing Molotov cocktails against protestors . . . together we have to protect the most important human right – the right to life'.[13] Her calls remained unanswered. After a period of intense violence, Yanukovych fled to Russia.

New elections were called which led to the establishment of a pro-Western government. This precipitated Russia's invasion of Crimea. Nina wrote later of the 'terrible tragedy that occurred in Odessa on the second of May'. She asked that all parties stop the confrontation and discontinue 'the use of violent methods for achieving their goal at the cost of human life. After all, we know from history that any confrontation always ends in reconciliation, but the loss of human life is irreparable ... government, politicians and society must stop the fratricidal confrontation now and start looking for the ways for such reconciliation.'[14]

By this time, Nina Karpachova was an international high-flyer. She represented Ukraine at various international forums: in 1993 as a delegate to the Second World Conference on Human Rights, held in Vienna; in 1995 to the Second World Conference of Women, held in Beijing; in 1999 she joined the European Ombudsman Institute and became head of the National Coordination Council for the Prevention of Human Trafficking; in 2000 she joined the International Ombudsman Institute; in 2005 she was a delegate to the World Conference against Racism and Xenophobia held in Durban, South Africa; in 2006 to an International Conference on the Right of the Child held in Athens; in 2009 to an International Conference on the Abolition of the Death Penalty held in Florence, Italy. As Ombudsman, Nina worked closely with international organisations such as the Red Cross and the Red Crescent. Her office provided relief to the victims of the Hurricane Katrina in New Orleans, to the victims of the Haitian earthquake, to Japanese children affected by the tsunami and the nuclear accident, to children in Somalia dying of starvation. In recognition, Nina received numerous national and international awards. Among them in 1997 Honoured Lawyer of Ukraine; in 2002 and 2007 the Yaroslave (the Wise) award for 'outstanding achievements in building a legal, democratic state'; the Officers' Cross by Poland; the Cuban Medal of Friendship.

Meanwhile, violent clashes between those who were pro-Russian and those who were pro-Western led to an outbreak of violence in Eastern Ukraine where Russophiles sought independence. In 2005 Nina was nominated for the Nobel Peace Prize for trying to solve the civil war. She did not win it, neither was the civil war resolved. In 2022, Russia invaded Ukraine.

Croatia: Vesna Girardi-Jurić (1944–2012)

The collapse of the Berlin Wall and the subsequent disintegration of the Soviet Union fuelled nationalism in other communist-controlled states and led to one of Europe's most turbulent periods. Yugoslavia, a federal state under communist control, was about to disintegrate. National tensions, which had been bubbling for years, exploded after the death of President Tito. Yugoslavia collapsed. New countries – Bosnia and Herzegovina, Croatia, Montenegro, North Macedonia, Serbia and Slovenia – emerged from the wreckage. It was complex. In 1991, three countries, Croatia, Slovenia and North Macedonia, were the first to declare independence. Croatia, a former part of the Yugoslavian communist state, faced three direct challenges: to build a new state, create a democracy, and fight a war against Serbia and Bosnia. Eight women were elected to the Sabor, the new established Croatian Parliament.[15] Only one woman, who was not directly elected, was appointed to a government post: Vesna Girardi-Jurić. Her responsibility as Minister of Education, Culture and Sport was to safeguard Croatia's cultural heritage after attempts to destroy it: as an archaeologist and a patriot, Vesna was very aware that if historical artefacts were damaged, historical memory was eradicated and a country's sense of itself extinguished.

Vesna Girardi Jurić was born on 15 January in the capital city, Zagreb. Her father, Eduard Girardi, and her mother, Marija Lorenzin, were both teachers. In 1947, when Vesna was three, her family moved to Pula, a coastal town in Istria, where she was educated.[16] At school she learned Italian, French and

English, becoming fluent in all three languages. In 1959 she became secretary of *Istarski Borac* (Istrian Fighter) and began writing regular articles for its journal.

In 1962, Vesna enrolled at the Faculty of Literature and Philosophy at the University of Zagreb. In 1968, while still a student, she married Mirko Jurić in Zagreb. In 1968, Vesna graduated from the University of Zagreb with a joint degree in English and Archaeology. Her thesis *Portraits from the Sepulchral Monuments of the Archaeological Museum of Istria*, marked her life-long commitment to archaeology. In 1969, Vesna gave birth to her first daughter, Kristina; in 1973 another daughter, Tamara, was born. This young mother lived and breathed classical antiquity – she spent 23 years working at the Archaeological Museum of Istria. Her home town of Pula is the site of many ancient Roman buildings, the most famous of which is the Pula Arena, one of the best-preserved Roman amphitheatres. In 1968 Vesna began work as a volunteer researcher; in 1974 she was appointed curator; in 1979 she was appointed Head of Department and a few months later became the Director. By now, she was a well-known academic. As curator, Vesna managed the Antique Collection, handled excavations, opened the first open-air archaeology park and worked on the restoration of Pula Arena. She was a prolific writer who authored around 400 scholarly works, curated more than 120 exhibitions, and founded three archaeological journals. Her linguistic fluency led to her selection as a tour guide for President of Yugoslavia Josip Tito's international guests (such as Queen Elizabeth II) when they visited Pula.

In 1990, Vesna became politicised. On 25 June 1991, Franjo Tuđman declared Croatia an independent country, free from Yugoslavia. Violence erupted as Serbian forces rejected the establishment of a new Croatia. Between 1991 and 1995 Croatia was at war, fighting for its independence. In 1992 Vesna was appointed Minister of Education, Culture and Sport of the Republic of Croatia. Part of her job was to protect the endangered cultural assets of the nation during the war. Vesna was all too aware of the indissoluble links between culture and identity. She had the unenviable task of evacuating cultural artefacts from museums, archives and libraries and moving them to safer locations, and of preserving items from looting or destruction. Perhaps her biggest challenge was protecting Dubrovnik. This beautiful, iconic old walled city was attacked, a deliberate and provocative assault on an important Croatian heritage site to undermine the morale of the country. On 6 December 1991, shelling by the Serbian army damaged or destroyed almost sixty per cent of Dubrovnik's old city buildings. Immediately, Vesna actively sought international support and strengthened Croatian ties with UNESCO to ensure funding for the preservation of Croatia's cultural heritage. For this, she was awarded the military rank of Major by President Tuđman. In 1995, the war officially ended. It had claimed 20,000 lives and displaced thousands of others: over 200,000 Serbs fled Croatia. Both sides committed atrocities.

Vesna was an academic, not a politician. In 1994 she left formal politics when she was appointed Ambassador to UNESCO, where she remained until 2001. In 2000 she was awarded her PhD for 'Cults in the Process of the Romanisation of Ancient Istria'. Vesna played a significant role in the restoration of Dubrovnik's old town, mobilising international funding for rebuilding the city and ensuring that the city retained its World Heritage status. Here, as a trained archaeologist, she liaised between Croatian and international experts to ensure that traditional materials – such as bringing terracotta tiles from France – were used to reconstruct the city sympathetically. By 2000, Dubrovnik's Old Town was restored. Vesna was also largely responsible for including the Basilica in Poreč, the Cathedral in Šibenik and the city of Trogir on UNESCO's World Heritage List. She was awarded seven of the highest national decorations, including the Homeland Thanksgiving

Medal, the Medal of the Societa Istriana di Archeologia e Storia Patria and the Order of Prince Branimir.

On 25 August 2012, Vesna Girardi Jurkić died suddenly of a heart attack at her home in Pula. She was 69 years old. On her desk was the manuscript of her new book. Her daughter Kristina, who was head of the Archaeological Museum in Pula, continued her mother's legacy by promoting the ancient heritage sites of her native Istria.

Bahrain: Mariam Al Jalahma (1961–)

In 2000, the seemingly ineluctable advance of democracy encouraged Emir Hamad bin Isa Al Khalifa, King of Bahrain, to appoint four women to his Consultative Council, the Shura Council, the upper House of Bahrain's bicameral government. They were the first women ever to hold a government post. Dr Mariam Al Jalahma was one of the four. [17] It was a momentous moment in the country's history, consolidating the new King's commitment to furthering women's political participation. Bahrain is a constitutional monarchy with a National Assembly which consists of two chambers: the elected Council of Representatives and the selected Shura Council. Shura members are chosen as representatives of various sections of Bahraini society such as businessmen, academics, professionals, medics. Members of the Council have the power to review and vote on forthcoming legislation, and amend laws as they see fit.

Mariam was born in this small island nation in the Persian Gulf. Bahrain has a population of about one and a half million. It is only 300 square miles, one of the smallest countries in Asia. It is oil rich but not as rich as other Arab nations and was forced to diversify its economy via banking and other services. The Bahrainian focus on education meant Mariam was well educated, finishing secondary education at the Al Hoora

Secondary School for Girls in Manama and winning a scholarship to study for a degree in medicine at Cairo University before focusing on family medicine and health care provision. She was a lifelong learner in medicine: in 1994 she gained a higher diploma in medicine from the University of Dundee; in 2000 a diploma in health care at the Royal College of Surgeons in Ireland.

In 2015 Mariam was appointed by the King of Bahrain as CEO of the National Health Regulatory Authority, set up a few years earlier. She was already a member of the Supreme Council of Health. In May 2023, Mariam was awarded the Nelson Mandela Award for Health Promotion by the Director General of the World Health Organisation, Dr Tedros Ghebreyesus for her decades-long work in promoting maternal, child and adolescent health. In 2023, Mariam was appointed Chief Executive of the Government Hospitals by His Majesty King Hamad bin Isa Al Khalifa.

Winnie Mandela has received a lot of historical attention, Nina Karpachova less so, and Vesna Girardi-Jurić none at all outside her home country. I am grateful to the Croatian Embassy for putting me in touch with Dr Wollfy Krašić at the Department of Demography and Croatian Diaspora, who helped me with sources and guided me through the complexities of the Croatian Parliament. Sometimes I came across a huge impenetrable block across the historical road. For instance, I could not find much information on the political shifts in Arab countries, particularly those with a significant patriarchal, autocratic government. Saudi Arabia, for example, does not have an elected parliament but a consultative body – the Shura Council – appointed by the King. In 2013, thirty women were appointed by King Abdullah to his previous all-male Assembly. Their history has yet to be written.

The 1990s marked, if not the final breakthrough, then a pivotal penultimate chapter in the global journey of women's struggle to gain political power. Three significant changes had occurred. Firstly, one of the last – and one of the particularly brutal – forms of colonial-style government was defeated. Secondly, the collapse of both the USSR and communist Yugoslavia led to the emergence of new countries. Thirdly, Arab Islamic states began to appoint women to their legislatures.[18]

By 2000, over 95 per cent of countries had elected or appointed women to its representative body. As well as the countries mentioned in this chapter, Comoros, Morocco and Wallis and Fortuna now had women in their legislature. The end of the twentieth century, of course, was not the end of history. Neither was it a journey's end for women's participation in government. Women make up half the world, but remain under-represented in the world's parliaments. It is heart-breaking to realise that many of the gains made in the twentieth century would often – violently – be taken away when democracy collapsed.

Conclusion:
You Can't Clap With One Hand

In 2000, after a century of struggle, two world wars, revolutions, freedom movements, civil wars and decolonisation, women were represented in most governments across the world. So many of the women politicians like Kollontai, Slachta and Machel were elected in these power vacuums, in periods of social and political turmoil, during the creation of independent nations and new constitutions and/or of transformations in their respective countries. Such women surfed the wave of history, swept along by the strong currents of reform. There was also a trend in women's representation which was one of gradual, steady – albeit very slow – progress. These women waded cautiously into male waters. Politicians like McCombs, Frey and Eigenmann were elected because democracy, and women's role within it, was gathering pace. By 2000, every country, apart from five, three in the Middle East (Saudi Arabia, Qatar and Kuwait) and two small island countries (Micronesia and Palau), had appointed or elected a woman representative.[1] Progress had been made. However, it is salutary to remember that overall, the numbers were uninspiring. In December 1999, the percentage of women in national parliaments globally was a mere 13.5 per cent.[2]

So, what did a new century, and a new millennium bring? In the first two and a half decades of the twenty-first century women's entry into governments doubled.[3] Once again, these figures mask geographical differences as you can see from the statistics below. In 2025, six countries in the world had fifty per cent or more women in their parliaments and the countries that now headed the list were all non-European. Even so, Nordic countries consistently had the highest representation of women with averages of 44.8 per cent, joined by a few countries in the Caribbean with averages of 42.5 per cent and countries in East Africa which had 32.4 per cent. Women remained the least represented in the Pacific at 20.1 per cent and in the Middle East at eighteen per cent.[4] Afghanistan, Myanmar and Sudan suspended their Parliaments. Our first politicians, Hilda Käkikoski, Alexandra Kollontai and Jeanette Rankin, might well be surprised and delighted by much of this progress.

Some of these statistics may be surprising. As Rosemary Skaine and others point out, there is little or no correlation between a country's wealth, its long-standing history of democracy and its appointment of women. In 2025, the all-powerful USA ranked 76th in the statistics whereas the four best for electing women – Rwanda, Cuba, Nicaragua and Mexico – were all economically developing countries. In 2003, Rwanda had replaced Sweden as the parliament with the most women politicians, and has continued with this progress, a shining example to the rest of the world. Equally surprising was that less democratic/more authoritarian countries elected more women to their legislative bodies than in America or Britain. The fifth best was the United Arab Emirates, an authoritarian federal monarchy consisting of seven emirates. Communist countries such as Cuba, ranked second in the world, elected a high number of women representatives, largely because of its equal rights policies. Surprising, too, that when countries became more democratic, such as those

Table 1. The percentage of women in Parliaments in 2025, compiled by the Inter-Parliamentary Union[5]

Rank	Country	Election Year	Seats	Women	Percentage
1	Rwanda	2024	80	51	63.8
2	Cuba	2023	470	262	55.7
3	Nicaragua	2021	91	50	55.0
4	Mexico	2024	500	251	50.0
5	United Arab Emirates	2023	28	14	50.0
5	Andorra	2023	28	14	50
11	Finland	2023	200	91	45.5
11	New Zealand	2023	123	56	45.5
14	South Africa	2024	390	174	44.6
17	Spain	2023	350	155	44.3
20	Argentina	2023	257	109	42.4
21	Ethiopia	2021	482	202	41.9
26	Britain	2024	650	263	40.5
31	Mozambique	2024	250	98	39.2
33	Angola	2022	220	86	39.1
35	Switzerland	2023	200	77	38.5
42	France	2024	575	208	36.2
43	Austria	2024	183	66	36.1
44	Germany	2021	733	262	35.7
57	Croatia	2024	151	50	33.1
58	Italy	2022	400	131	32.8
68	Canada	2021	337	104	30.9
70	Zimbabwe	2023	279	84	30.1
75	Iraq	2021	329	95	28.9
76	USA	2024	435	125	28.7
81	Liechtenstein	2021	25	7	28.0
84	Egypt	2020	592	164	27.7
91	China	2023	2977	790	26.5
101	Israel	2022	120	29	24.2
104	Greece	2023	300	70	23.3
112	Indonesia	2024	580	127	21.9
118	Ukraine	2019	401	85	21.2
122	Bahrain	2022	40	8	20.0
124	Turkey	2023	593	118	19.9
132	Brazil	2022	513	93	18.1
133	Bahamas	2021	39	7	18.0
136	Pakistan	2024	311	53	17.0
139	Russia	2021	450	74	16.4
141	Japan	2024	465	73	15.7
143	Hungary	2022	197	30	15.2
144	Zambia	2021	167	25	15.0
149	Cyprus	2021	56	8	14.3
151	India	2024	544	75	13.8
166	Syria	2024	250	24	9.6
175	Iran	2024	285	14	4.9
182	Tuvalu	2024	16	0	0,0
	Pitcairn			0	0.0
	Turks & Caicos			0	0.0

in Eastern Europe, then women's representation declined. In 2025, Hungary, at 143rd, sat near the bottom. Before it broke away from the USSR, women made up between twenty and thirty per cent of parliamentarians; in 1990, when Hungary transitioned to democracy, this dropped to seven per cent.[6]

Historians, like myself, always keen to tidy up the past, often find that history is too messy and that women do not always fit the pattern we create for them. Women's history certainly unravels the well-woven carpet of male parliamentary history, a dominant narrative of white male politicians usually wearing ties and dark suits. At the beginning of the twentieth century and throughout the world, ideas about traditional gender roles encouraged assumptions about government being a male preserve. Women's roles were historically linked to the home while men dominated the public sphere of work and politics. At times, as *Trailblazers* points out, these deeply rooted patriarchal attitudes, sometimes religiously based, limited women's potential. Some countries, Hughes and Paxton argue, such as those in authoritarian Middle East and North African regimes are still reluctant to give women the opportunity to stand for election, largely because of 'negative cultural beliefs towards women' based on religious or cultural attitudes.[7] In countries such as Saudia Arabia and Iran, conservative religious authorities wield significant influence. In some Muslim countries men have more power in marriage and divorce, polygamy is legal, women inherit half of what men inherit, women's legal testimony is worth half that of men's, child marriage is legal, honour killings are legal, women are required by law to dress in certain ways and are prohibited from working or even leaving the home unaccompanied. Under a guardianship system, women in a number of Arab countries are considered minors and require the permission of their male guardians to travel, to marry and to enter business contracts. Some scholars conservatively interpret certain Quranic verses and Hadiths to justify women's political exclusion. However, Islamic religion does not prohibit women from political involvement. Other scholars insist that Islam supports gender equality in governance. Brave Muslim women like those in Afghanistan, Cyprus, Indonesia, Iran, Egypt, Pakistan, and Turkey, all countries mentioned in this book, re-interpreted Quranic texts to argue their case for women's participation. Indeed, several Muslim-majority countries like Bangladesh, Pakistan, Indonesia and Turkey have chosen female heads of government. Moreover, women are making significant inroads in several Arab states.

Was women's entry into government inevitable? The simple answer is no. A report by the Inter-Parliamentary Union argues that the increase in the number of women politicians was not automatic but a consequence of electoral engineering.[8] Affirmative action, they argued, worked.

There were – and are – three crucial institutional determinants for women's electoral success. Firstly, proportional representation; secondly, gender-based electoral quotas; thirdly, the commitment of political parties. Proportional representation systems generally led to higher female representation than majoritarian or first-past-the-post systems. This is because proportional systems encouraged parties to nominate diverse candidates. The countries with the highest representation of women – the Nordic countries of Sweden, Norway, Finland and Denmark, and later those of South America and sub-Saharan Africa – all benefitted from a proportional representation system. The strategy has been enormously successful. In 2004, thirteen of the fifteen countries with the highest percentage of women parliamentarians had proportional representation in place.

Undoubtedly, quota systems also favoured women. In countries with gender quotas, that is, mandating a minimum percentage of seats for women, there was higher female representation. For example, South Africa and Mozambique adopted women-friendly policies and fast-tracked women into their governing bodies. After independence FRELIMO insisted that women candidates form thirty per cent. In Latin America too, eleven countries required a minimum twenty per cent of women to be nominated as candidates. In 1991 Argentina adopted a thirty per cent quota as well as a PR system: in 2025 women constituted 42.0 per cent of those elected. The United Arab Emirates, by presidential decree, ruled that women have a fifty per cent quota in Parliament. In the United Kingdom, Clare Short recommended all-women short-lists in Labour safe seats. In 1993, her recommendations were put into practice. In 1997, 79 years after women were granted the right to stand for Parliament, this policy was introduced for the general election that year and the number of women who entered Parliament doubled. Other parties followed Labour's example. In 2025, women formed 40.5 per cent of the British House of Commons.

As the IPU 2005 report argued, 'it is at the party level that the principle of equality must be put into practice'.[9] Political parties were, and still are, the gatekeepers to elected office, and their level of support significantly impacted women's chances of winning elections. Without a political party behind them, it was difficult for women to stand for election, let alone win it. Parties played a major role in recruiting, funding, educating and promoting candidates. Certainly, women such as Constance Markievicz, He Xiangning and Eugénie Éboué Tell, were supported by their respective parties. When countries gained their freedom from colonialism, many of the parties adopted women-friendly policies. In countries which emerged from violent conflict – Mozambique, South Africa, Zimbabwe – women were encouraged to be a part of the governing body. Women like Joice Mujuru, Graça Machel and Winnie Mandela had played a key part in these independence struggles and were rewarded for their help in defeating colonialism.

Women's participation in armed conflict also disrupted traditional gender relations, paving their way to political power once the conflict ceased.[10] For example, Mozambique women, who had fought against the Portuguese dictatorship, were rewarded by the 1975 Constitution, which declared that women's emancipation was 'one of the essential tasks of the state'. In 2003, after a brutal civil war, Rwanda reserved thirty per cent of its seats for women. In contrast, the lack of a strong gender equality policy both in the last century and in this one, generally meant that fewer women stood for election, let alone entered the legislature, as witnessed by Ukraine, Pakistan and Hungary.

In democracies, parliaments are supposed to represent the people. Yet throughout the twentieth century, women were grossly under-represented and are only just catching up. Governments which exclude half of their population and which do not reflect the demographics of the country can hardly be thought of as truly legitimate, as after all the ideal of government is 'by the people, for the people'. Parliaments across the globe can only consider themselves inclusive when women make up half the elected politicians. Only then will their democracy be a true democracy.

Governing bodies, as Sonia Palmieri points out, mirror our societies.[11] They are places where the country's policy direction is set for good – or less than good. Ideally, there should be gender-sensitive parliaments, ones where men and women have equal rights and together set a positive role model for society. These are, she argues, ones which have less aggressive language and behaviours, have more family-friendly sitting hours, have childcare facilities and parental leave, health care and social safety nets and gender-sensitive programmes for all politicians.

Parliament, however, is not there for the parliamentarians. It is the legislative body of a country and can make or amend laws as it sees fit. It can, as the IPU points out, 'repeal discriminatory legislation . . . can ensure that budgets are allocated . . . to advance gender equality and the rights of women and girls. Parliaments can represent the claims and priorities of women and girls in their constituencies and place them high on the agenda of parliament.'¹² Women's political representation is therefore not just essential for democratic justice but for effective governance. The proverb, 'you cannot clap with one hand' is a traditional saying which emphasises the need for both men and women in governing bodies to co-operate. It suggests that just as clapping requires two hands, building a successful and representative political system requires both men and women to participate. Indeed, a nation cannot progress effectively without women's participation. To exclude women excludes the talents, perspectives and priorities of fifty per cent of the population; having women represented improves the quality of decision making. When women make up a significant number in their legislative bodies, issues such as childcare and violence against women become part of the mainstream. So very many of the politicians in *Trailblazers* used their positions to advance the rights of women. Research suggests that a 'critical mass' of women is around thirty per cent, as this is the point at which women's presence is significant enough to effect change.

The trailblazers in this book, almost without exception, tried their very best to improve the lives of their countrywomen. They often fought alone, sometimes in small groups, always relying on the support of their male colleagues. The courage of women like Alexandra Kollontai, Clara Campoamor, Umi Sardjono and Graça Machel was remarkable. Nordic countries such as Finland, Norway, Sweden and Denmark initially led the field. All these countries had a long history of active feminist movements that began in the nineteenth and twentieth centuries, all advocating for women's rights across the spectrum, from suffrage to education through to working practices and politics. Today these countries promote egalitarian values, have strong welfare systems that provide paid parental leave and affordable childcare thus encouraging women to balance careers and family life. The removal of structural barriers, the promotion of egalitarian values, the embrace of gender quotas and their enviable welfare policies help women to achieve their political potential.

In the twenty-first century, Rwanda's female-dominated Parliament strengthened gender-based violence laws, improved health care for women and children, extended equal inheritance rights, criminalised marital rape and domestic violence and began economic programmes to help women start up business and become landowners. Women in South Africa framed abortion, pornography, domestic violence, genital mutilation, reproductive rights and equality of opportunity laws. African women parliamentarians, who belong to the Network of Women Parliamentarians of Central Africa, work together across national boundaries to improve the position of women in their respective countries. In 2003, *The Protocol on the Rights of Women in Africa* was adopted at the African Union summit. In 2005, 45 of the Union's 53 members signed the protocol.[13] Only eight did not.[14] In 2019, Finland was led by Sanna Marin and a majority-female Cabinet which enacted laws to help women. Parental leave was reformed, giving equal leave to mothers and fathers; free education and childcare was expanded; climate laws strengthened; and progress was made to improve gender equality more generally. In 2025, Finland was ranked the happiest country in the world. Is there a correlation between this and women's equality? Did Hilda Käkikoski begin a trend?

One dispiriting aspect is that women's progress, as *Trailblazers* shows, was not a straight railway track heading towards a destination but more of a roller-coaster with scary rides and speedy downward slides. Afghani and Iranian women remain stranded on a roller-coaster plunging down into oblivion. Across the world, despotic behaviour by elected politicians also threatens good governance. Will future generations look back on the twentieth century as the age of democracy, an exceptional moment in history now giving way to new systems of power? Political decay, polarisation and government paralysis are all too common. In 2019, Boris Johnson tried illegally to prorogue the British Parliament; in 2021 Donald Trump allegedly encouraged a seditious rebellion, menacingly warning that he would 'go after his enemies', destroy the constitution and govern autocratically. In 2024 Trump was re-elected and is already undermining political institutions, threatening constitutional norms, inciting division by targeting racial, ethnic and political groups, calling the media 'the enemy of the people', and admiring authoritarian leaders like Putin. The Hungarian President, Viktor Orban calls his regime an illiberal democracy and gleefully undermines its conventions by eliminating any opposition and placing his cronies into positions of power. In parts of Africa, political power became centralised, constitutions were abandoned and 'opposition' political parties made illegal. Into this stepped the 'big men' who became presidents for life in a single party state. Here elections served as referenda – only those who belonged to the ruling party were allowed to stand. Some women – usually married to the leader – held senior political positions. In 2025, we seemed to be at the start of a global authoritarian counter-revolution aimed at reversing the gains made by women, gays and ethnic minorities.

Meanwhile, trust in politics is on a downward slope, weird conspiracy theories replace reason, and admiration for populist strong men (very rarely women) who favour authoritarianism continues apace. In February 2025, the actor, comedian and writer, David Mitchell warned of the threat to democracy, citing a report that Gen Z – those aged between 13 and 27 – thought 'the UK would be a better place if a strong leader was in charge who does not have to bother with parliament or elections'.[15] Democracies only work because the electorate believes in this form of government. This book is intended as an apposite reminder that democracy or any representative system, long fought for, is fragile. Women's rights are precarious. Time and again, women's achievements are threatened:

successes in Afghanistan and Iran were wiped out by overtly patriarchal governments.

Politics remains dangerous. Violence against women, especially those who challenge patriarchal norms, continues. In 2003, Anna Lindh, Sweden's Foreign Minister, was fatally stabbed and Iraqi politician Aquila Al-Hashimi was shot; in 2007, the former Prime Minister of Pakistan, Benazir Bhutto was assassinated; in 2012 the Afghan politician Hanifa Safi was murdered by a bomb planted in her car; in 2014 Saado Ali Warsame was shot by Somali gunmen; in 2016, the British MP Jo Cox was murdered by a white supremacist. Most politicians enter politics to make life better for their constituents, their country and the world. Democratically elected, they do not expect to be killed in the process. The women mentioned in this book were murdered by those who held extremist ideologies and it is a frightening thought that in Britain alone, there are men who stoke division by gratifying people's basest instincts: Lee Anderson, Nigel Farage, George Galloway and Azhar Ali, are all masters at extinguishing nuance, a key element of democratic debate. Matteo Salvini in Italy, Marine le Pen in France, Narendra Modi in India, Recep Erdogan in Turkey, Jair Bolsanoro in Brazil, Viktor Orban in Hungary and Donald Trump in the United States share similar traits.

There are glimmers of hope. I find it intriguing that while old established democracies are threatened, older autocratic regimes seem to be – albeit slowly – allowing women into their governing bodies. At the beginning of the twenty-first century women were elected in several countries, known for their religiously based masculinities: Djibouti in 2003, United Arab Emirates in 2007, Kuwait in 2009, Brunei in 2011, Saudia Arabia in 2013, Qatar in 2017 and Micronesia in 2021. In 2018 Bahrain's Parliament elected Fawzia Zainai as speaker, the first time a woman had held this post; in UAE women comprise half the governing body. This poses an intriguing question as to why women's representation is growing here and not in other more traditional legislatures. Is it because these newly elected women were all from the upper echelons of their society and posed little threat to the status quo?

There is also some international push-back against patriarchal strong-men governments. The 1979 United Nations Convention on the Elimination of all Forms of Discrimination against Women (CEDAW) had set a tone for the equal participation of women in all forms of government. In 1995, at the Fourth World Conference on Women held in Beijing, a Platform for Action outlined thirteen different strategic objectives and actions, one of which was to increase women's participation in governance.[16] In 2006 the IPU published *Gender Equality: Making a Difference through Parliament,* showing how to achieve gender equality world-wide.

There is hope too in that women have made progress in leadership roles across the world. In the years between 1900 and 2000 only 25 women ever held the highest office. In 2006 alone women led the governments of eleven countries: Bangladesh, Chile, Finland, Germany, Ireland, Latvia, Liberia, Mozambique, New Zealand, the Philippines and São Tomé and Príncipe.[17] Sometimes, women are elected leaders when female representation remains low such as India's Indira Gandhi.[18] This is because female politicians, it is argued, were more likely to be 'dynastic politicians', often preceded by a member of the family. In the 2004, 2009 and 2014 parliaments around two thirds of female parliamentarians were from dynastic political families 'gaining entry because of name, recognition and contacts'.[19] India was no exception: female elites across the world have been elected, and continue to be so, through kin-based appointments, a system known as 'wifeism'.

This book ends with another story of hope, a story that widens the scope of women's achievement, a story that looks at women in trans-national bodies. It is a story of a Muslim woman from a conservative country: Sheikha (Princess) Haya from Bahrain. Sheikha Haya was born on 18 October 1952 into the Bahraini ruling Al Khalifa family. She was well educated. In 1974 she gained a BA in law at the University of Kuwait; in 1986 a Diploma in Civil Rights Law from the University of Alexandria and in 1988 a Diploma in Comparative Law from Ain Shams University, Egypt. Fluent in Arabic, French and English, Shaikha Haya was Bahrain's ambassador to France, Belgium, Switzerland and Spain between 2000 and 2004. She was Bahrain's first female ambassador and the country's permanent delegate to UNESCO.

In 1979, Shaikha Haya was one of the first two women to be admitted to the Bahraini Bar. She set up her own practice, the Haya Rashed Al Khalifa Law Firm, determined to deliver high-quality legal services, uphold justice and promote international legal standards. It provided a range of legal services from corporate and commercial law, banking and finance to family and personal law. In 2024, the firm employed four women and nine men. Her foundation provides scholarship, mentorship and general support to young women professionals, helping to 'equip them with the tools they need to make a meaningful impact in society'.[20] She is also legal advisor to the Royal Court. Between 1997 and 1999, Shaikha Haya was vice-chair of the International Bar Association, a global association of legal practitioners with its head office in London.

Shaikha Haya has had an illustrious diplomatic career, a prominent figure in both domestic and international affairs. On 6 June 2006, she became the first Arab and the first Muslim woman to chair the United Nations Assembly, where she played a pivotal role in shaping international arbitration, spearheading efforts to promote the peaceful resolution of disputes and strengthen multilateral co-operation internationally. In her acceptance speech, Shaikha Haya spoke of being 'moved by a deep feeling of pain caused by the tragedies occurring throughout the world at both the human and environmental levels'.[21] She wanted to address the human suffering caused by political disputes, war, terrorism, poverty and malnutrition and the environmental crises caused by pollution, global warming and the depletion of natural resources. In her view, the UN faced challenges that threatened global security, particularly 'the greatest evil of our time: terrorism', which she felt was exacerbated by poverty, unemployment, illiteracy and extremism. In her statement presented at the First Session she underlined the fact that 'over half the world's population, namely women, typically have less access to health care, employment, decision making and property ownership. This disparity needs to be addressed.'[22] Peace and security, she argued, were essential to promoting human rights and eradicating poverty. These were impaired by human conflicts and the destructive power of disasters like earthquakes and floods. We live, she argued, in a world 'afflicted by violent armed conflicts, hunger and disease; a world threatened by international terrorism, organised crime and the proliferation of all types of weapons . . . a world where the enjoyment of human rights is still an unrealised dream'.[23]

During Shaikha's Presidency she led a range of UN initiatives, including help for the least developed countries, a commitment to end world poverty, studies on women and violence, the launching of a peace-building fund, conferences on trafficking in women and girls, and, in Shaikha Haya's view the implementation of the Millenium goals to eradicate poverty was the overarching theme of her Presidency. She ended her term quoting Gandhi, who said, 'We need to be the change we want to see in the world.'

Acknowledgements

Thanks to my editor Elise Heslinga for inviting me to write this book, commenting on my proposal, and helping me improve the book in all its stages. It has been quite a journey. It proved challenging to locate information, particularly on many of the lesser-known women trailblazers in this book, so I wrote to embassies, libraries and universities asking for information. Many responded to my pleas and I would like to thank the following: Eva-Patricia Sturm at the Austrian Embassy; Tammy Hill at the Belgium Embassy; Joaquim Aurelion Correia de Araujo Neto at the Brazilian Embassy; the Croatian Embassy; Wollfy Krašić, University of Zagreb, Croatia; Marios Theocharous, Cultural Counsellor, Cyprus High Commission; Esra Emin, Press Attaché, Turkish Republic of Northern Cyprus; Sevim Erol, Eastern Mediterranean University; Pirjo Pellinen at the Finnish Embassy; Stefanos Dimitriadis at the Greek Embassy; Konstantina Pentarchou from the Library of Gender and Equality, Greece; Anastasia Ragkou, Library of Hellenic Studies, who provided copies of Elena Skoura's parliamentary contributions; the New Zealand High Commission; Trine Berg Kopperud at the Norwegian Embassy; Calma Clarinda at the Polish Embassy; Sonia Morcillo Garcia at the

Spanish Embassy; Angela Zollinger at the Swiss Embassy; staff at the Turkish Embassy.

Friends and friendly colleagues across the globe have helped too. Thank you to the following. Teréz Kleisz for recommending material on Hungary, Mary Jane Mossman for sending me material on Canada, Michela Minesso and Barbara Kirkham Trancuido for information on Italy, Cornelius Goop for sending me Liechtenstein newspaper articles, Judy Cheadle for sending me material on China and Rozina Visram for her help on India. Thanks to Alissa Walter, Seattle Pacific University for trying to help me with Iraqi women. Sue Morgan and three anonymous reviewers read my proposal and made many useful suggestions to improve the book. Two anonymous reviewers also commented helpfully on the entire manuscript. Sue Morgan used her analytical eyes to spot gaps and problems in both my proposal and in the draft manuscript; Jackie Rowley's journalistic skills helped me liven up the text. Bridget Sorrel-Cameron, Cathy Loxton and Dawn Rumley read the entire manuscript. I would like to thank them all. Thanks too to Diane Atkinson, Clare Short and Laura Schwartz for their intellectual support.

The library staff at the University of Warwick are amazing, tracing out-of-print books, ordering online documents and helping in diverse ways. Warwick staff also tracked down and obtained inter-library loans from across the world. Thank you especially to the University of Michigan and the University of Ontario for sending these books and to Sidney and David at the Oral Archives, University of Columbia, for providing me with a transcript of an interview of Delia Parodi. Huge thanks to the Women's History Network, simply for existing and generating interest in women's stories. Thank you to all those academics, journalists, Wikipedia writers and other authors for collecting and publishing information on their countrywomen.

Thanks to Béatrice Parrain, Ordre de la Libération, France; Berni Metcalfe, National Library of Ireland; Piro Pellinen,

Finland; Layanan Arsip, Indonesia; Almira Medaric, Fürsten-tum Liechtenstein for providing me with photographs.

My greatest thanks, as ever, are to my husband, Jonathan Dudley. He fell in love with several of the trailblazers as he read their stories. His critical editorial eye improved my writing. The book is dedicated to my darling wonderful granddaughters.

Notes

Introducing the Trailblazers

1 See June Hannam, Mitzi Auchterlonie and Katherine Holden's, *International Encyclopedia of Women's Suffrage, ABC-Clio*, 2000 and Jan Adams, *Women and the Vote: A World History*, Oxford University Press, 2016.

2 The Vatican City is a sovereign state. Its head is the Pope, who is elected by a conclave of male bishops and archbishops.

3 'Women in Parliaments, 1945–1995, A World Statistical Survey', *Inter-Parliamentary Union*, Geneva.

4 Melanie M. Hughes and Pamela Paxton, 'The Political Representation of Women Over Time', *Palgrave Handbook of Political Rights*, Palgrave Macmillan, 2020.

1 The First Trailblazers, 1900–1918

1 Yksi Kamari, *Kaksi Sukupuolta*, Eduskunnan Kirjasto, Helsinki, 1997.

2 Previously, only seven per cent of the population – and only men – had the vote, whereas franchise reform gave the vote to 85 per cent of the population, including women.

3 Risto Alapuro, *State and Revolution in Finland*, Brill, 2019, p. 107.

4 Aura Korppi-Tommola, 'A Long Tradition of Equality: Women's Suffrage in Finland', in Blanca Rodriguez Ruiz and Ruth Rubio Marin (eds) *The Struggle for Female Suffrage in Europe*, Brill, 2012.

5 Eeva Ahtisaari, 'Hilda Kakikoski: Opettaja, Puhuja Ja Politiitikko Naisen Asialla', in Yksi Kamari, *Kaksi Sukupuolta*, Eduskunnan kirjasto, Helsinki, 1997

6 John Martin Crawford, *The Kalevala, the Epic Poem of Finland*, Columbian Publishing, 1891.

7 Thanks to Sir Stanley Wells for information about Finlandia.

8 I am very grateful to Pirjo Pellinen, Special Advisor, Culture and Public Diplomacy, Embassy of Finland, for this reference and others who have helped me write this section.

9 Robert Aldrich and Garry Wotherspoon, *Who's Who in Gay and Lesbian History*, Psychology Press, 2002.

10 The Social Democrats emerged as the largest party with 80 seats; the Finnish Party came second with 59.

11 Elisa Rolle and Hilda Käkikoski, *Live Journal*, published online 31 January 2017.

12 Natalia Novikova and Kristen Ghodsee, 'Alexandra Kollontai (1872–1952): Communism as the Only Way Towards Women's Liberation', in F. de Haan (ed.) *Palgrave Handbook of Communist Women Activists around the World*, Palgrave, 2023.

13 The others were Yevgenia Bosch, Catherine Breshkovsky, Vera Figner, Olha Matveevskaya, Maria Perveeva, Elena Rozmirovich, Anastasia Sletova-Chernova, Maria Spiridonova, Varvara Yakovleva.

14 Alexandra's mother had been married before and already had three children, two daughters and one son. The daughters lived with their mother; the son with his father.

15 Natalia Novikova and Kristen Ghodsee, 'Alexandra Kollontai (1872–1952): Communism as the Only Way Towards Women's Liberation', in F. de Haan (ed.) *Palgrave Handbook of Communist Women Activists Around the World*, 2023, p. 62.

16 Alexandra Kollontai, *The Autobiography of a Sexually Emancipated Communist Woman*, Herder and Herder, 1971.

17 Quoted in Natalia Novikova and Kristen Ghodsee, 'Alexandra Kollontai (1872–1952): Communism as the Only Way Towards Women's Liberation', p. 62.

18 Alexandra Kollontai, *The Autobiography of a Sexually Emancipated Communist Woman*.

19 Quoted in Natalia Novikova and Kristen Ghodsee, 'Alexandra Kollontai (1872–1952): Communism as the Only Way Towards Women's Liberation', p. 66.

20 See Paula Bartley, *Labour Women in Power*, Palgrave Macmillan, 2019.

21 Alexandra Kollontai, *Mezhdunarodnyi den'rabotni tz*, Moscow, 1920.

22 Quoted in Natalia Novikova and Kristen Ghodsee, 'Alexandra Kollontai (1872–1952): Communism as the Only Way Towards Women's Liberation', p. 72.

23 Cathy Porter, *Women in Revolutionary Russia*, Cambridge University Press, 1987.

24 See Anne McShane's 'Women at the Heart of the Revolution', *Jacobin*, November 2019.

25 Native American, Asian American, women of Latino origin and African American women all had to fight for their right to vote. Native Americans were not allowed to be US citizens, thus prohibiting them from voting; others were excluded by discriminatory immigration laws and literacy tests. In 1924 the Indian Citizenship Act gave Native Americans the right to vote.

26 Kevin Giles, *Flight of the Dove, the Story of Jeannette Rankin*, Touchstone Press, Beaverton, 1980.

27 James J. Lopach and Jean A. Luckowski, *Jeannette Rankin: A Political Woman*, University Press of Colorado, 2005. See also Norma Smith, *Jeannette Rankin, America's Conscience*, Montana Historical Society Press, 2002 and Corrine J. Naden, *Jeannette Rankin*, Marshall Cavendish Bendick, 2012.

28 *Jeannette Rankin, First Lady in Congress*, Hannah Josephson, Bobbs-Merrill, 1974, p. 48.

29 Ibid., p. 51.

30 Jeanette Rankin, *On this Day, Jeanette Rankin's History-Making Moment*, NCC staff, April 2024.

31 Kevin S. Giles, *Flight of the Dove, the Story of Jeannette Rankin*, Touchstone Press, 1980, p. 17.

32 Ibid., p. 11.

33 Jeanette Rankin, *On this Day, Jeanette Rankin's History-Making Moment*.

34 See *Generations of Courage, The Women's International League for Peace and Freedom, from the 20th Century into a New Millennium*.

35 Kevin S. Giles, *Flight of the Dove, the Story of Jeannette Rankin*, p. 153.

36 Ibid., p. 153.

37 Ibid., p. 171.

38 James J. Lopach and Jean A. Luckowski, *Jeannette Rankin, A Political Woman*, University Press of Colorado, 2005.

39 Jeanette Rankin, 1941 quoted in Mary Barmeyer O'Brien, *Jeannette Rankin: Bright Star in the Big Sky*, Rowman and Littlefield,

40 Norma Smith, *Jeannette Rankin, America's Conscience*, Montana Historical Society Press, 2002, p. 184.

41 Kevin S. Giles, *Flight of the Dove, the Story of Jeannette Rankin*, p. 184.

42 These three women were not the only women to be elected: a conservative–liberal suffragist and women's rights activist, Anna Rogstad, was elected in Norway (1911) while a Bolshevik activist, Anna Leetsmann, was elected in Estonia (1917) during its brief independence from Russia.

2 The Aftermath of War, 1918–1930

1 In 1960 First Nations women could vote and stand for Parliament.

2 David Thomson, *Europe since Napoleon*, Penguin 1971.

3 In 1981 the law was changed. If an MP was convicted of a crime and received a prison sentence of one year or more they were disqualified from sitting in Parliament.

4 Lauren Arrington, *Revolutionary Lives*, Princeton University Press, 2019, p. 2.

5 Ibid.

6 Sean O'Faoláin, *Constance Markievicz*, Sphere Books, 1934.

7 Lauren Arrington, *Revolutionary Lives*, Princeton University Press, 2019, p. 35.

8 Court trial, quoted in Sean O'Faoláin, *Constance Markievicz*, Sphere Books, 1934, p. 157.

9 NA, HO 144/1580/316818 quoted in Lauren Arrington, *Revolutionary Lives*, Princeton University Press, 2019, p. 198.

10 Lauren Arrington, *Revolutionary Lives*, Princeton University Press, 2019, p. 203.

11 Margaret Stewart and Doris French, 'Aggie was a terror', *Chatelaine Magazine*, April 1979. See the Agnes Macphail website, Grey Highlands Public Library for further information.

12 See Margaret Stewart, *Ask No Quarter: A Biography of Agnes Macphail*, Longmans, Green and Company, 1959; Tabitha de Bruin, 'Agnes Macphail', *Canadian Encyclopaedia*, April 2008. Thanks to my lovely friend Mary Jane Mossman, Professor Emerita, Osgoode Hall Law School, for help with this section and for sending me a copy of Macphail's biography.

13 She later discovered that this was because of a bet.

14 *Telling Times* video, Agnes Macphail.

15 Ontario Women's History.

16 Agnes Macphail, quoted in T. A. Crowley, *Agnes Mcphail and the Politics of Equality*, Lorimer, 1990, p. 90.

17 *The KP Telegraph*, February 1938.

18 House of Commons, Ottawa, 26 March 1928.

19 Agnes Macphail, House of Commons, 9 April 1927, quoted in Doris Pennington, *Agnes Mcphail: Reformer*, Simon and Pierre, 1990, p. 72.

20 Ibid., p. 103.

21 Surprisingly, there is no full-length biography of Clara Zetkin. Karen Honeycutt's, 'Clara Zetkin: A Left-wing Socialist and Feminist in Wilhelmian Germany', Columbia University, PhD, 1975 is a useful start.
22 Ibid.
23 In some short biographies, it is claimed that Clara met Ossip in Paris.
24 Letter to Karl Kautsky, quoted in Karen Honeycutt, 'Clara Zetkin: A Left-Wing Socialist and Feminist in Wilhelmian Germany', p. 62.
25 Quoted in Karen Honeycutt, 'Clara Zetkin', p. 223.
26 Kautsky quoted in Karen Honeycutt, 'Clara Zetkin', p. 246.
27 Ibid., p. 406.
28 Ibid., p. 239.
29 Helen Boak, *Women in the Weimar Republic*, Manchester University Press, 2013, p. 97.
30 Clara Zetkin quoted in Dalia Nassar and Kristin Gjesdal (ed.), *Women Philosophers in the Long Nineteenth Century: The German Tradition*, Oxford University Press, 2021, p. 175.
31 Adelheid Popp, *The Autobiography of a Working Woman*, T. Fisher Unwin, 1911.
32 Ariadne, Frauen in *Bewegung, 1848–1938*, Osterreichsische Nationalbibliothek, 2019.
33 Adelheid Popp, *Parlamentskorrespondenz*, VOM 28, April 2009.
34 I am grateful to another lovely friend, Dr Teresz Kleisz, University of Pécs, Hungary, for providing articles for this section.
35 The best piece in English about Margit Slachta is Margit Balogh and Ilona Mona's article 'Slachta, Margit (1884–1974)' in Francisca de Haan et al. (eds), *A Biographical Dictionary of Women's Movements and Feminisms: Central, Eastern, and South Eastern Europe, 19th and 20th Centuries*, Central European University Press, 2006. Rita Maria Kiss, 'Slachta Margit arcai. 2. Rész: A keresztény feminista', *Barankovics Alapitvany* was also a useful source.

36 Quoted in Rita Maria Kiss, 'Slachta Margit arcai. 2. Rész: A keresztény feminista', *Barankovics Alapitvany*.

37 Quoted Paul Hanebrink, *In Defense of Christian Hungary*, Cornell University, 2009, p. 221.

38 Quoted in Maria Schmidt, 'Margit Slachta's Activities in Support of Slovakian Jewry, 1942–43', *Holocaust and Genocide Studies*, 5 (1), 1990: 69.

39 Slachta Margit, Yad Vashem.

40 It was common for Chinese women to have multiple names, including courtesy names, family names. I have used He Xiangning throughout. This section is based on Lily Xiao Hong Lee et al. (eds), *Biographical Dictionary of Chinese Women, 1912–2000*, Hong Kong University Press, 2003; Shelly Chan, *A Maidservant of the Revolution, He Xiangning and Chinese Feminist Nationalism in the 1920s and 1930s*, Occasional Papers, Hong Kong Institute of Asia-Pacific Studies, 2007.

41 I am grateful to Judy Cheadle for providing websites in Chinese.

42 Quoted in https://mp.weixin.gg.com

43 Ibid.

44 Ibid.

45 I wrote to the Chinese Embassy for help but received no reply. I went on to ask DeepSeek AI, the Chinese AI service, for information about He's role in the cultural revolution but the site replied 'Sorry, that's beyond my scope. Let's talk about something else.'

46 Elsewhere too, women were making a political mark in In Armenia, Belgium, Czechoslovakia, Denmark, Estonia, Georgia, Guernsey, Iceland, Latvia, Lithuania, Luxembourg, Poland, Slovakia, Sweden.

3 The Great Depression, 1930–1940

1 During this period, fourteen more countries elected the first women to their Parliaments: Brazil, Burma, Ceylon, Cuba, Indonesia, Isle of Man, Kenya (white women only), New Zealand (Maoris were excluded), Portugal, Puerto Rico, South Africa (white women only), Spain, Suriname and Turkey.

2 Thanks to the Archivo del Congresso de los Diputados and Sonia Morcillo-Garcia for providing information. Some of this chapter is based on Alba González, *Clara Campoamor: la lucha polÄtica por los derechos de la mujer*, Ministerio de la Presidencia, 2022; See also *Clara Campoamor. La Mujer olvidada*, 2011, a tv movie about her life.

3 In Spain individuals use a combination of their father's and mother's surnames. The father's name comes first.

4 *Salient Women*, Biographies of extraordinary women from salien twomen.com.

5 Miranda Samblancat, 'Clara Campoamor Rodrigues', *Diccionario Biográfico de la Real Academia de la Historia*.

6 Alba González, *Clara Campoamor: la lucha polÄtica por los derechos de la mujer*, Ministerio de la Presidencia, 2022.

7 Merbrure Gőnenç, Tűrkan Örs Baştuğ, Sabiha Erbay, Huriye Öniz Baha, Nakiye Elgűn, Fakihe Öymen, Bahire Bediş, Morova Aydelik, Mihri Pektaş, Meliha Ulaş, Fatma Esma Nayman, Sabiha Gőrkey, Hatice Özgener. In 1936 Hatice Özgener won her seat in a by-election.

8 Hati Cirpan, Şekibe Insel.

9 Benal Nevzat Iştar Ariman.

10 Seniha Hizal.

11 Dr Ayten Sezer, 'The First Female Members of Parliament in Turkey and their Work in Parliament; Bahar Toparlak, 'Fatma Memik, One of the First Female Members of Parliament of the Republic', *International Journal of Historical and Social Research*, 12, 2014: 71–81.

12 Savaş Sertel, 'The Republic of Intellectual in Parliament', *Journal of Faculty of Letters*, June 2015.

13 Atatűrk Ansiklopedisi.

14 Savaş Sertel, *Atatűrk Ansiklopedisi*, 22 March 2021.

15 Bahar Toparlak, 'Fatma Memik, One of the First Female Members of Parliament of the Republic', *International Periodical for History and Social Research*, 12, 2014: 71–81.

16 I am grateful to Joaquim Aurelio Correia de Araujo Neto from the Brazilian Embassy for providing information.

17 Quoted in Carlita Pereira de Querios, *Speech by the First Woman Elected to Congress in Brazil*, p. 336. Carlita donated 30 archival boxes to Fundação Getulio Vargas's School of Social Sciences. It has yet to be explored. Brazilian historiography has favoured men's history. In the country's official history, women, blacks, Indians, workers and other so-called social minorities are absent.

18 This section is based on Jean Garner, 'McCombs, Elizabeth Reid, 1873–1935', *Dictionary of New Zealand Biography*, 1998 and Jenny Coleman, *From Suffrage to a Seat in the House: The Path to Parliament for New Zealand Women*, Otago University Press, 2016.

19 *Star* (Christchurch), 27 July 1901, p. 7.

20 *Evening Post*, 15 September 1933, p. 8.

21 Ibid., p. 7.

22 Jenny Coleman, *From Suffrage to a Seat in the House: The Path to Parliament for New Zealand Women*, Otago University Press, 2016, p. 5.

23 *NZ Truth*, 27 January 1927, p. 6.

24 Sandra Wallace, 'Members for Everywoman? The Campaign Promises of Women Parliamentary Candidates', *New Zealand Journal of History*, 1991, 27: 188.

25 Joan W. Scott, 'Gender, a Useful Category of Analysis', *American Historical Review*, December 1986, 91: 1072.

4 War and Peace, 1940–1950

1 Michela Minesso, *Diritti e politiche sociali*, Franco Angeli, 2016.

2 Dan A. D'Amelio, 'Italian Women in the Resistance World War II', *Italian America*, 19 (2), 2001: 127–41.

3 Thanks to Michela Minesso, whose inspirational talk at a conference in Milan celebrating Matteoti and whose book *Diritti e politiche sociali*, Franco Angeli, 2016, has served as a basis for this section.

4 Dan A. D'Amelio, 'Italian Women in the Resistance World War II'.

5 Giuseppe Sircana, 'Merlin, Angelina', *Dizionario Biografico degli Italiani*, 73, 2009.

6 Graziella Gaballo, 'Lina Merlin', *enciclopediadelledonne.it.*

7 Ibid.

8 Jane Slaughter, *Women and the Italian Resistance, 1943–1945*, Arden Press, 1997, p. 36.

9 Michela Minesso, *Diritti e politiche sociali*, Franco Angeli, 2016, p. 9.

10 Ibid.

11 Ibid.

12 Ibid., p. 90.

13 See Molly Tambor, *The Lost Wave: Women and Democracy in Postwar Italy*, Oxford University Press, 2014 for an in-depth analysis of the reform of prostitution in Italy.

14 Michela Minesso, *Diritti e politiche sociali*, Franco Angeli, 2016.

15 Graziella Gaballo, 'Lina Merlin', *enciclopediadelledonne.it*

16 Lorelle Semley, *To be Free and French, Citizenship in France's Atlantic Empire*, Cambridge University Press, 2017.

17 Arlette Capdepuy, 'Quelle place pour Madame Éboué dans le gallisme de la Ve République?' *Histoire@politique*, 2012; Annette K Joseph-Gabriel, *Reimagining Liberation: How Black Women Transformed Citizenship in the French Empire*, University of Illinois Press, 2019.

18 Two were her biological children and two were Felix's from previous relationships.

19 Jean-Damascene Gasanabo, 'Madame Eugénie Tell Éboué (1891–1972)', *Black Past*, 29 January 2012.

20 Tokuko, Ōgai, 'The Stars of Democracy: The First Thirty-Nine Female Member of the Japanese Diet', *US-Japan Women's Journal English Supplement*, University of Hawaii Press, No 11, 1996, p. 3.

21 Five Liberal Party, six Progressive Party, eight Socialist Party, one Communist Party, nine Independents and 10 from minor parties.

22 Tokuko, Ōgai, 'The Stars of Democracy: The First Thirty-Nine Female Member of the Japanese Diet', *US-Japan Women's Journal English Supplement*, University of Hawaii Press, No 11, 1996.

23 This section is based on Tokuko, Ōgai, 'The Stars of Democracy: The First Thirty-Nine Female Member of the Japanese Diet', *US-Japan Women's Journal English Supplement*, University of Hawaii Press, No 11, 1996; Carmen Blacker, 'Obituary, Shizue Kato', *Guardian*, 1 February 1992; 'Shidzué Ishimoto Kato', *Museum of Contraception and Abortion*; Sujin Lee, 'Differing Conceptions of "Voluntary Motherhood: Yamakawa Kikue's Birth Strike and Ishimoto Shizue's Eugenic Feminism'*, U.S–Japan Women's Journal*, No. 52, 2017, pp. 3–22; Baroness Shidzué Ishimoto, *Facing Two Ways: The Story of My Life*, Cassell, 1935.

24 Shidzué writes a lot about her mother in her autobiography but never mentions her name. She is listed in the index as Mrs Hirota.

25 Baroness Shidzué Ishimoto, *Facing Two Ways: The Story of My Life*, Cassell, 1935, p. 153.

26 Ibid., p. 165.

27 This section is based on M. Reza Pirbhai, '"From Purdah to Parliament," the Twentieth Century According to Shaista Ikramullah', *Journal of Women of the Middle East and the Islamic World*, 14, 2016; Siobhan Lambert Hurley, 'Ikramullah, Begum Shaista', *Oxford Encyclopaedia of Women in World History*, Oxford University Press, 2008; Pakistan Institute of International Affairs, 'Shaista S Ikramullah: 1915–2000', *Pakistan Horizon*, 61, 2008; Amna Munawar Khan, 'The Role and Impact of Women Legislators in Pakistan's Parliament', *Defence Journal*, 26, 2024; Shaista Suhrawardy Ikramullah, *From Purdah to Parliament*, Oxford University Press, 2000.

28 *Los Angeles Times*, 16 June 1951, p. 3.

29 Shaista quoted in M. Reza Pirbhai, '"From Purdah to Parliament," the Twentieth Century According to Shaista Ikramullah', *Journal of Women of the Middle East and the Islamic World*, 14, 2016: 281.

30 Shaista Suhrawardy Ikramullah, *From Purdah to Parliament*, Oxford University Press, 2000, p. 95.

31 Ibid., p. 70.

32 Shaista quoted in M. Reza Pirbhai, '"From Purdah to Parliament," the Twentieth Century According to Shaista Ikramullah', *Journal of Women of the Middle East and the Islamic World*, 14, 2016: 292.

33 Shaista Suhrawardy Ikramullah, *From Purdah to Parliament*, Oxford University Press, 2000, p. 192.

34 Shaista quoted in M. Reza Pirbhai, '"From Purdah to Parliament," the Twentieth Century According to Shaista Ikramullah', *Journal of Women of the Middle East and the Islamic World*, 14, 2016: 305.

35 Shaista Suhrawardy Ikramullah, *From Purdah to Parliament*, Oxford University Press, 2000.

36 This section is based on Letty Cottin Pogrebin, 'Golda Meir', *The Halvi/Hyman Encyclopaedia of Jewish Women*; Deborah E. Lipstadt, *Golda Meir*, Yale University Press, 2023; Meron Medzini, *Golda Meir*, De Gruyter, 2008; Seth Thompson 'Golda Meir, A Very Public Life', in *Women as Political Leaders*, Routledge, 2013.

37 Golda Meir, quoted in Seth Thompson, 'Golda Meir, A Very Public Life', p. 181.

38 Golda Meir, quoted in Letty Cottin Pogrebin, 'Golda Meir', *The Halvi/Hyman Encyclopaedia of Jewish Women*.

39 Golda Meir, quoted in Deborah E. Lipstadt, *Golda Meir*, Yale University Press, 2023, p. 69.

40 Other countries that elected women include Albania, Algeria, Australia, Bangladesh, Barbados, Bermuda, Bulgaria, Cook Islands, Curacao, Dominica, Dominican Republic, Ecuador, Guam, Jamaica, Malta, Mauritius, North Korea, North Macedonia, Panama, Philippines, Romania, Seychelles, South Korea, Taiwan, Thailand, Trinidad and Tobago, Uruguay, Venezuela and Vietnam.

41 See Martin Conway, *Western Europe's Democratic Age*, 1945–1968, Princeton University Press, 2020 for a fascinating, thought-provoking study of this topic.

5 New Horizons, 1950–1960

1 This section is based on Jennie Natalia Palacios, *Delia Parodi y la organización cívica femenina en la provincia de San Luis Acción administrative?*, ISNC, December 2019; Carolina Berry, 'Delia Degliuomini de Parodi, el desafio de reemplazar lo irresmplazable', *La Segunda línea del liderazgo Peronista 1945–1955*, Eduntref-Pueblo Heredro, 2013; *Reminiscences of Delia*, interviewed by Romero, Columbia University Library recording.

2 *Reminiscences of Delia.*

3 Ibid.

4 Carolina Berry, 'Delia Degliuomini de Parodi, el desafio de reemplazar lo irresmplazable', *La Segunda línea del liderazgo Peronista 1945–1955*, Eduntref-Pueblo Heredro, 2013, p. 300.

5 This section is based on Katharine McGregor and Ruth Indiah Rahayu, 'Umi Sardjono (1923–2011) and the Quest to Build a New Society for Indonesian Women', *Palgrave Handbook of Communist Women Activists around the World*, 2023; Firliana Purwanti, 'Umi Sarjono: Pembuka Jalan Gerakan', *Historia*, June 2014; Munawar Setiyadi, 'Perjuangan Umi Sardjono, Pendiri Gerwani', *Arah Juang*, 62; Annie Pahlman, *Women, Sexual Violence and the Indonesian Killings of 1965–66*, Routledge, 2017.

6 Quoted in Katharine McGregor and Ruth Indiah Rahayu, 'Umi Sardjono (1923–2011) and the Quest to Build a New Society for Indonesian Women', *Palgrave Handbook of Communist Women Activists around the World*, 2023, p. 383.

7 This section is based on E. S. Buzz, 'Here's the Story of Rawya Ateya: First Parliamentarian in the Arab World', *Egyptian Streets*, 16 October 2020; Arthur Jr Goldschmidt, *Biographical Dictionary of Modern Egypt*, Lynne Rienner Publishers, 2000.

8 Jomana Qaddour, 'Women's Quotas: Making the Case for Codifying Syrian Women's Political Participation', *Journal of Race, Gender and Social Justice*, 26 (3), 2019: 564.

9   E. S. Buzz, 'Here's the Story of Rawya Ateya: First Parliamentarian in the Arab World', *Egyptian Streets*, 16 October 2020; Ne'maat Magdi, 'Rawya Ateya: The First Egyptian Female Deputy', *Al Rai*, August 2009.

10 This section is based on Stergiou P. Leptokaridis, *The First Greek Member of Parliament, The Female Rebel*, Demand Publications, 2003.

11 Quoted in Stergiou P. Leptokaridis, *The First Greek Member of Parliament*, p. 69.

12 Tasoula Vervenioti, 'Charity and Nationalism. The Greek Civil War and the Entrance of Right-Wing Women into Politics', in Paola Bacchetta and Margaret Power (eds), *Right-Wing Women from Conservatives to Extremists Around the World*, Routledge, 2002.

13 *Greek Reporter*, 18 January 2023.

14 *The Greek Herald*, 18 January 2021.

15 Quoted in Stergiou P. Leptokaridis, *The First Greek Member of Parliament, The Female Rebel*, Demand Publications, 2003, p. 117.

16 Ibid., p. 125.

17 Eyewitness quoted in Minale Adugna, *Women and Warfare in Ethiopia*, Gender Issues Research Report,13: 27.

18 *The Ethiopian Herald*, 19 September 2007.

19 This section is based on Reidulf K. Molvaer, 'Siniddu Gebru: Pioneer Woman Writer, Feminist, Patriot, Educator, and Politician', *Northeast African Studies*, 1997, 4 (3); Richard Pankhurst, 'Senedu Gebru', *Dictionary of African Biography*, Oxford University Press, 2012; *The Courageous Life of Senedu Gebru*. AWIB Ethiopia, YouTube video; *The Ethiopian Herald*.

20 *The Ethiopian Herald*, 23 August 1998.

21 *Ethiopian Times*, 24 July 2005.

22 This section is based on Rajitha T., 'Role of Annie Mascarene in the Freedom Movement in Travancore', *International*

Journal of Innovative Knowledge Concepts, VII, May 2019; Rozina Visram, *Women in India and Pakistan*, Cambridge University Press, 1992; Angellica Aribam and Akash Styawali, 'Anna Mascarene: A Trailblazer Who Wanted Women to Get Their Political Due', *Mint*, September 2024; Aribam, Angellica, and Styawali, *The Fifteen, The Lives and Times of the Women in India's Constituent Assembly*, Hachette, 2024.

23 Rozina Visram, *Women in India and Pakistan*, Cambridge University Press, 1992, p. 43.

24 Quoted in Angellica Aribam and Akash Styawali, 'Anna Mascarene: A Trailblazer Who Wanted Women to Get Their Political Due', *Mint*, September 2024.

25 *The Times of India*, 12 April 1953.

26 Angellica Aribam and Akash Styawali, 'Anna Mascarene: A Trailblazer'.

27 Antigua and Barbuda, Bolivia, Burkino Faso, Cambodia, Cameroon, Chile, Costa Rica, Ghana, Gibraltar, Grenada, Guatamala, Greenland, Guyana, Honduras, Laos, Malaysia, Mali, Mexico, Nepal, Nicaragua, Papua New Guinea, Peru, Saint Lucia, Saint Vincent and the Grenadines, Sierra Leone, Singapore, Tanzania, Uganda and the Virgin Islands.

6 Decolonisation and Beyond, 1960–1970

1 Roquia Abubakr, Khadija Ahrari, Masuma Esmati-Wardak, Aziza Gardizi, Anahita Ratebzad, Homeira Seljuqi.

2 This section is based on Tim Wheeler, 'Remembering Anahita Ratebzad, Socialist Leader and Mother of Afghan Women's Liberation', *People's World*, 19 August 2021; an interview given by Dr Anahita Ratebzad, Reddit; Anahita Ratebzad, *Times of India*, 28 January 1980.

3 There were four delegates from Afghanistan representing Afghan National Association of Women: the other three were Mrs Homayra Saljuqui, Miss Kubra Nourzay, Miss Ayesha Mohammed Ali.

4 In 1959 the Prime Minister Solomon Bandaranaike was assassinated. In 1960 his wife Sirimavo Bandaranaike became the world's first female Prime Minister.

5 Afghanistan, Burma, Ceylon, China, Egypt, Ghana, India, Indonesia, Iran, Japan, Mongolia, Pakistan, Philippines, Singapore, Thailand, Tunisia, Turkey, Uganda, Vietnam, as well as observers from UNESCO, UNICEF, WHO, ILO and Women's International League for Peace and Freedom.

6 *The First Asian-African Conference of Women*, Report of the Proceedings, 15–24 February, 1958, p. 120.

7 Valentie Moghadam, *Modernizing Women: Gender and Social Change in the Middle East*, Lynne Reiner, 1993, p. 232.

8 Francis Fukuyama, *The End of History and the Last Man*, Hamish Hamilton, 2012.

9 This section is based on Susan Love Brown, 'Johnson, Doris Louise', *Dictionary of Caribbean and Afro-Latin American Biography*, Oxford University Press, 2016.

10 'Dr Doris Johnson Helped Shape the Quiet Revolution', *Punch*, January 2011.

11 Dr Doris Johnson, speech on Women's Suffrage to the Members of the House of Assembly,1959.

12 Ibid.

13 K'adir night, known as the Night of Power, is the holiest in the Islamic calendar. It commemorates the night when the Quran was first revealed to the Prophet Muhammad.

14 This section is based on Ana Sayfa, 'YDP Gençik Kollari Kadriye Hulusi Hacibulgur'un Kabristanini Ziyaret Etti', *Hakikat*, 19 August 2021; Dr Filiz Besim, 'Bugunden Dune', *Yazarlar*, 12 December 2017; Ülker Vanci Osam (ed.) 'Ís Birakmiş Kibrisli Türjler', *Iz Birakmis Symposium*, Doğu Akdeniz Üniversitesi Yaninlari, 2021. Many thanks to the university for sending me a copy of the symposium papers.

15 This section is based on *Iranian Influential Women: Farrokhru Parsa, 1922–1980*, Iran Wire, 31 October 2023; Malmaz Afkhami,

The Other Side of Silence, A Memoir of Exile, Iran and the Global Women's Movement, UNC Press, 2022; Faranak Rafiei, *Like a Phoenix from the Ashes*, Goethe Institute, March 2022.

16 The others were Mehrangiz Dowlatshahi, Nayereh Ebtehaj-Samii, Showkat Malek Jahanbani, Mehrangiz Manouchehrian, Shams ol-Moluk Mosahab, Nezhat Nafisi and Hajar Tarbiat.

17 Mahnaz Afkhami, 'Iran: a Future in the Past – The "Prerevolutionary" Women's Movement' in Robin Morgan, *Sisterhood is Global: The International Women's Movement Anthology*, Open Road Integrated Media, 1996, p. 427.

18 This section is based on 'Gwendoline Chomba Konie – Zambia', *Gender Links for Equality and Justice*, 1 July 2012; Karen L Kinnear, *Women in Developing Countries: a Reference Handbook*, Bloomsbury, 2011; Gwendoline Konie, 'Gaining Political Power', *Africa Report*, 28, 1 March 1983; Robin Morgan, *Sisterhood is Global: The International Women's Movement Anthology*, Open Road Integrated Media, 1996.

19 Gwendoline Konie, 'Zambia: Feminist Progress – More Difficult than Decolonisation' in Robin Morgan, *Sisterhood is Global: The International Women's Movement Anthology*, p. 928.

20 Ibid., p. 929.

21 Gwendoline Konie, 'Gaining Political Power', *Africa Report*, 28, 1 March 1983.

22 Gwendoline Konie, quoted in *Gender Links for Equality and Justice*, 1 July 2012.

23 President Kaunda, Reflecting on Gwendoline Konie's life, 22 March 2009.

24 The first women took their seats in Aruba, Belize, British Virgin Islands, Cayman Islands, Central African Republic, Chad, Congo, Equatorial Guinea, Eswatini, Faroe Islands, Fiji, Gabon, Gambia, Haiti, Hong Kong, Ivory Coast, Lebanon, Lesotho, Liberia, Madagascar, Malawi, Monaco, Montserrat, Nigeria, Paraguay,

Rwanda, Senegal, Solomon Islands, Sudan, Syria, Togo and Vanuatu.

7 Global Challenges, 1970–1980

1 Anguilla, Benin, Bhutan, Botswana, Cape Verde, DR Congo, Guinea Bissau, Kiribati, Marshall Islands, Mauritania, New Caledonia, Niue, Northern Mariana Islands, Palau, Samoa, San Marino, Săo Tomé and Principe, Somalia, Tonga, Yemen all elected their first women.

2 Elizabeth Blunschy, Tilo Frey, Hedi Lang, Lise Girardin, Josi Meier, Gabrielle Nanchen, Martha Ribi, Hanna Sahfeld-Singer, Liselotte Spreng, Hanny Thalmann, Lilian Uchtenhagen, Nelly Wick.

3 The first women took their seats in Aruba, Belize, British Virgin Islands, Cayman Islands, Central African Republic, Chad, Congo, Equatorial Guinea, Eswatini, Faroe Islands, Fiji, Gabon, Gambia, Haiti, Hong Kong, Ivory Coast, Lebanon, Lesotho, Liberia, Madagascar, Malawi, Monaco, Montserrat, Nigeria, Paraguay, Rwanda, Senegal, Solomon Islands, Sudan, Syria, Togo and Vanuatu.

4 This section is based on 'Elizabeth Blunschy ist tot', *BLICK*, 2 May 2015; Raya Badraun, 'Elizabeth Blunschy: Erste Präsidentin des Nationalrats ist 90 Jahre alt', *Tagblatt*, 13 July 2012; 'Sie war die erste National-rats-Präsudentin: Elizabeth Blunschy verstorben', *Watson*, 2 May 2016; Elizabeth Blunschy, Josi J Meier, Judith Stamm, *Drei Wege Ins Bundeshause*, Comenius, 2023.

5 Elizabeth Blunschy, Josi J. Meier, Judith Stamm, *Drei Wege Ins Bundeshause*, Comenius, 2023, p. 17.

6 Ibid., p. 20.

7 Ibid., p. 22.

8 Ibid., p. 23.

9 Ibid., p. 24.

10 Ibid., p. 26.

11 Judy Fayald, 'Swiss Me', *WWD*, December 1977.

12 Elizabeth Blunschy, Josi J. Meier, Judith Stamm, *Drei Wege Ins Bundeshause*, Comenius, 2023, p. 33.
13 University of Lucerne, 18 May 2015.
14 Elizabeth Blunschy, Josi J. Meier, Judith Stamm, *Drei Wege Ins Bundeshause*, Comenius, 2023, p. 33.
15 This section is based on Monika Schärer, 'Tilo Frey, Die schwarze Schweizer Polit-Pionierin', *Dienstag*, 24 September 2019; Jovita dos Santos Pinto et al., *Un/doing Race*, Seismo Verlag, 2022; Von Carlos Hanimann, 'Der sonderbare Fall der Tilo Frey, *Republik*.
16 'Un pionnière s'en est allé', *ARCinfo*, 28 June 2008.
17 Alex Fernandes, *Observer*, 21 April 2024.
18 The other colonies were Angola, Cape Verde, São Tomé and Principe.
19 Alcinda Abreu, Maria Arruvaia, Monica Chitupila, Carlota Chiwanga, Cecelia Chongo, Celeste Cossa, Justina Gaspar, Helena da Gloria, Melita Guambe, Maria Laice, Rosinha Lisboa, Graca Machel, Celeste Manhica, Isabel Martins, Salome Moiane, Felipa Muniveda, Esperanca Muthemba, Teresa Nhalingue, Marina Pachinuapa, Felizarda Paulino, Maria Rafael, Ana Sansao, Leopoldina dos Santos, Cristina Tembe, Teresa Tembo, Maria Veloso.
20 This section is based on Claude-Hélène Mayer, 'Angela Merkel and Graça Machel: The Comparative Heroine's Journeys of Two Women Leaders Beyond WEIRD', *Beyond WEIRD: Psychobiography in Times of Transcultural and Transdisciplinary Perspectives*. Springer 2023; Frances B. Henderson, 'Machel, Graça', *Dictionary of African Biography*, Oxford University Press, 2012; Kathleen Sheldon, 'Machel, Graça', *The Oxford Encyclopedia of Women in World History*, Oxford University Press, 2008; 'Graça Machel', *Learning for Justice Newsletter*; Graça Machel, in *Insurrectionary Uprisings, A Reader in Revolutionary Nonviolence and Decolonization*, Daraja Press, 2018; 'Graça Machel', *The Monitor*, 8 March 1997; Graça Machel, https://theelders.org
21 *Observer*, 30 June 2013, p. 28.

22 'Graça Machel', *Learning for Justice Newsletter*.
23 https://childrenandarmedconflict.un.org/1996/08/1996-graca -machel-report-armed-conflict-children
24 Graça Machel, in *Insurrectionary Uprisings, A Reader in Revolutionary Nonviolence and Decolonization*, Daraja Press, 2018, p. 169.
25 Ibid., p. 172.
26 Gary Younge, *Guardian*, 8 July 1997, p. 7.
27 *Pacific Islands Monthly*, February 1974.
28 Interview with Kathy Marks, in *FreshAir*, 28 April 2009. See also Luke Jones, 'Pitcairn Files', *Sunday Times*, 12 January 2025.
29 Ibid.
30 Ibid., p. 33.
31 Ibid., p. 35.
32 *Guardian*, 30 September 2014.
33 *Independent*, 30 July 1998.
34 *Independent*, 29 September 2004.
35 *BBC News*, 25 October 2004.
36 Pitcairn Island Tourism, 2024.
37 Anguilla, Benin, Bhutan, Botswana, Cape Verde, DR Congo, Guinea Bissau, Kiribati, Marshall Islands, Mauritania, New Caledonia, Niue, Northern Mariana Islands, Palau, Samoa, San Marino, São Tomé and Principe, Somalia, Syria, Tonga and Yemen all elected women for the first time.
38 Quoted in Jomana Qaddour, 'Women's Quotas: Making the Case for Codifying Syrian Women's Political Participation', *Journal of Race, Gender and Social Justice*, 26 (3), 2019: 585.

8 Navigating the 1980s

1 Prince Hans Adam, *Wahlurkunde*, Landtagsabgeordneten, 16 April 1986.
2 *Wahlurkunde*, Landtagsabgeordneten, 16 April 1986.
3 *Volksblatt*, 30 October 2010.
4 *Liechtenfteiner Volksblatt*, 16 April 1986.
5 Ibid.

6   Liechtensteinishce Landesbibliothek, 1978–1988.

7   *Volksblatt*, 30 October 2010.

8   This section is based on *Dr Rosita Beatrice Missick Butterfield, SCM, MBE 1991–1993*, Turks and Caicos Island website; 'A life with purpose and charisma', *Turks and Caicos Weekly News*, 7–13 February 2015.

9   *Turks and Caicos Weekly News*, 3 October 2023.

10 Parliamentary tributes to Rosita Butterfield, quoted in *TCI Sun*, 28 January 2015.

11 This section is based on 'Maria Mambo Café', *Blackpast*, 4 November 2023; 'Maria Mambo Café, In Memoria', *ClubK*, 13 February 2014; Mayra de Lassalette, 'Perdeu – se uma grande filha de Angola', *VAO Portuguese*, 2 December 2013;

12 Secretary General, OMA quoted in *Jornal de Angola*, 4 December 2013.

13 MPLA political bureau, 'Morreu Maria Mambo Café', *Jornal de Angola*, 12 December 2013.

14 The war ended when the leader of the opposition group was assassinated and international support disappeared. In 1989 the Berlin Wall fell and the Soviet Union collapsed; in 1994 South African white minority rule ended.

15 Angola was one of three sources of 'conflict diamonds'. The opposition group, UNITA was said to earn at least $3.72 billion from illicit diamonds, money used to fund their armed struggle. See 'A Peace Dividend 20 Years in the Making: the Angola Case Study', *World Diamond Council*, March 2024 for an analysis of Angola's diamond trade.

16 See Paula Christina Roque, 'Angola's Façade Democracy', *Journal of Democracy*, October 2009 for a pessimistic analysis of Angolan politics.

17 Aili Mari Tripp, *Women and Power in Post-Conflict Africa*, Cambridge University Press, 2015.

18 Victoria Chitepo, Ruth Chinamano, Naomi Nhiwatiwa, Tenjiwe Lesabe, Nyasha Kumbula, Evelyn Masaiti, Mavis Chidzonga. All were ZANU representatives.

19 This section is based on *Joice Mujuru*, Pindula.co.zw; Karousos M., Joice Mujuru (1955-), *BlackPast*.org, 9 December 2023; Sam Masters, 'Joice Mujuru: Zimbabwe's Former Vice-president Forms New Party to Challenge Robert Mugabe's Zanu-PF', *Independent*, 1 March 2016.

20 Some mention 1958 as a birth date but 1955 is cited in most sources and biographies.

21 *The Herald*, Zimbabwe, 17 December 2014.

22 Quoted in article by Linda Mujuru and Gamuchirai Masiyiwa, 'Joice Mujuru: The Fighter', *Global Press Journal*, 22 July 2018.

23 *Washington Post*, 26 July 2005.

24 Nadje Al-Ali, 'Reconstructing Gender: Iraqi Women between Dictatorship, War, Sanctions and Occupation', *Third World Quarterly*, 26 (4–5), 2005: 739.

25 *Peace Women*, Women's International League for Peace and Freedom, 19 March 2013.

26 MEMRI TV, Special Dispatch, No 489, March 2003.

27 Nadje Al-Ali, 'Reconstructing Gender: Iraqi Women between Dictatorship, War, Sanctions and Occupation', *Third World Quarterly*, 26 (4–5), 2005.

28 Quoted in *Peace Women*, Women's International League for Peace and Freedom, 19 March 2013.

29 This section is based on 'Hon Naamal Maheu Latasi', *Pacific Women in Politics*; Susi Saitala Kofe and Fakavae Taomia, *Advancing Women's Political Participation in Tuvalu, A Research Project commissioned by the Pacific Islands Forum Secretariat*.

30 *Pacific Monthly*, May 1990, p. 56.

31 In this decade, Andorra, Iraq, Jordan, Nauru, Niger, Saint Kitts and Nevis, also elected women for the first time.

9 The Journey's End? 1990–2000

1 This is based on Emily Bridger, 'From "Mother of the Nation" to "Lady Macbeth": Winnie Mandela and Perceptions of Female Violence in South Africa, 1985–91', *Gender and History*, 27 (2),

2015; Emma Gilbey, *The Lady. The Life and Times of Winnie Mandela*, Jonathan Cape, 1993.

2 Winnie Madikezela-Mandela and Ashmed Kathrada, *491 Days: Prisoner Number 1323/69*, Ohio University Press, 2014, p. 284.

3 Ibid.

4 Ibid.

5 Helen Suzmann, quoted in Brenna Munro, 'Nelson, Winnie, and the Politics of Gender', in *The Cambridge Companion to Nelson Mandela*, Cambridge University Press, 2014, p. 102.

6 Winnie Mandela, quoted in Brenna Munro, 'Nelson, Winnie, and the Politics of Gender', in *The Cambridge Companion to Nelson Mandela*, p. 101.

7 Winnie Mandela quoted in Emily Bridger, 'From "Mother of the Nation" to "Lady Macbeth": Winnie Mandela and Perceptions of Female Violence in South Africa, 1985–91', *Gender and History*, 27 (2), 2015: 449.

8 Kwesi Quartey, 'Tribute to Winnie Madikizela-Mandela', *Journal of Pan African Studies*, 11 (7), May 2018.

9 About half of candidates were not independent, members of any political party. In 1917, Ukrainians had a short experience of national self-determination when the country freed itself from Russian domination and formed its own autonomous government. Ukrainians, buoyed up by the Bolshevik's public commitment to the principle of national self-autonomy, declared a new People's Republic. In 1917, Yevgenia Bosch (1879–1925), a Bolshevik revolutionary, was elected Minister of the Interior, effectively the head of government. She was the first female Prime Minister in the world. The new regime she headed was short-lived. When the treaty of Brest-Litovsk gave Ukraine to Germany, she resigned from the government and took up arms against the German invasion. In 1925, upset by Trotsky's removal from the Soviet leadership, weakened by prison, exile and tuber-culosis, she committed suicide. After the Second World War, Ukraine reverted to being part of the Russian Empire, this time called the Union of Soviet Republics. Ukrainians were elected to

the Supreme Soviet of the Soviet Socialist Republic of Ukraine and to the USSR Parliament.

10 This is based on Nina Karpachova, *1000 Peace Women*; 'The First Ombudsman of Ukraine: Nina Karpachova', *Ombudsman of Ukraine*, 10 July 2012; Sarah Birth, 'Women and Political Representation in Contemporary Ukraine', in Richard E. Matland and Kathleen Montgomery (ed), *Women's Access to Political Power in Post-Communist Europe*, Oxford Scholarship Online, 2003.

11 *TV5*, Kiev, 2 August 2004.

12 Nina Karpachova, quoted in 'Ukrainian Ombudsperson Condemns Ex-Premier's Itinerant Hearing', *BBC Monitoring Former Soviet Union*, 8 December 2011.

13 Nina Karpachova, 18 February 2024.

14 Nina Karpachova, 'Appeal of the First Ukrainian Parliament Commissioner for Human Rights', *Europäisches Ombudsman Institute*, 2018/19.

15 Figures vary. The Inter Parliamentary Union (1995) suggests that eight women and 130 men were elected to the House of Representatives, the Zastupnicki Dam. I have only found seven of them: Barbara Bešinić, Savka Dabčević Kučar, Katarina Fuček, Mira Ljubićć-Lorger, Milanka Opačić, Vera Pivčević-Stanić, Gordana Turić.

16 This section is based on Museum Documentation Center, MDR .HR; 'Vesna Girardi Jurkić', https://www.istrianet.org; Zvjezdana Nasić, 'Vesna Girardi Jurkić', *Kroatologija* 3, 2012.

17 The others were Dr Nada Haffadh, Bahia Al Jishi and Ms Alice Samaan. This section is based on Dr Mariam Al Jalahma, WHO Global Co-ordination Mechanism on the Prevention and Control of NCDs.

18 Countries include Bosnia, Croatia, Slovenia newly created from the former Yugoslavia; Comoros, an island country in South-eastern Africa in 1993; Morocco, North Africa 1993; Oman and Bahrain in 2000, Wallis and Futuna in 1992; South Africa in 1994.

Conclusion

1 Pamela Paxton and Melanie M. Hughes, *Women, Politics and Power: A Global Perspective*, Sage, 2014.

2 See www.archive.ipu.org for statistics on women in parliaments across the globe.

3 See *Women in National Parliaments*, Inter-Parliamentary Union, 2025.

4 *Global and Regional Averages of Women in National Parliaments*, Inter-Parliamentary Union, 2025

5 These statistics are from www.archive.ipu.org. I have included the top five; after that I have chosen the countries, I have looked at in the book. For a full breakdown see the archive.

6 Melanie M. Hughes and Pamela Paxton, 'The Political Representation of Women Over Time', *Palgrave Handbook of Political Rights*, Palgrave Macmillan, 2019.

7 Ibid., p. 39.

8 *Women in National Parliaments*, Inter-Parliamentary Union, 2005, p. 7

9 Ibid., p. 7.

10 Gretchen Bauer and Hanna E. Britton, *Women in African Parliaments*, Lynne Rienner Publishers, 2006.

11 Sonia Palmieri, *Gender-Sensitive Parliaments*, IPU, 2011.

12 *The Convention on the Elimination of All Forms of Discrimination against Women and its Optional Protocol*, IPU, 2023, p. 21

13 Twenty countries both signed and ratified. Rosemarie Skaine, *Women Political Leaders in Africa*, McFarland and Co, 2008, p. 28.

14 The eight were Angola, Botswana, Central Africa Republic, Egypt, Eritrea, São Tomé and Principe, Sudan and Tunisia.

15 David Mitchell, *Guardian*, 2 February 2025.

16 This section comes from Rosemarie Skaine, *Women Political Leaders in Africa*, McFarland and Co, 2008.

17 Ibid.

18 Francesca R. Jensenius, 'India: A Contradictory Record', in Melanie M. Hughes and Pamela Paxton, 'The Political

Representation of Women Over Time', *Palgrave Handbook of Political Rights*, Palgrave Macmillan, 2019.

19 Ibid.

20 Ya Oussas, *Shaikha Haya Rashed Al Khalifa*, yaoussas.com, 2022.

21 Acceptance Speech of H. E. Ms Sheikha Haya Rashed Al Khalifa, President-Elect of the 61st Session of the General Assembly, United Nations General Assembly, 8 June 2006.

22 Statement of H. E. Ms Sheikha Haya Rashed Al Khalifa, President of the 61st Session of the General Assembly, at the Opening of the 61st Session, United Nations General Assembly, 12 September 2006.

23 Ibid.

Bibliography

1 Joan Wallah Scott, 'Gender: A Useful Category of Historical Analysis', *American Historical Review*, December 1986.

Bibliography

Interestingly, and surprisingly, I could find no book that examined the first women who broke into high politics across the world. Joan W. Scott's article, written just over forty years ago, still has resonance today. Political history, she argues, 'has been the stronghold of resistance to the inclusion of material or even questions about women and gender'.[1] Suffrage histories dominate. Books like June Hannam, Mitzi Auchterlone and Katherine Holden's *International Encyclopedia of Women's Suffrage* and Jad Adams' *Women and the Vote: A World History* both deal with how women gained the vote. I was fortunate in discovering Michael Genovese and Janie S. Steckenreider's *Women as Political Leaders*, which is a fascinating study of women who have headed governments across the world. I did not aspire to writing anything ambitious like these excellent academic compendiums, but merely hoped to introduce some remarkable women to a wider audience. Nonetheless, with virtually nothing to build upon, I was faced with the challenging task of both researching the facts and trying to come up with some overall conclusions.

I bought a world map. I decided to choose a representative section from across the globe. Not just rich and powerful countries but also small island nations. I did not wish to focus on the Western hemisphere, on countries with a well-established historiography but aimed to include the global south, often which had a different trajectory and very different histories. I began to climb a steep and vertiginous learning path.

I chose the countries I wanted to focus on. Many were left out, and deserve inclusion but *Trailblazers* is designed to be representative, not inclusive. It was (relatively) easy to access information from countries such as Germany, Russia, America and Britain, which has a well-established feminist research base written in English. Others like Finland and Turkey, where there was so very little, I wrote to embassies and consulates. Some did not answer, but those who did were extraordinarily helpful and researched material for me. This ranged from autobiographies, biographies, contemporary sources, conference papers, oral interviews, newspaper accounts and parliamentary records. For instance, the press attaché of the Turkish Republic of Northern Cyprus told me about a conference that had been held on Turkish Cypriot women. The university, where it was held, sent me a PDF of the conference paper. In this fractious modern world, it was heart-warming to know that there were so many good people, willing to help foreign strangers. More detail about my source material is included in the notes.

One of my joys is meeting other historians working in similar fields. I was invited to speak at two conferences organised by Dr Michela Minesso, University of Milan. Here I met experts in European political history: Michela Minesso, Brigitte Studer (Switzerland) and Carmen de la Guardia Herrero (Spain), all of whom gave inspirational lectures on their countries' first female politicians.

I discovered the Inter-Parliamentary Union (IPU) archives. For anyone interested in women in high politics, this is an essential database. The IPU, for those like me who had never heard of it before writing *Trailblazers*, is a global organisation of national parliaments whose slogan is 'For democracy. For everyone.' It has five objectives: to build effective and empowered parliaments, promote inclusive and representative parliaments, support resilient and innovative parliaments, catalyse collective parliamentary action and strengthen the accountability of the IPU. It works to increase women's representation in parliament and empower women MPs. Each year it publishes an analysis of women in Parliament which makes for salutary reading.

The following indicative bibliography includes only the books, articles, newspapers and interviews I have directly used in writing *Trailblazers*.

Adam, Prince Hans, *Wahlurkunde*, Landtagsabgeordneten, 16 April 1986.

Adams, Jad, *Women and the Vote: A World History*, Oxford University Press, 2016.

Adugna, Minale, *Women and Warfare in Ethiopia*, Gender Issues Research Report, 13.

Afkhami, Mahnaz, *The Other Side of Silence, A Memoir of Exile, Iran and the Global Women's Movement*, UNC Press, 2022.

Afkhami, Mahnaz, 'Iran: a Future in the Past – The "Pre-revolutionary" Women's Movement' in Robin Morgan, *Sisterhood is Global: The International Women's Movement Anthology*, Open Road Integrated Media, 1996.

Ahtisaari, Eeva, 'Hilda Kakikoski: Opeṭṭaja, Puhuja Ja Politiitikko Naisen Asialla', in Yksi Kamari, *Kaksi Sukupuolta*, Eduskunnan kirjasto, 1997.

Al-Ali, Nadje, 'Reconstructing Gender: Iraqi Women between Dictatorship, War, Sanctions and Occupation', *Third World Quarterly*, 26 (4–5), 2005.

Alapuro, Risto, *State and Revolution in Finland*, Brill, 2019.

Aldrich, Robert and Wotherspoon, Garry, *Who's Who in Gay and Lesbian History*, Psychology Press, 2002.

Anon, *Adelheid Popp*, Parlamentskorrespondenz, VOM 28, April 2009.

Anon, 'Shidzué Ishimoto Kato', *Museum of Contraception and Abortion*, 2024.

Anon, *The First Asian–African Conference of Women*, Report of the Proceedings, 15–24 February, 1958.

Aribam, Angellica and Styawali, Akash, *The Fifteen, The Lives and Times of the Women in India's Constituent Assembly*, Hachette, 2024.

Aribam, Angellica and Styawali, Akash, 'Anna Mascarene: A Trailblazer Who Wanted Women to get their Political Due', *Mint*, September 2024.

Arrington, Lauren, *Revolutionary Lives*, Princeton University Press, 2019.

Badraun, Raya, 'Elizabeth Blunschy: Erste Präsidentin des Nationalrats ist 90 Jahre alt', *Tagblatt*, 13 July 2012.

Balogh, Margit and Ilona Mona, Ilona, 'Slachta, Margit (1884–1974)' in Francisca de Haan et al. (eds), *A Biographical Dictionary of Women's Movements and Feminisms: Central, Eastern, and South Eastern Europe, 19th and 20th Centuries*, Central European University Press, 2006.

Baroness Shidzué Ishimoto, *Facing Two Ways: The Story of My Life*, Cassell, 1935.

Bauer, Gretchen, and Britton, Hannah, *Women in African Parliaments*, Lynne Rienner, 2006.

BBC News, 25 October 2004.

Berry, Carolina, 'Delia Degliuomini de Parodi, el desafio de reemplazar lo irresmplazable', *La Segunda línea del liderazgo Peronista 1945–1955*, Eduntref-Pueblo Heredro, 2013.

Besim, Dr Filiz, 'Bugunden Dune', *Yazarlar*, 12 December 2017.

Birth, Sarah, 'Women and Political Representation in Contemporary Ukraine' in Richard E. Matland and Kathleen Montgomery (eds), *Women's Access to Political Power in Post-Communist Europe*, Oxford Scholarship Online, 2003.

Blacker, Carmen, 'Obituary, Shizue Kato', *Guardian*, 1 February 1992.

Boak, Helen, *Women in the Weimar Republic*, Manchester University Press, 2013.

Bridger, Emily, 'From "Mother of the Nation" to "Lady Macbeth": Winnie Mandela and Perceptions of Female Violence in South Africa, 1985–91', *Gender and History*, 27 (2), 2015.

Britton, Hannah E., *Women in African Parliaments*, Lynne Rienner Publishers, 2006.

Brown, Susan Love, 'Johnson, Doris Louise', *Dictionary of Caribbean and Afro-Latin American Biography*, Oxford University Press, 2016.

Bruin, Tabitha, 'Agnes Macphail', *Canadian Encyclopaedia*, April 2008.

Buzz, E. S., 'Here's the Story of Rawya Ateya: First Parliamentarian in the Arab World', *Egyptian Streets*, 16 October 2020.

Capdepuy, Arlette, 'Quelle place pour Madame Éboué dans le gallisme de la Ve Bruin, République?' *Histoire@politique*, 2012.

Chan, Shelly, *A Maidservant of the Revolution, He Xiangning and Chinese Feminist Nationalism in the 1920s and 1930s*, Occasional Papers, Hong Kong Institute of Asia-Pacific Studies, 2007.

Clara Campoamor. La Mujer olvidada, a tv movie, 2011.

Clements, Barbara Evans, *A History of Women in Russia from Earliest Times to the Present*, Indiana University Press, 2012.

Clements, Barbara Evans, *Bolshevik Feminist, The Life of Aleksandra Kollontai*, Indiana University Press, 1979.

Coleman, Jenny, *From Suffrage to a Seat in the House: The Path to Parliament for New Zealand Women*, Otago University Press, 2016.

Conway, Martin, *Western Europe's Democratic Age*, 1945–1968, Princeton University Press, 2020.

Crawford, John Martin, *The Kalevala, the Epic Poem of Finland*, Columbian Publishing, 1891.

Crowley, T. A., *Agnes Mcphail and the Politics of Equality*, Lorimer, 1990.

D'Amelio, Dan A., 'Italian Women in the Resistance World War II', *Italian America*, 19 (2), 2001.

Ethiopian Herald.

Evening Post, 15 September 1933.

Fairfax, Kathy, *Comrades in Arms: Bolshevik Women in the Russian Revolution*, Resistance Books, 1999.

Fayald, Judy, 'Swiss Me', *WWD*, December 1977.

Frauen, Ariadne, in *Bewegung, 1848–1938*, Osterreichsische Nationalbibliothek, u/d.

Gaballo, Graziella, 'Lina Merlin', *enciclopediadelledonne.it*, 2024.

Galili, Ziva, 'Women and the Russian Revolution', *Dialectical Anthropology*, 1990, 15 (2/3).

Garner, Jean, 'McCombs, Elizabeth Reid, 1873–1935', *Dictionary of New Zealand Biography*, 1998.

Gasanabo, Jean-Damascene 'Madame Eugénie Tell Éboué' (1891–1972), *Black Past*, 29 January 2012.

Genovese, Michael A., Steckenrider, Janie S., *Women as Political Leaders*, Routledge, 2013.

Emma Gilbey, *The Lady. The Life and Times of Winnie Mandela*, Jonathan Cape, 1993.

Giles, Kevin, *Flight of the Dove, the story of Jeannette Rankin*, Touchstone Press, Beaverton, 1980.

Goldschmidt, Arthur Jr, *Biographical Dictionary of Modern Egypt*, Lynne Rienner Publishers, 2000.

González, Alba, *Clara Campoamor: La lucha politica por los derechos de la mujer*, Ministerio de la Presidencia, 2022.

The Greek Herald, 18 January 2021.

Greek Reporter, 18 January 2023.

Guardian, 30 September 2014.

Hanebrink, Paul, *In Defense of Christian Hungary*, Cornell University, 2009.

Hannam, June, Auchterlone Mitzi and Holden, Katherine, *International Encyclopedia of Women's Suffrage*, ABC-Clio, 2000.

Henderson, Frances B, 'Machel, Graça', *Dictionary of African Biography*, Oxford University Press, 2012.

The Herald, Zimbabwe, 17 December 2014.

Hetherington, Sheila, *Katharine Atholl, 1874–1960*, Aberdeen University Press, 1991.

Honeycutt, Karen, 'Clara Zetkin: A Left-Wing Socialist and Feminist in Wilhelmian Germany', Columbia University, PhD, 1975.

Hopper, Helen, *A New Woman of Japan: A Political Biography of Katö Shidzue*, Boulder, 1996.

House of Commons, Ottawa, 26 March 1928.

Hughes, Melanie M. and Paxton, Pamela, 'The Political Representation of Women Over Time', *Palgrave Handbook of Political Rights*, Palgrave Macmillan, 2020.

Hurley, Siobhan Lambert, 'Ikramullah, Begum Shaista', *Oxford Encyclopaedia of Women in World History*, Oxford University Press, 2008.

Ikramullah, Shaista Suhrawardy, *From Purdah to Parliament*, Oxford University Press, 2000.

Independent, 30 July 1998

Independent, 29 September 2004.

Inter-Parliamentary Union archives, 'Women in Parliaments, 1945–1995, A World Statistical Survey', *Inter-Parliamentary Union. u/d.*

Jalalzai, Farida, *Shattered, Cracked or Firmly Intact? Women and the Executive Glass Ceiling Worldwide*, Oxford University Press, 2013.

Johnson, Dr Doris, 'Speech on Women's Suffrage to the Members of the House of Assembly, 1959', *Bahamian Politics*, 27 November 2012.

Jones, Luke, 'Pitcairn Files', *Sunday Times*, 12 January 2025.

Joseph-Gabriel, Annette K, *Reimagining Liberation: How Black Women Transformed Citizenship in the French Empire*, University of Illinois, 2019.

Josephson, Hannah, *Jeannette Rankin, First Lady in Congress*, Bobbs-Merrill, New York, 1974.

Kamari Yksi, *Kaksi Sukupuolta*, Eduskunnan Kirjasto, Helsinki, 1997.

Karousos M, 'Joice Mujuru (1955–)', *BlackPast.org*, 9 December 2023.

Karpachova, Nina, 'Ukrainian Ombudsperson Condemns Ex-premier's Itinerant Hearing', *BBC Monitoring Former Soviet Union*, 8 December 2011.

Karpachova, Nina, 'Appeal of the First Ukrainian Parliament Commissioner for Human Rights', *Europäisches Ombudsman Institute*, 2018/19.

Khan, Amna Munawar, 'The Role and Impact of Women Legislators in Pakistan's Parliament', *Defence Journal*, 26, 2024.

Kinnear, Karen L, *Women in Developing Countries: A Reference Handbook*, Bloomsbury, 2011.

Maria Kiss and Rita Maria, 'Slachta Margit arcai. 2. Rész: A keresztény feminista', *Barankovics Alapitvany*, 2024.

Kofe, Susi Saitala and Taomia, Fakavae, *Advancing Women's Political Participation in Tuvalu, A Research Project commissioned by the Pacific Islands Forum Secretariat*.

Kollontai, Alexandra, *The Autobiography of a Sexually Emancipated Communist Woman*, Herder and Herder, 1971.

Kollontai, Alexandra, *Mezhdunarodnyi den'rabotni tz*, Moscow, 1920.

Konie, Gwendoline, 'Zambia: Feminist Progress – More Difficult than Decolonisation', in Robin Morgan, *Sisterhood is Global: The International Women's Movement Anthology*, Open Road Integrated Media, 1996.

Konie, Gwendoline. 'Gaining Political Power', *Africa Report*, 28, 1 March 1983.

Konie, Gwendoline, *Gender Links for Equality and Justice*, 1 July 2012.

Korppi-Tommola, Aura, 'A Long Tradition of Equality: Women's Suffrage in Finland', in Blanca Rodriguez Ruiz and Ruth Rubio Marin (eds), *The Struggle for Female Suffrage in Europe*, Brill, 2012.

The KP Telegraph, February 1938.

Lassalette, Mayra de, 'Perdeu – se uma grande filha de Angola', *VAO Portuguese*, 2 December 2013.

Lee, Sujin, 'Differing Conceptions of "Voluntary Motherhood": Yamakawa Kikue's Birth Strike and Ishimoto Shizue's Eugenic Feminism', *U.S.-Japan Women's Journal*, No. 52, 2017.

Leptokaridis, Stergiou P., *The First Greek Member of Parliament, The Female Rebel*, Demand Publications, 2003.

Liechtenfteiner Volksblatt, 16 April 1986.

Lily Xiao Hong et al. (eds), *Biographical Dictionary of Chinese Women, 1912–2000*, Hong Kong University Press, 2003.

Lipstadt, Deborah E., *Golda Meir*, Yale University Press, 2023.

Lopach, James J. and Jean A Luckowski, Jean A., *Jeannette Rankin, a Political Woman*, University Press of Colorado, 2005.

Los Angeles Times, 16 June 1951.

Graça Machel, in *Insurrectionary Uprisings, A Reader in Revolutionary Nonviolence and Decolonization*, Daraja Press, 2018; 'Graça Machel', *The Monitor*, 8 March 1997.

Madikezela-Mandela, Winnie and Kathrada, Ashmed, *491 Days: Prisoner Number 1323/69*, Ohio University Press, 2014.

Magdi, Ne'maat, 'Rawya Ateya: The First Egyptian Female Deputy', *Al Rai*, August 2009.

Masters, Sam, 'Joice Mujuru: Zimbabwe's Former Vice-President Forms New Party to Challenge Robert Mugabe's Zanu-PF', *Independent*, 1 March 2016.

Mayer, Claude-Hélène, 'Angela Merkel and Graça Machel: The Comparative Heroine's Journeys of Two Women Leaders Beyond WEIRD', *Beyond WEIRD: Psychobiography in Times of Transcultural and Transdisciplinary Perspectives*, Springer 2023.

Medzini, Meron, *Golda Meir*, De Gruyter, 2008.

Minesso, Michela, *Diritti e politiche sociali*, Franco Angeli, 2016.

McDermid, Jane and Hillyar, Anna, *Midwives of the Revolution: Female Bolsheviks and Women Workers in 1917*, Taylor and Francis, 1999.

McGregor, Katharine and Rahayu, Ruth Indiah, 'Umi Sardjono (1923–2011) and the Quest to Build a New Society for Indonesian Women', *Palgrave Handbook of Communist Women Activists around the World*, 2023.

McShane, Anne, 'Women at the Heart of the Revolution', *Jacobin*, November 2019.

Moghadam, Valentie, *Modernizing Women: Gender and Social Change in the Middle East*, Lynne Reinner Publishers, 2013.

Molvaer, Reidulf K., 'Siniddu Gebru: Pioneer Woman Writer, Feminist, Patriot, Educator, and Politician', *Northeast African Studies*, 1997, 4 (3): 61–75

Mossman, Mary Jane, *Quiet Rebels: A History of Ontario Women Lawyers*, WLU Press, 2024.

Mujuru, Linda and Masiyiwa, Gamuchirai, 'Joice Mujuru: The Fighter', *Global Press Journal*, 22 July 2018.

Munro, Brenna, 'Nelson, Winnie, and the Politics of Gender', in *The Cambridge Companion to Nelson Mandela*, Cambridge University Press, 2014.

Naden, Corrine J., *Jeannette Rankin*, Marshall Cavendish Bendick, New York, 2012.

Novikova, Natalia and Ghodsee, Kristen, 'Alexandra Kollontai (1872–1952): Communism as the Only Way Towards Women's Liberation', in F. de Haan (ed.), *Palgrave Handbook of Communist Women Activists around the World*, 2023.

NZ Truth, 27 January 1927.

Observer, 30 June 2013.

O'Brien, Mary Barmeyer, *Jeannette Rankin: Bright Star in the Big Sky*, Rowman and Littlefield.

O'Faoláin, Sean, *Constance Markievicz*, Sphere Books, London, 1934.

Ögai, Tokuko, 'The Stars of Democracy: The First Thirty-Nine Female Members of the Japanese Diet', *US –Japan Women's Journal English Supplement*, University of Hawaii Press, No. 11, 1996.

Osam, Ülker Vanci (ed.), 'İs Birakmiş Kibrisli Türjler', Iz Birakmis Symposium, Doğu Akdeniz Üniversitesi Yaninlari, 2021.

Pacific Islands Monthly, February 1974.

Pacific Monthly, May 1990

Pakistan Institute of International Affairs, 'Shaista S Ikramullah: 1915–2000', *Pakistan Horizon*, 61, 2008.

Palacios, Jennie Natalia, *Delia Parodi y la organización cívica femenina en la provincia de San Luis Acción administrative?* ISNC, December 2019.

Pahlman, Annie, *Women, Sexual Violence and the Indonesian Killings of 1965–66*, Routledge, 2017.

Pankhurst, Richard, 'Senedu Gebru', *Dictionary of African Biography*, Oxford University Press, 2012.

Pawbahamas, 'Dr Doris Johnson Helped Shape the Quiet Revolution', *Punch*, 20, January 2011.

Pennington, Doris, *Agnes Mcphail: Reformer*, Simon and Pierre, 1990.

Pirbhai, M. Reza, '"From Purdah to Parliament," the Twentieth Century According to Shaista Ikramullah', *Journal of Women of the Middle East and the Islamic World*, 14, 2016.

Pogrebin, Letty Cottin, 'Golda Meir', *The Halvi/Hyman Encyclopaedia of Jewish Women*.

Popp, Adelheid, *The Autobiography of a Working Woman*, T. Fisher Unwin, 1911.

Porter, Cathy, *Women in Revolutionary Russia*, Cambridge University Press, 1987.

Purwanti, Firliana, 'Umi Sarjono: Pembuka Jalan Gerakan', *Historia*, June 2014.

Qaddour, Jomana, 'Women's Quotas: Making the Case for Codifying Syrian Women's Political Participation', *Journal of Race, Gender and Social Justice*, 26 (3), 2019.

Quartey, Kwesi, 'Tribute to Winnie Madikizela-Mandela', *Journal of Pan African Studies*, 11 (7), May 2018.

Rafiei, Faranak, *Like a Phoenix from the Ashes*, Goethe Institute, March 2022.

Rajitha T., 'Role of Annie Mascarene in the Freedom Movement in Travancore', *International Journal of Innovative Knowledge Concepts*, VII, May 2019.

Rankin, Jeanette, *On this Day, Jeanette Rankin's History-Making Moment*, NCC Staff, April 2024.

Ratebzad, Anahita, *Times of India*, 28 January 1980.

Rolle, Elisa, 'Hilda Käkikoski', *Live Journal*, 31 January 2017.

Romero, *Reminiscences of Delia*, interview, Columbia University Library recording.

Roque, Paula Christina, 'Angola's Façade Democracy', *Journal of Democracy*, October 2009.

Samblancat, Miranda, 'Clara Campoamor Rodrigues', *Diccionario Biográfico de la Real Academia de la Historia*. Pinto, Jovita dos et al., *Un/doing Race*, Seismo Verlag, 2022.

Sayfa, Ana, 'YDP Gençik Kollari Kadriye Hulusi Hacibulgur'un Kabristanini Ziyaret Etti', Hakikat, 19 August 2021.

Schärer, Monika, 'Tilo Frey, Die schwarze Schweizer Polit-Pionierin', *Dienstag*, 24 September 2019.

Schmidt, Maria, 'Margit Slachta's Activities in Support of Slovakian Jewry, 1942–43', *Holocaust and Genocide Studies*, 5 (1), 1990.

Scott, Joan Wallah, 'Gender: A Useful Category of Historical Analysis', *American Historical Review*, December 1986.

Semley, Lorelle, *To be Free and French, Citizenship in France's Atlantic Empire*, CUP, 2017.

Sertel, Savaş, 'The Republic of Intellectual in Parliament', *Journal of Faculty of Letters*, June 2015.

Setiyadi, Munawar, 'Perjuangan Umi Sardjono, Pendiri Gerwani', *Arah Juang*, 62.

Sezer, Ayten, Dr, 'The First Female Members of Parliament in Turkey and their Work in Parliament.'

Sircana, Giuseppe, 'Merlin, Angelina', *Dizionario Biografico degli Italiani*, 73, 2009.

Slachta Margit, Yad Vashem.

Smith, Norma, *Jeannette Rankin, America's Conscience*, Montana Historical Society Press, 2002.

Smith, Paul, *Feminism and the Third Republic: Women's Political and Civil Rights in France, 1918–1945*, Oxford University Press, 1996.

Star (Christchurch), 27 July 1901.

Stewart, Stewart, *Ask No Quarter: A Biography of Agnes Macphail*, Longmans, Green and Company, 1959.

Stewart, Margaret and French, Doris, 'Aggie was a Terror', *Chatelaine Magazine*, April 1979.

Sunday Times Magazine, 12 January 2025.

Tambor, Molly, *The Lost Wave: Women and Democracy in Postwar Italy*, Oxford University Press, 2014.

Thompson, Seth, 'Golda Meir, A Very Public Life', in Michael Genovese et al., *Women as Political Leaders*, Routledge, 2013.

Tipton, Elise, 'Ishimoto Shizue: The Margaret Sanger of Japan', *Women's History Review*, 6 (3): 1997.

Tokuko, Ōgai, 'The Stars of Democracy: The First Thirty-Nine Female Member of the Japanese Diet', *US-Japan Women's Journal English Supplement*, University of Hawaii Press, No 11, 1996.

Toparlak, Bahar, 'Fatma Memik, One of the First Female Members of Parliament of the Republic', International *Journal of Historical and Social Research*, 12, 204.

Tripp, Aili Mari, *Women and Power in Postconflict Africa*, CUP, 2015.

Turks and Caicos Weekly News, 7–13 February 2015.

Turks and Caicos Weekly News, 3 October 2023.

Vervenioti, Tasoula, 'Charity and Nationalism. The Greek Civil War and the Entrance of Right-wing Women into Politics', *Right-Wing Women from Conservatives to Extremists Around the World*, ed Paola Bacchetta and Margaret Power, Routledge, 2002.

Visram, Rozina, *Women in India and Pakistan*, CUP, 1992.

Volksblatt, 30 October 2010.

Wallace, Sandra, 'Members for Everywoman? The Campaign Promises of Women Parliamentary Candidates', *New Zealand Journal of History*, 1991, 27.

Wheeler, Tim, 'Remembering Anahita Ratebzad, Socialist Leader and Mother of Afghan Women's Liberation', *People's World*, 19 August 2021.

Younge, Gary, *Guardian*, 8 July 1997

Zewde, Bahru, *A History of Modern Ethiopia*, Boydell and Brewer, 2017.